SELF-REGULATION *and* INQUIRY-BASED LEARNING *in the* PRIMARY CLASSROOM

SELF-REGULATION *and* INQUIRY-BASED LEARNING *in the* PRIMARY CLASSROOM

Brenda Jacobs

CANADIAN SCHOLARS

Toronto | Vancouver

Self-Regulation and Inquiry-Based Learning in the Primary Classroom
Brenda Jacobs

First published in 2022 by
Canadian Scholars, an imprint of CSP Books Inc.
425 Adelaide Street West, Suite 200
Toronto, Ontario
M5V 3C1

www.canadianscholars.ca

Library and Archives Canada Cataloguing in Publication

Title: Self-regulation and inquiry-based learning in the primary classroom /
    Brenda Jacobs.
Names: Jacobs, Brenda (Lecturer in education), author.
Description: Includes bibliographical references and index.
Identifiers: Canadiana (print) 20220177082 | Canadiana (ebook) 20220177090 |
    ISBN 9781773383224 (softcover) | ISBN 9781773383231 (PDF) |
    ISBN 9781773383248 (EPUB)
Subjects: LCSH: Inquiry-based learning. | LCSH: Self-culture. | LCSH:
    Web-based instruction. | LCSH: Education, Primary.
Classification: LCC LB1027.23 .J32 2022 | DDC 371.39—dc23

Cover art: Photo of Collaborative Valley Art by Brenda Jacobs
Cover design by Rafael Chimicatti
Page layout by S4Carlisle Publishing Services

22 23 24 25 26   5 4 3 2 1

Printed and bound in Ontario, Canada

Canadä

For Felix,
Whose ability to self-regulate at such a young age astonishes Oma!

CONTENTS

FOREWORD

As someone who worked closely with Brenda Jacobs when she was a graduate student in our Faculty of Education at York University, I am delighted to provide the foreword for her book on self-regulation and inquiry-based learning. When I was a professor in the faculty, I supervised both her master's research project and her doctoral dissertation because of our shared interest in emergent curriculum and the influence of the Reggio Emilia experience on early learning in North America. Jacobs first astonished me as a Master of Education student, when she completed nine graduate courses in a single year, while also raising four children, the youngest but three years of age. She completed an interesting research project then, which appears as the chapter "Children's Conversations about the Sun, Moon, and Earth" in *Emergent Curriculum in the Primary Classroom*. That book is a collection of lovely examples of emergent curriculum created by teachers while they taught in systems that followed a standardized curriculum (Wien, 2008). Jacobs's chapter showed her own capacity to teach young children using strong participatory structures, genuine inquiry, and expansive time frames that allow children agency, and she generated a vibrant emergent curriculum. She then became intrigued by the work of Stuart Shanker on young children's self-regulation and undertook doctoral research to explore its relationship with emergent curriculum and inquiry-based learning.

This book builds on that research. You will see her strength in framing the research in the first chapter, where she sets out the literature on self-regulation with which she aligns her work. She then builds her book upon four insights revealed in the data generated during her research. These insights concern a relationship between play and inquiry-based learning, and insights on emotion, oral language, and how to scaffold children's thinking. A foreword should not "steal the author's thunder" so I but give you a heads-up to watch for these, signalling their importance. While her book is an argument in favour of inquiry-based learning as a support for self-regulation, she also considers the relationship between her insights and educating children with exceptionalities, and the relationship between her insights and online learning.

I wish to highlight three aspects of the book's content that I found particularly meaningful. These three areas concern how educators attend to children's emotions, the design of environments that support self-regulation, and how participatory structures foster play and inquiry.

THE ROLE OF POSITIVE EMOTION IN LEARNING

A significant emphasis in the book is the necessity of taking care to address children's emotional development in schools. The notion that taking care of everyone's thoughts and feelings is a significant aspect of success in learning may be an unfamiliar notion to those who think school is about standardized curriculum, but the importance of emotion to learning has long been recognized in early childhood education (e.g., Ontario Ministry of Education, 2014, 2016). Jacobs notes that an insight from the field of social and emotional learning is "that positive emotions generate energy while negative emotions consume energy" (p. 17). The proportion of positive to negative emotions matters for healthy development, too. Fifty years ago in education we used to say that, in order to avoid damage, the proportion was four to one—that is, four or five positive interactions were necessary to counter one interaction that produced negative emotions. I do not know whether researchers today would agree, but Jacobs's point that too much negative emotion damages mental health and impedes the ability to learn is powerful.

The very idea that we can learn to regulate our emotions may be somewhat unfamiliar. Certainly, adults are accustomed to suppressing emotion, sending feelings underground where rumination on negative thoughts can lead to bad stuff. In contrast, the idea that emotions should be communicated—but not imposed—requires significant understanding and empathy in teachers. Jacobs shows us, through her examples from these four superb classrooms, the ways these teachers support children in thinking about what they are feeling, how they control negative feelings, and how they reconnect with a peer after an interaction has gone wrong. We see children's sense of belonging and how that helps them thrive, as well as their freedom to be themselves (rather than being on an obedience frame without options for making their own decisions). Readers will find many examples to compare with their own experience.

THE ROLE OF THE ENVIRONMENT IN SUPPORTING SELF-REGULATION

Jacobs portrays ways the four teachers developed their classroom environments to support children's self-regulation and potential to learn. She argues that such strong learning occurs in environments that facilitate children's interests and autonomy. Schools in provinces or states with standardized curriculum most frequently use direct instruction on a timed schedule as their "delivery mode," a transmission model of learning that makes the fallacious assumption that if something has been taught, it has been learned. There are always legions of teachers who understand such a belief to be untrue. Particularly when educating young children, teachers understand that many strategies are required to provide an environment rich enough to include multiple opportunities for indirect learning: in a rich environment, teachers do not control learning; they support it.

There are two basic options for organizing curriculum: one structures *time* and leaves space less defined; the other structures *space* and offers expansive time frames. When time is the organizing principle, you know what is being taught if you know what time it is on the schedule: if it's 9:15 it's reading time, and if it's 10:10 it's math, and so forth. Most of us have grown up with such schedules for the bulk of our formal learning. However, if space is the organizing principle, as in Montessori classrooms, then you know what a child is learning by the space they occupy in the room: language materials are organized in one area, mathematics materials in another, gross motor activities across the room. If many activities and interactions are occurring simultaneously, space is highly structured and time is expansive, less determined.

Expansive time frames are long periods of time for multiple activities that involve play, inquiry, and arts-making: instruction is folded inside them as needed. An expansive time frame could be anywhere from close to an hour to a full morning. Expansive time frames allow children to experience, and develop, sustained concentration for self-chosen tasks. Self-chosen tasks allow children to feel powerful because they are the decision-makers in charge of their own activity.

Over 100 years ago, Maria Montessori expressed the notion of self-regulation through her term *normalization* (Montessori, 1964). As a doctor, she understood this mental state and recognized when children were calm, alert, and learning in contrast to times they were merely obedient or were actively misbehaving. She was asked to intervene in a tenement renovation where children had been gathered into a room to protect the building from damage and was initially renowned for turning these semi-feral children into productive and positive learners. Montessori, in her approach, found ways and means to support children in autonomous activity through which they became normalized—in contemporary terms, self-regulated—and able to learn well.

In this book, Jacobs shows us how strong teachers offer structures in their environments that help children self-regulate. Notice how Sharon draws the children into thinking further about the river valley they were studying, and how she brings the valley inside the classroom. And take note of Lauren's description of how she decides to organize spaces in her classroom: she thinks through the routines she wants the children to follow and, from this imagined activity, constructs the spaces that will contain those routines. It is a profound act of deep knowledge and experience in how to coordinate the organization of time and space for optimal learning and living together. Most programs for young children are an amalgam of organization of time and of space, but anyone who thinks a tight time schedule is appropriate for young children is missing an understanding of how organization of space supports self-regulation, and how children build concentration through the self-selected activity of play and inquiry. Readers of this book will encounter many marvelous strategies for creating supportive environments.

THE ROLE OF PARTICIPATORY STRUCTURES

Participatory structures are organizational designs that offer multiple ways for members of a group to be active and to belong. Participants have the power to make decisions, a sense of ownership in the setting, and multiple ways of knowing they belong. Participation is choosing what to do, whom to do it with, and for how long. Of course, children require lots of support. Teachers orchestrate, make suggestions, offer ideas and questions, and direct with authority when necessary but permit a wide range of acceptable activity. Such an approach allows children and teachers to be authentic and to respond to each other with genuine interest, and it permits curriculum to emerge as a reflection of what is most significant at the time to the children and educators.

Jacobs shows how the four teachers in her research invited children's play and inquiry into their programs and makes the connection between the presence of these and Mihaly Csikszentmihalyi's notion of flow (2008). Csikszentmihalyi spent his career as a psychologist studying what made people happy. He found it did not matter what the activity was—whether reading braille or mountain climbing, the mental state was the same. It was a state of total concentration on an autotelic (self-motivating) activity that was challenging to the player, and in which the player had the necessary skills to meet the challenge. He called this state *flow* because the sense of time disappears or is altered and argued that people emerge from such activity happy and satisfied. We are too busy concentrating for such feelings to arise during the activity, but we feel happy afterwards because, he argues, we have made ourselves more integrated.

Jacobs shows how these four teachers support play and inquiry so that the children are frequently in states we would describe as flow. Their enjoyment of school is embedded in such activity. What they are learning arises from many sources—materials to explore and create with, friends to interact and negotiate with, books and blocks to think with, questions and problems to explore, stories and images to create, and, running through it all, the deep feeling that leads events to be memorable. Remembered.

As a reader, you will encounter four pairs of educators creating classrooms in which learning is profound, rich, and shared by the collective of children and educators. The specific inquiries that developed in each classroom show how curriculum emerges from the authentic interactions that occur and shows the wonderful range of possible inquiries. In each case, readers will see how teachers are able to sustain children's collective inquiry through strategies they have developed. They might alter the environment, they might ask a question, they might share what others have done—they have a thousand strategies, and you will delight in finding them and comparing them to your own. I thank Jacobs for revealing the work of these teachers to us, for taking the photographs that document and bring to life the children's activities, and for sustaining her own capacity to bring to us in such sharp detail how these teachers make children's learning so rich and powerful. I take the liberty of mentioning one of my favourite moments when the children catch Darlene (absorbed with necessary preparations for lunch) to tell her they want to run: it's not something she can organize at that moment and she responds with, "What's your plan?" Ah, you better have a plan if you want to do something.

Jacobs has given us, through her comprehensive documentation skills, a portrait of four teachers and of four classrooms, as each engaged in an inquiry that emerged from authentic moments of play and conversation in the children's activity. She shows us what the children did and how the adults supported their interactions, and from this builds her own theory of how such complex projects occur. You as a reader may compare these episodes to experiences in your own classrooms, finding aspects that are parallel and perhaps finding new ideas for supporting your own children in functioning well in large learning groups. This book is Jacobs's inquiry into how self-regulation might occur in classrooms for young children and, through her own thoughtful conversations with the teachers and documentation of processes, she has provided a set of answers to consider. Taking care of the emotions of members of the group, observing how the design of the environment supports how teachers want children to act, and building participatory structures that allow a sense of belonging and community are a few of the complex processes you will encounter here. The commitment to high-quality education for young children from everyone involved in this book is a commitment to patience and beauty in creating caring relationships as a foundation for learning. I have profound gratitude for that commitment.

Carol Anne Wien, PhD
Faculty of Education, York University

PREFACE

The origins of this book can be traced to my interest in emergent curriculum, inquiry-based learning, and self-regulation as a teacher, parent, graduate student, and professor. Although I had already taught in public schools for 15 years, I first learned about emergent curriculum as a graduate student while working on my Master of Education. This new knowledge led to a rich four-month-long ethnographic research study in my kindergarten classroom that focused on children's conversations during an emergent curriculum inquiry (Jacobs, 2008). My interest in inquiry-based learning ultimately led me to teach at an independent school for four years where I had the freedom to explore emergent curriculum inquiries with my grade 1 students. I found the last few years I spent teaching young children to be the most exhilarating, as this type of curriculum planning was much closer to my own personal beliefs about exemplary teaching and learning.

In 2010, I attended a conference where Dr. Stuart Shanker was a keynote speaker talking about the importance of self-regulation. His address had a huge impact on me because it helped me to understand why my youngest son, Noah, had had difficulty self-regulating at school. Noah at the time found it hard to form social relationships with his peers, reacted impulsively, and as a result got into trouble. This left him feeling ashamed and embarrassed, extremely anxious, and uncomfortable in his own skin. It also had a huge impact on him academically, as he had difficulty paying attention in class and learning how to write. A year before Shanker's keynote I had moved Noah to a gifted program in a public school where he started to flourish. As a parent, I regretted that I had not heard Stuart speak about self-regulation years earlier, as it would have helped me to understand what Noah was going through at the time. I came home from that conference feeling like I had experienced an epiphany in terms of my own understanding of self-regulation. As a result, I was able to reflect on and think about how self-regulation had impacted both my personal life and professional career over the years.

It was my interest in inquiry-based learning and Stuart's keynote address about self-regulation that inspired me to write this book. My hunch at the time was that one of the very significant, but largely unexplored, benefits of emergent curriculum as a teaching practice is that it supports the children's ability to self-regulate, which, as Pascal (2009) states, "is the central building block of early learning" (p. 4). By studying four classroom environments where teachers co-construct emergent curriculum inquiries with the children, I hoped to discover insightful research findings that would help educators to better appreciate the potential of emergent curriculum inquiries to support children's ability to self-regulate at an optimal learning level. The empirical research findings I ultimately report on in this book offer new evidence of a relationship between self-regulation and inquiry-based learning.

Brenda Jacobs, PhD
Faculty of Education, Ontario Tech University

ACKNOWLEDGEMENTS

I am grateful to all the teachers, Early Childhood Educators, and children for their participation in the research that led to this book. It was an absolute delight to work with them on the emergent curriculum inquiries. Thank you to the teachers and Early Childhood Educators for allowing me to immerse myself in their classrooms and taking the time to share their thinking about self-regulation and inquiry-based learning. Without their generosity, this book would not have been possible. Thank you to all the children for their boundless enthusiasm to participate in the emergent curriculum inquiries and share their ideas, questions, and theories. They were a constant reminder that only by being attentive to what children say and do can we truly see that they are "rich in potential, strong, powerful, competent, and most of all connected to adults and other children" (Malaguzzi, 1994).

I would like to thank Dr. Carol Anne Wien, Dr. Stuart Shanker, and Dr. Jacqueline Lynch for their invaluable contributions to this book. Throughout the years, Dr. Carol Anne Wien has been a mentor and a friend. I value her knowledge and passion for the field of early childhood education and all things Reggio-inspired. Carol Anne's ability to push me to think more deeply about my research and express my ideas in a succinct manner have made the arguments and insights in this book stronger. Most importantly, she has taught me that there are many different ways to slice a cake. Dr. Stuart Shanker's work has helped me to truly understand the meaning of self-regulation as arousal regulation and I thank him for sharing his knowledge, positive feedback, and advice over the years. Dr. Jacqueline Lynch has provided continued support, words of encouragement, and helpful suggestions.

Two of my former B.Ed. students, Bryden MacDonald (OCT) and Shangavi Raveendran (OCT), contributed to the epilogue. In the fall of 2020, we offered a workshop called "Inquiry-based Learning in an Online Primary Classroom" at the Sharing Excellence in Online and Blended Learning conference for K–12 teachers at Ontario Tech University. The inspiration for this workshop came about because of the COVID-19 pandemic. As you will see in this book, inquiry-based learning is an effective way to support children becoming self-regulated learners. Yet there is very little guidance for educators about how to implement inquiry-based learning in a virtual classroom. Bryden and Shangavi researched and demonstrated a range of online educational platforms as we explored the four components of emergent curriculum with the participants.

I would also like to recognize the continued love and support of my family throughout this journey. Thank you to my mother, Geraldine, my husband, Les, and our four children, Aaron, Grace, Oliver, and Noah. Les's encouragement to pursue this research and his reassurance throughout the process gave me the strength to see the writing through to completion. Lastly, a special thank you to Noah for being the true inspiration behind my quest to better understand self-regulation and write this book.

INTRODUCTION

> Self-regulation is the cornerstone of development and is the central building block of early learning. Self-regulation is the ability to adapt one's emotions, behaviours and attention to the demands of the situation. Attention skills, working memory and cognitive flexibility underlie planning and problem-solving. The capacity to make inferences about others' mental states, such as intentions, emotions, desires and beliefs, is used to interpret behaviour and regulate social interactions. The regulation of attention is essential to children's learning dispositions or habits of mind and action, including persistence, curiosity and approaching new experiences with confidence.
> —Charles Pascal, 2009, p. 4

This book is designed to explore the relationship between self-regulation and inquiry-based learning in primary classrooms. Self-regulation can be understood as a reflective learning process where children become aware of what it feels like to be overstressed, recognize when they need to up-regulate or down-regulate, and develop strategies to reduce their stress and restore their energy. This process enables children to see themselves as self-regulated learners in a manner that has long-term implications for their capacity to learn. Self-regulation is an increasingly prominent issue because children are experiencing much more stress than in the past, especially since the beginning of the COVID-19 pandemic. This has resulted in many more social, emotional, behavioural, cognitive, physical, and mental health problems (Cost et al., 2021; Offord Centre for Child Studies, 2020; Statistics Canada, 2020; Vaillancourt, McDougall et al., 2021; Vaillancourt, Szatmari et al., 2021). There is a broad consensus in educational research that how well students do in school depends on how well they can self-regulate (Blair & Diamond, 2008; Blair & Razza, 2007; Fitzpatrick & Pagani, 2013; Jones et al., 2017; McClelland et al., 2006; McClelland & Cameron, 2011; Ponitz et al., 2009; Rimm-Kaufman et al., 2009; Shanker, 2013b, 2016; Welsh et al., 2010). Many professionals consider self-regulation to be a better indicator of school success than IQ. As the statement from Charles Pascal (2009) above suggests, self-regulation has come to be recognized as fundamental to learning in the primary years.

Inquiry-based learning is an approach to teaching and learning in the primary classroom that places students' observations, questions, ideas, and theories at the centre of intellectually stimulating learning experiences. It encourages active learning and critical thinking through collaborative student-led investigations guided by interesting questions or problems. As inquiries evolve, students and teachers co-construct knowledge by sharing multiple perspectives. Inquiry-based learning enables students "to address curriculum content in integrated and 'real world' ways and to develop—and practice—the higher-order thinking skills and habits of mind that lead to deep learning" (Ontario Ministry of Education, 2011). Banchi and Bell (2008) identify a continuum of inquiry-based learning from low-level structured inquiry to high-level open inquiry. The continuum is organized around how much information is given to the students and how much guidance is provided by the teacher. Open inquiry involves students formulating and investigating their own questions.

Emergent curriculum, also known as negotiated curriculum, is a particular type of curriculum planning or teaching practice that supports inquiry-based learning. It focuses on what the children are learning, while an inquiry-based approach explains how the children will go about it. Emergent curriculum inquiries, like open inquiries, are a specific kind of inquiry-based learning. They are sustained investigations that emerge from either the children's or teachers' interests, encounters with materials in the classroom, or unexpected events. The curriculum is built around the children's interests and is co-constructed between the teachers and children as the inquiry unfolds. The topic under investigation develops and moves fluidly and organically as it expands. Its path is determined by the connections the children and teachers make as they bring their ideas and theories to the topic under investigation. Emergent curriculum inquiries by their nature are culturally relevant and responsive because they respect the learners' cultures and lived experiences (UNESCO, 2021).

This book shows how inquiry-based learning enables children to become self-regulated learners in the primary classroom by focusing on four examples of emergent curriculum inquiries. These inquiries were undertaken in Canadian primary classrooms and are used to illustrate concretely the relationship between self-regulation and inquiry-based learning. Three of the inquiries involved educators working in a large district school board in the Greater Toronto Area (GTA). Lauren, Darlene, and Sharon are experienced teachers who are inspired by the Reggio Emilia approach, and their programs are an interpretation of those principles and practices. They all have expertise generating and studying pedagogical documentation based on the emergent curriculum inquiries they co-construct with the children in their classrooms. Mikayla is both a certified teacher and an Early Childhood Educator (ECE). She is also Reggio-inspired and has a strong background in early childhood development. Vanessa and Kerri are ECEs who likewise bring their knowledge of early childhood development to the inquiry process. The other emergent curriculum inquiry was undertaken at a well-established independent school for girls in the GTA. Kathryn and Victoria are both experienced teachers. Kathryn is also Reggio-inspired and has expertise generating and studying pedagogical documentation. Victoria was just learning about pedagogical documentation for the first time. There were 103 children from diverse backgrounds who participated in the inquiries. Fifty-six percent of the children came from racialized communities, including Black, East Asian, Middle Eastern, and South Asian. One-third of the children were English Language Learners (ELLs). Just over half of the students were girls. This diversity in the student population is reflective of the GTA. The emergent curriculum inquiries were all culturally relevant and responsive to the students.

There are four compelling insights about the relationship between self-regulation and inquiry-based learning introduced and explored in this book. The first insight is that children learn how to self-regulate during inquiry-based learning in the same way they do during play. Inquiries support the children's ability to self-regulate in the same way as play does because they emerge from the children's interests, they are enjoyable and intrinsically rewarding, and there is a sense of control over the activity. The organization of physical space and

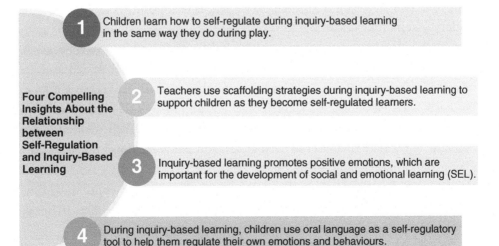

Four Compelling Insights About the Relationship between Self-Regulation and Inquiry-Based Learning

1 Children learn how to self-regulate during inquiry-based learning in the same way they do during play.

2 Teachers use scaffolding strategies during inquiry-based learning to support children as they become self-regulated learners.

3 Inquiry-based learning promotes positive emotions, which are important for the development of social and emotional learning (SEL).

4 During inquiry-based learning, children use oral language as a self-regulatory tool to help them regulate their own emotions and behaviours.

materials for the purpose of facilitating children's interests and autonomy during play and inquiry enables them to stay focused, consider other perspectives, and figure out their own thinking. Classroom environments can be designed so that children can independently choose where to go so they can up-regulate or down-regulate their energy levels. Expansive time frames give children more time to develop skills such as independence, resourcefulness, risk-taking, perseverance, problem-solving, initiative, and creativity in the multiple domains of self-regulation. Children stay immersed in play and inquiry while working collaboratively and inclusively with others, as they are in a state of experiential flow and can ignore distractions. Children can concentrate and feel capable of meeting the demands that an inquiry places on them.

The second insight is that teachers use scaffolding strategies during inquiry-based learning to support children as they become self-regulated learners. Scaffolding reduces children's stress levels and their aversion to risk-taking so they can move to a higher level of cognitive functioning. When teachers use documentation to scaffold children's thinking, it also strengthens their memory as they review previous thinking, self-correct, find confirmation and denials, and make comparisons with the theories and ideas of others. Teachers adapt and extend their classroom environments to enhance children's self-regulation by planning provocations that enable children to think through their ideas and theories. Reciprocal actions that are challenging, but not overwhelming, support self-regulation because they enable the children to feel more confident and stay focused on the investigation.

The third insight is that inquiry-based learning promotes positive emotions, which are important for the development of social and emotional learning (SEL). A central finding from the field of SEL is that positive emotions such as elation, inspiration, pride, and curiosity generate energy, while negative emotions such as fear consume energy, making it difficult for students to concentrate and pay attention (Jones & Kahn, 2017). When children feel valued and are invested in an inquiry, they learn to listen to others and have a greater ability to modulate their emotions, work collaboratively, and take pride in their achievements. During inquiries, children become more aware of their own emotions and how to regulate them as the need arises. Authentic relationships that create a sense of belonging and the capacity for empathy promote positive behaviours in the prosocial domain. Daily routines that are predictable help children become more independent as they can anticipate transitions, which enable them to up- or down-regulate knowing what activity is coming next.

The fourth insight is that during inquiry-based learning children use oral language as a self-regulatory tool to help them regulate their own emotions and behaviours. Oral language enables thinking to become more complex and flexible. It allows children to imagine, manipulate, and create new ideas, as well as to share their ideas and theories with others. When children express their thinking during inquiry-based learning, speech is used to help them understand, clarify, and focus their thoughts. Conversation provides children with opportunities to use their cognitive processes to solve difficult tasks and social conflicts, which is important for self-regulated learning. Children draw on their cognitive processes like reasoning, problem-solving, flexible thinking, multitasking, and working memory to clarify their thinking when revisiting documentation. This helps strengthen children's executive functions so they can reduce the tension created by stress. In the next chapter, I position these four insights in relation to current scholarship on self-regulation.

OVERVIEW OF CHAPTERS

Chapter 1 defines self-regulation in terms of how it is understood as arousal regulation, describes the five domains that are sources of stress, explains how children develop self-regulation, and examines research on self-regulation in schools. It also discusses educational policy across Canada and differences in how the provinces embrace SEL and self-regulation more generally.

Chapter 2 initially frames emergent curriculum and then provides a detailed explanation of the four components of emergent curriculum I discovered, which are inquiry design, design of the environment, conversation, and documentation. Inquiries undertaken in Canadian primary classrooms—the Invisibility Inquiry, the Office Inquiry, the Running Club Inquiry, and the Community Inquiry—are described and then used to illustrate each of these components in chapters 3 to 6.

Chapter 3 focuses on self-regulation and the inquiry design component of emergent curriculum. The inquiries introduced in chapter 2 are used here to illustrate concretely the relationship between self-regulation and inquiry design, which is one of the components that support inquiry-based learning. Inquiry design has five aspects—building the curriculum, engaging in reciprocal actions, taking ownership over the direction of the inquiry, promoting positive emotions such as excitement and curiosity, and encouraging collaboration and inclusivity—that when considered together clearly demonstrate how inquiry design enables children to become self-regulated learners in the classroom. The insights about the relationship between self-regulation and inquiry-based learning outlined above are interwoven throughout this chapter.

Chapter 4 focuses on self-regulation and the design of the environment, which is another component of emergent curriculum that supports inquiry-based learning. As in chapter 3, inquiries are used to illustrate concretely the relationship between self-regulation and the design of the environment. This design component has six aspects—organizing the classroom space and materials, keeping the environment uncluttered and neutral, adapting and extending beyond the classroom, developing daily routines, using expansive time frames, and building authentic relationships—that show that the design of the environment enables children to become self-regulated learners. Once again, the insights about the relationship between self-regulation and inquiry-based learning are interwoven into the discussion.

Chapter 5 focuses on self-regulation and the conversation component of emergent curriculum. The conversation component has four aspects—encouraging children to participate, expressing their different ideas and theories, nurturing their reasoning and problem-solving capabilities, and supporting their awareness of how to regulate their emotions—that illustrate that conversation enables children to become self-regulated learners in the primary classroom. The inquiries provide illustrations of the relationship between self-regulation and conversation. As explained above, one compelling insight about the relationship between self-regulation and inquiry-based learning is that children use oral language as a self-regulatory tool to help them regulate their own emotions and behaviours. This insight is evident and interwoven throughout this chapter.

Chapter 6 focuses on self-regulation and the documentation component of emergent curriculum, which also supports inquiry-based learning. The inquiries provide concrete examples of the relationship between self-regulation and documentation. The first three aspects involve teachers revisiting documentation with the children to keep them invested in the inquiry, scaffold their thinking, and help them better understand their own theories and ideas. The other aspect involves the teachers studying the documentation to reflect on the children's thinking and their engagement in the inquiry. When these four aspects are considered together, they demonstrate how the documentation component enables children to become self-regulated learners. The insights about the relationship between self-regulation and inquiry-based learning are also interwoven into the discussion of documentation.

Chapter 7 concludes that inquiry-based learning helps children to become self-regulated learners in innovative and unanticipated ways. I then discuss future directions by exploring how self-regulation might play an especially critical role in helping children with exceptionalities address their needs. I identify how the four insights about inquiry-based learning and self-regulation can inform our thinking about exceptional learners in the classroom. I suggest that inquiry-based learning has extraordinary potential to help children with exceptionalities become self-regulated learners, but more research needs to be done.

In the epilogue, I address the major disruption in education we have experienced because of the COVID-19 pandemic. Children are being educated online in virtual classrooms, which has left educators scrambling to come up with new and innovative ways to deliver curriculum and hold children's attention. I introduce four key elements, mirroring the four components of emergent curriculum, that must be present in a virtual classroom setting to enable educators to implement an inquiry-based approach to teaching and learning. I then review some online educational platforms to demonstrate how it is possible to engage in inquiry-based learning, which is an effective way to support children becoming self-regulated learners in virtual classrooms.

Chapter One

What Is Self-Regulation?

> In essence, "self-regulation" refers to a child's ability to deal with stressors effectively and efficiently and then return to a baseline of being calmly focused and alert. The more smoothly a child can make the transitions from being hypo-aroused (necessary for recovery) to hyper-aroused (necessary to meet a challenge) and return to being calmly focused and alert, the better is said to be his or her "optimal regulation."
> —Stuart Shanker, 2012b, p. 12

The term *self-regulation* has no universal definition and has been used in many different ways, depending on the discipline and the interests of researchers (Rimm-Kaufman & Wanless, 2012; Shanker, 2016; Wasik & Herrmann, 2004). However, there are significant overlaps among most researchers about how they understand self-regulation. Some researchers think about self-regulation as executive functions (see Blair & Diamond, 2008; Blair & Razza, 2007; Blair & Ursache, 2011; Bodrova & Leong, 2008; Diamond et al., 2007; Fitzpatrick & Pagani, 2013; McClelland et al., 2006; McClelland & Cameron, 2011; Ponitz et al., 2009; Welsh et al., 2010). Other researchers think about self-regulation as self-control (see Bauer & Baumeister, 2011; Duckworth & Carlson, 2013; Rimm-Kaufman et al., 2009; Rimm-Kaufman & Wanless, 2012). Still other researchers think about self-regulation as self-regulated learning (see Grolnick et al., 1999; Horner & Shwery, 2002; Schunk & Zimmerman, 2007). My own understanding of self-regulation aligns with the many researchers who think about it as arousal regulation (Lillas & Turnbull, 2009; Mastrangelo, 2012; Porges, 2011, 2015a; Shanker, 2013a, 2013b, 2016, 2020; Vohs & Baumeister, 2011).

Despite the absence of agreement on how precisely to define self-regulation, there is a broad consensus in the research that how well students do in school depends on how well they can self-regulate (Blair & Diamond, 2008; Blair & Razza, 2007; Fitzpatrick & Pagani, 2013; Jones et al., 2017; McClelland et al.,

2006; McClelland & Cameron, 2011; Ponitz et al., 2009; Rimm-Kaufman et al., 2009; Shanker, 2013b, 2016; Welsh et al., 2010). In recent years, self-regulation has received a lot of attention from teachers, researchers, and policy makers because it is so beneficial to children's learning.

SELF-REGULATION AS AROUSAL REGULATION

Self-regulation, in my view, is a reflective learning process where children become aware of what it feels like to be overstressed, recognize when they need to up-regulate or down-regulate, and develop strategies to reduce their stress and restore their energy. This view is in alignment with scholarship on self-regulation as arousal-regulation. Vohs and Baumeister (2011), for example, describe self-regulation as the ability to:

1.   Attain, maintain, and change one's level of energy to match the demands of a task or situation.
2.   Monitor, evaluate, and modify one's emotions.
3.   Sustain and shift one's attention when necessary and ignore distractions.
4.   Understand both the meaning of a variety of social interactions and how to engage in them in a sustained way.
5.   Connect with and care about what others are thinking and feeling— to empathize and act accordingly. (cited in Shanker, 2013b)

The adoption here of this understanding of self-regulation in terms of arousal regulation follows other important educational research on self-regulation in Canada (Hawes et al., 2012; Pelletier, 2014a; Timmons et al., 2016).

Arousal regulation requires drawing a distinction between self-control and self-regulation. Self-control is about inhibiting impulses, whereas self-regulation is about identifying the causes of stress, reducing their intensity and, if necessary, having enough energy to resist (Rimm-Kaufman & Wanless, 2012). Self-regulation occurs when a child deals effectively and efficiently with everyday stressors like noise, movement, light, or frightening experiences and then recovers, whereas self-control requires a child to delay gratification and resist an impulse or to comply with a norm by suppressing a behaviour to avoid punishment or receive a reward (Shanker 2013b, 2020). Self-regulation involves identifying hidden stressors and reducing the causes of problems in children's moods, thoughts, and behaviours. Self-control only identifies surface behaviours and seeks to inhibit or manage problems only when they occur. Self-regulation is what makes self-control possible or even unnecessary. A child needs to be calmly focused and alert to learn the skills that underpin self-control. Children's self-control skills can be significantly enhanced, but first we have to work on their self-regulation. Pascal (2009) explains, "Self-regulation is not about compliance with external authorities—it is about establishing one's own internal motivation for adapting to and understanding emotional and social demands. In fact, for many children, requiring compliance undermines their own abilities to self-regulate" (p. 4).

Shanker (2016), a leading Canadian expert in arousal regulation, explains that the original psycho-physiological reference is "to how we manage the stresses that we are under. And 'stress' in its original sense refers to all those stimuli that require us to expend energy to maintain some kind of balance" (p. 5). When a child is able to maintain this balance, they are self-regulated. Optimal regulation is the capacity to recover back to baseline when making gradual and rapid changes along the arousal continuum as well as to modulate the highs and lows of energy within each level. It includes six critical elements: (1) when feeling calmly focused and alert, the ability to know that one is calm and alert; (2) when one is stressed, the ability to recognize what is causing that stress; (3) the ability to recognize stressors both within and outside the classroom; (4) the desire to deal with those stressors; (5) the ability to develop strategies for dealing with those stressors; and (6) the ability to recover efficiently and effectively from dealing with stressors.

Stressors for children can be psychosocial, environmental, positive or negative emotions, patterns that are hard to recognize, and the stress of others. The sympathetic nervous system works by releasing adrenaline and cortisol, thereby activating energy to up-regulate, whereas the parasympathetic nervous system works by releasing acetylcholine and serotonin to down-regulate. Shanker (2016) argues that arousal-regulation "is a function of the complementary forces of sympathetic nervous system (SNS) activation, which makes us more aroused, and parasympathetic nervous system (PNS) inhibition, which slows everything down" (p. 19). We constantly shift up and down this arousal scale: as arousal goes up, so does energy consumption; as it goes down, we are able to restore our reserves. The autonomic nervous system is the system that regulates the transitions between these arousal states.

Throughout the day, because of the sympathetic and parasympathetic nervous systems, children move through different arousal states. These systems meet the demands for energy expenditure and then replenishing energy and recovery. When a child is overstressed, their brain finds it harder to manage these transitions and the recovery function is less resilient, so the child becomes stuck in an aroused state. When a child is in chronic hypo-arousal or hyper-arousal, they have difficulty attending to and processing internal and external sensations both physically and emotionally. When this happens, they are highly susceptible to impulsivity and aggression (Berger, 2011; Shanker, 2016).

Some children need to work much harder to block out stressors (Shanker, 2010). Focusing attention over a long period of time drains children's energy, which diminishes their ability to sustain their attention. The harder they have to work the less energy they have left over to learn. Children need to be able to access the appropriate arousal level (asleep, drowsy, hypo-alert, calmly focused and alert, hyper-alert and flooded) for the situation in which they are engaged. When a child is hyper-alert and their nervous system is overloaded, they feel fatigued and it can be difficult for them to focus on a task or listen to what someone else is saying. When a child is hypo-alert, and their nervous system is overloaded, they might be withdrawn and show a lack of engagement in learning tasks or daydream for prolonged periods of time. A hypo-alert child is less inclined to become engaged in social interactions and is more likely to miss out on shared learning experiences with their peers. A hyper-alert child, on the other hand, is less able to remain engaged in social interactions and cannot sustain the necessary focus to learn (Shanker, 2013b). By reducing the stressors on the nervous system, children have more resources to control their impulses and can access the arousal level appropriate for the learning situation.

Self-regulation is a prominent issue today because it has been found that children are experiencing much more stress than in the past. In his review of research, Shanker (2012a, 2013b) found that a major new worry for researchers is "that urbanization brings with it all sorts of physical and psychological stresses that test a child who might have coped better in a more rustic setting" (p. 106). In cities, there are lots of visual, auditory, and social stimuli and a lack of green space. Many stressors are also affecting children who live outside cities. There have been fundamental changes in family and social patterns in recent decades. Children are experiencing a decline in exercise and participation in sports, as well as a change in eating and sleeping habits. There are fewer experiences with nature and a dramatic increase in the amount of time children spend playing video games. Children are also exposed to violent or troubling emotional themes in the media. In addition, young children are spending longer periods of time in formal education settings, and many children are having trouble meeting this challenge, which has led to more behavioural problems.

The COVID-19 pandemic has magnified many stressors that children face. Virtually all aspects of children's development have been affected by the pandemic. For example, according to the Offord Centre for Child Studies (2020), the COVID-19 pandemic imposed unprecedented levels of stress and adversity on Canadian families due to prolonged isolation resulting from closures of schools, extracurricular programs, outdoor recreational spaces, and social events. Forty percent of parents indicated that their child's mood or behaviour had deteriorated. Statistics Canada (2020) found that many parents were concerned about their children's social engagement during the pandemic. Three-quarters were concerned about their children's opportunities to socialize with friends, and half about their children's loneliness or social isolation. Two-thirds of parents were similarly concerned about managing their children's emotions, behaviours, stress levels, and anxiety. The younger the children, the greater their concerns.

Vaillancourt, Szatmari, et al. (2021) report that emergency room visits at Toronto's Hospital for Sick Children for mental health concerns rose 120 percent during the pandemic. They explain, "factors like the lack of contact with peers and teachers, the fear of health and death of family members, and the decreased structure in daily living seem to have contributed to increased anxiety, depression, and behavioural problems in many children" (p. 16). Cost et al. (2021) found that 70 percent of school-aged children experienced deterioration in at least one aspect of mental health, including depression, anxiety, irritability, attention, hyperactivity, obsessions, and compulsions. Deterioration in anxiety and irritability were highest among children in the primary grades. This deterioration is strongly associated with stress related to social isolation.

THE FIVE DOMAINS OF SELF-REGULATION

Stressors can be organized around the five-domain model. This model is based on the claim that too much stress is an important explanation for why a child might be having difficulty paying attention, ignoring distractors, inhibiting impulses, modulating their emotions, or staying calmly focused and alert. While the sources of stressors can be biological, cognitive, emotional, social, or prosocial, the underlying mechanisms for self-regulation reside in the biological domain. Often a child's stressors come from a combination of some or all of these domains. The five domains are linked in complex ways and influence one

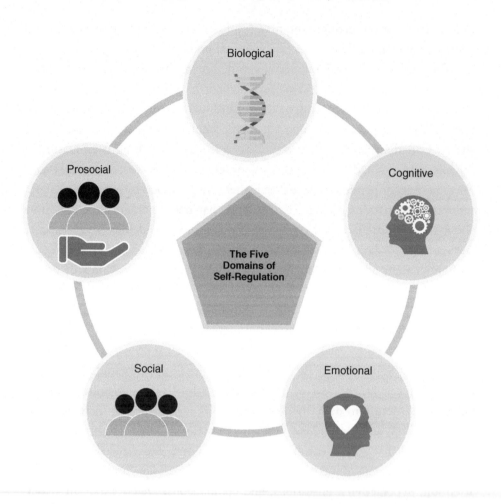

another, so that a problem in one domain can exacerbate problems in the others (Shanker 2013b, 2016). The multiplier effect occurs when one stress makes the child more sensitive to other stressors.

The biological domain is the level of energy in the human nervous system that varies depending on a child's disposition and the situation they are in. Lewis and Todd (2007) state that the brain is designed to regulate bodily processes and is the fundamental organ of self-regulation. The brain regulates our nervous system by releasing chemicals to control arousal. In order for the brain to perform this function, it needs to know what is important and be in tune with the ever-changing stream of events in the world. Shanker (2013a, 2016) explains that when a child encounters stress, they burn energy. The brain will then deal with the stressor by releasing adrenaline and cortisol, which will get their heart racing, increase the pace of their breathing, and raise their blood pressure so that they can deal with the stress. This can lead to hyper-alertness and a rapid depletion of energy, so the child needs to down-regulate. Then the brain will release acetylcholine and serotonin to calm the system down. This can lead to hypo-alertness, so the child needs to up-regulate.

Children who fidget or flit from one activity to another are self-regulating to allow for optimal functioning where they can change their arousal level quickly to match the energy level needed to fit with different learning situations in an efficient manner. Some children need more energy to reach a state of equilibrium and then have less energy to attend to other demands on them. Some of these children, for example, are hypersensitive to sensory input in the environment. Their nervous system becomes quickly overloaded and either shuts out the stimuli by withdrawing (hypo-alert) or becomes overstimulated (hyper-alert). Children who are hypo-alert need to up-regulate by increasing their level and expenditure of energy, so they are aroused sufficiently enough to learn. Children who are hyper-alert need to down-regulate by decreasing their level and expenditure of energy. In the biological domain, stressors include poor nutrition, lack of sleep, not enough movement or exercise, motor and sensorimotor challenges, sensory stimuli, allergens, pollution, and extreme temperatures (Shanker, 2016).

The cognitive domain of arousal regulation refers to thinking and learning, which includes mental processes such as memory, attention, problem-solving, and the acquisition and retention of information. Self-regulation here means that children can efficiently sustain and switch attention, sequence their thoughts, keep different pieces of information in their mind simultaneously, ignore distractions, and inhibit impulsive behaviour. Metacognition (the awareness and understanding of one's own thinking) and executive functions (cognitive processes that regulate areas like planning, working memory, mental flexibility, multitasking, and problem-solving) are both important for self-regulation. Self-regulation serves as a critical foundation for the effectiveness of executive functions. The more regulated a child is, the better they can develop and exercise their executive functions. Cognitive processes like perception and awareness are the foundation for the development and operation of executive functions. In the cognitive domain, stressors include limited awareness of external and internal stimuli, sensory information that is difficult for a child to process, sensory experiences that are hard for a child to understand, too much information presented too quickly or slowly, information that is too abstract, and information that requires too much concentration (Shanker, 2016).

Diamond et al. (2007) explain the link between self-regulation and executive functions. There are three components of executive functions: inhibition, working memory, and cognitive flexibility (see also Blair & Razza, 2007; Blair & Ursache, 2011). Inhibitory control, or effortful control, is the ability to resist doing one thing in order to do something else that is more appropriate or needed. In general, you avoid giving in to your first impulse and provide a more considered response. Our ability to inhibit attention to distractions makes it possible to sustain attention and remain focused. Inhibition allows us control over our attention and actions. Working memory is the ability to hold on to information and be able to work with or manipulate that information. It means the ability to hold information in mind despite distraction or while you do something else. The information can be newly learned or retrieved from long-term storage. Cognitive flexibility or attentional set-shifting is the ability to adjust to new priorities and consider something from a new perspective or "think outside the box." It builds on inhibition and working memory. These three aspects of cognition are important for planning, monitoring of behaviour, and future-directed thinking (Blair & Ursache, 2011).

Self-regulation involves in part the ability to control our impulses and inhibit doing something, as well as the capacity to do something even if we don't want to (Bodrova & Leong, 2008). Children who can self-regulate can delay gratification and suppress impulses in order to think ahead about the possible consequences of their actions and consider alternative choices. Executive functions refer to aspects of cognition that are called upon when the brain and behaviour cannot run on automatic. Blair and Diamond (2008) subsequently found that maladaptive cognitive and emotional regulation skills can undermine a child's performance in the primary classroom. Children who are angry, frustrated, and exhibit impulsive behaviour have difficulty concentrating in the classroom and are more aggressive towards their peers and teachers. This affects the child's self-perception and confidence around academic and social challenges. Having difficulty following instructions and cooperating with others at the start of school is likely to forecast later academic and social problems.

The international movement known as social and emotional learning (SEL) is encapsulated by the emotional, social, and prosocial domains of self-regulation. The Collaborative for Academic, Social, and Emotional Learning (CASEL) defines SEL as "the process of acquiring and effectively applying the knowledge, attitudes, and skills necessary to recognize and manage emotions; developing caring and concern for others; making responsible decisions; establishing positive relationships; and handling challenging situations capably" (Zins & Elias, 2007). Five core competencies are at the heart of the SEL movement and are seen as critical for a child's well-being as well as their educational success. These core competencies include self-awareness, self-management, social awareness, relationship skills, and responsible decision-making. This movement has been embraced across Canadian schools as they begin to introduce SEL programs into their curriculum.

SEL programs reflect the understanding that SEL competencies are as important and can be learned in the same way as academic skills. CASEL recognizes that there are barriers that prevent some students from developing these competencies and that in order for SEL to benefit all students it must advance the goals of equity and excellence in ways that are most meaningful to local diverse communities (CASEL, 2022a). In other words, SEL must be culturally relevant and responsive. Students learn, practice, and apply SEL skills in and out of the classroom by engaging in positive experiences and activities. Research has shown positive outcomes for these programs that have both psychological and academic benefits (Jones et al., 2017). Generally, there are improved social-emotional skills and academic achievement; attitudes toward school, self, and others; social behaviours and classroom environment; and mental health with the reduction of stress and anxiety. Vaillancourt, McDougall, et al. (2021) note that, since the COVID-19 pandemic, children are facing so many unprecedented and prolonged stressors that now more than ever they need to feel like they matter and build positive relationships with their teachers and peers. Many children's ability to learn and relate positively to others has or will be negatively affected. They argue it is important to invest in children's social and emotional development by implementing SEL programs at schools, as this will address the mental health and well-being of children in the wake of COVID-19.

The emotional domain is the realm of feelings and moods such as overexcitement, frustration, or fear, which are generally easy to identify. A central insight from the field of SEL is that positive emotions generate energy while negative emotions consume energy, making it difficult for students to concentrate and pay attention (Jones & Kahn, 2017). Excessive negative emotions can damage a child's mental health and impede their ability to learn. We must recognize that emotions are not just an aspect of the mind that needs to be controlled or suppressed. Cultivating a child's positive and prosocial emotions is just as important to self-regulation as learning how to control negative ones. Without positive affective interactions, we run the risk of reducing emotion regulation to behaviour management. Children can communicate their negative emotions through affect signals, which include tone of voice, gestures, and facial expressions, and modulate their emotions in response to others. These affect signals instill confidence in the child because they have a strategy to deal with disruptive emotions. The more difficulties a child has in other domains, the more likely they are to have negative emotions and low self-esteem. Cognitive abilities are dependent on how a child is functioning emotionally. In the emotional domain, stressors include new and confusing emotions, intense emotions, and complicated relationships (Shanker, 2016).

In the social domain, children who are optimally regulated understand, assess, and act on social cues and behave in a socially appropriate manner. Children who have strong social intelligence are good at co-regulation. This is a process where two people can adjust their own behaviour to help each other remain calm, focused, and alert. They understand what the other person is thinking and can interpret their affect cues and gestures. This process can be very difficult for some children. When these children experience problems in the social domain, it also effects their biological and emotional regulation in a profound way, and the reverse is also true. A child might be anxious, so they become tense, and this depletes their energy. They find it harder to pick up on subtle social cues and become even more anxious and less able to connect with friends. When their energy is low, it is harder for them to manage their impulsivity. The child finds it hard to explain with their words, and too much stress shows in their behaviour, mood, and inability to get along with or listen to others. When children become chronically stressed, they rely on adrenaline and cortisol to keep going and they become hyper or manic. In the social domain, stressors include difficult social situations, interpersonal conflicts, trauma, being victimized or witnessing acts of aggression, and social conflicts that arise from not understanding how our words and actions affect others (Jones & Doolittle, 2017; Jones & Kahn, 2017; Shanker, 2016).

The prosocial domain for self-regulation is where children engage in behaviours that are positive and helpful. These behaviours promote social acceptance, friendship, and empathy. A lack of skills in the prosocial domain can cause dysregulating effects across the other domains. Children who are optimally regulated in the prosocial domain have a heightened ability to stay calmly focused and alert when faced with stressors in the other domains. Empathy means to care about someone else's emotions, to try and help others deal with their emotions, and to be able to distinguish between others' emotions and your own. Empathy is based on a child's own experiences of what it feels like to be in the same situation as well as the ability to empathize more with some emotions rather than others. Children who lack empathy can experience emotional, psychological, or behavioural problems such as low self-esteem and/or bullying. Often these children have difficulty joining in social interactions with others, which makes school very difficult for them. When children co-regulate, they turn to one another for support, and this encourages the development of empathy. Children find the prosocial domain stressful because they must make the effort to resist selfish impulses and put the interests of others before their own (Shanker, 2013b).

Stressors in the prosocial domain include dealing with other people's emotions, putting the needs of others ahead of your own, tensions between differing values, feelings of guilt, and moral uncertainty. It is important to remember that these are potential stressors; what makes it a stressor is how it affects us and then how we respond. Stressors from any of the domains can trigger a stress cycle, especially when a child is in a low energy and high tension state. When a child is in this state, "the more difficult he is going to find any one domain or, in some cases, all of these domains. And the more challenging he finds one of these domains, the more this is going to deplete even further his overall energy reserves" (Shanker, 2016, p. 82).

THE DEVELOPMENT OF SELF-REGULATION

Children learn how to self-regulate by first being regulated by others (Florez, 2011; Greenspan & Shanker, 2004; Shanker, 2016, 2020). A baby's brain and their caregiver's brain share an intuitive channel of communication, which is sometimes called the *interbrain*. The interbrain is established and maintained by shared emotion, touch, eye contact, and voice. Babies have limited self-soothing reflexes, and they have difficulty moving between arousal states smoothly, so they need a caregiver to help them make these transitions. The caregiver reads the baby's cues—facial expressions, movements, and sounds—and adjusts their own behaviour to help up-regulate or down-regulate the baby as needed. These responses are physiological, so the caregiver feels what their baby is feeling. These intimate exchanges help set the baby's baseline state of arousal. The more stress a baby endures, the higher their baseline level of arousal, and the more reactive they are to stress. Some babies are more susceptible to heightened arousal and harder to calm.

The interbrain remains a feature of the parent-child relationship and is the foundation for other social relationships. The interbrain helps a child develop the ability to self-regulate. Shanker (2016) states that "It is by being regulated a child develops the ability to self-regulate. Regulating a child … [is] concerned with managing the child's arousal states until such time as the child can do this on her own" (p. 69). Greenspan and Shanker (2004) note that when a child is around 18 months old, they begin to make the transition from being regulated by others to self-regulation. This happens when they can convey their own emotions to others and understand their parents' emotional signals. The toddler starts to take a more active role in the self-regulatory process using emotionally expressive gestures such as tone of voice, body posture, or facial expressions and language to convey their feelings. Children begin to engage in back-and-forth emotional gesturing during conversations. It is the continuous flow of emotional gesturing that organizes and maintains these symbolic exchanges and provides a constant source of new emotions that stirs up the next sequence of ideas or words.

When children are between the ages of two and three, they begin to use oral language as a self-regulatory tool. Bodrova and Leong (2007) explain that for toddlers and preschoolers, "thinking and speech merge.… When children become capable of thinking as they talk, speech actually becomes a tool for understanding, clarifying, and focusing what is in their minds" (pp. 67–68). The origins of this idea can be traced back to the pioneering work of Lev Vygotsky (1978), who believed that oral language is fundamental to learning how to self-regulate. He explained that the "human capacity for language enables children to provide for auxiliary tools in the solution of difficult tasks, to overcome impulsive action, to plan a solution to a problem prior to its execution, and to master their own behavior" (p. 28). Bodrova and Leong (2007) note that for Vygotsky language makes "humans more efficient and effective problem solvers" (p. 64).

Vygotsky distinguishes between speech as a means of communication with others and egocentric or private speech. Private speech is defined by Kohlberg et al. (1968) in a seminal child development study as "speech which is not addressed or adapted to a listener (other than the child) and which is carried on with apparent satisfaction in the absence of any signs of understanding by a listener" (p. 692). Private speech is prevalent in children's conversations. It is not failed communication with others but rather it has the different function of "cognitive self-guidance." Oral language is used by children during private speech as a tool for self-regulation. Bodrova and Leong (2007) explain, "Speech directed outward enables us to communicate with other people, while speech directed inward allows us to communicate to ourselves, to regulate our own behavior and thinking" (p. 65). Children use private speech to think out loud and organize their thoughts while they work through problems independently. Private speech for children increases as tasks become more challenging and stressful (Diamond et al., 2007). Over time, self-directing private speech dissipates and becomes verbal thought (Kohlberg et al., 1968). Vygotsky believed that for young children "the speech used for communication and for private speech is not easily distinguished and occurs simultaneously in the same context. Public and private speech gradually separate into two distinct strands in older children and adults" (Bodrova & Leong, 2007, p. 69).

When children are between the ages of three and six, the rapid development of oral language plays a pivotal role in social development (Dickinson et al., 2013). Porges (2011) uses the term *neuroception* "to describe how neural circuits distinguish whether situations or people are safe, dangerous, or life-threatening … neuroception takes place in the primitive parts of the brain, without our conscious awareness" (p. 11). It is a neural process where our body reacts to features in the environment and will shift arousal states to deal with any potential risk (Porges, 2015b). Neuroception explains why social interaction can be both a stressor in itself and also the first line of defense to deal with stress. Self-regulation is concerned with neuroception and the social engagement system. When a neuroception of safety is triggered, our body calms down so we can attend to or socially engage with others. When a neuroception of danger is triggered, our body prepares to move. Porges (2011) explains that we might not be aware of danger on a cognitive level. However, our body has already started neural processes to signal a fight, flight, or freeze response. Even if cognitively we know there is no need to be frightened, our bodies betray us with an increase in heart rate, trembling, perspiring, or becoming dizzy. When our neuroception detects safety, it promotes physiological states that support positive social engagement behaviours. In order for the nervous system to switch effectively from defensive to social engagement strategies, it must assess the risk and, if the environment seems safe, it must inhibit the defensive reactions to fight, flee, or freeze.

Play is an especially valuable opportunity to exercise our nervous system in order to foster SEL. Play, for Porges (2015b), is a neural exercise where neuroceptions of danger and safety alternate. The social engagement system uses a prosodic voice, head gestures, and facial features to help us calm down. Play can transition into aggressive behaviour if the social engagement systems do not down-regulate a neuroception of danger. Play as a neural exercise improves the efficiency of the neural circuit to down-regulate a fight or flight behaviour. It enables children to transition efficiently from active to calm states. The ability to move rapidly to a calm state optimizes spontaneous and reciprocal social behaviours as well as facilitates efficient learning. Play strengthens our neural circuits that can down-regulate our defense systems. During play, children can down-regulate because of the social engagement system, although the effectiveness of this system requires practice. As the neural regulation of our social engagement system grows stronger, we become more resilient and can deal with challenges.

Play is also a major mechanism for developing executive functions and using oral language as a self-regulatory tool. During dramatic play, children engage in learning that is within their zone of proximal development and on the edge of their capabilities (Diamond et al., 2007). Children can plan their play scenario together ahead of time using conversations and private speech. Teachers are then able to approach play scenarios and prompt a discussion of what the children will do next. Role-playing facilitates the internalization of rules and expectations and imposes constraints on behaviour.

The influential psychologist Mihaly Csikszentmihalyi (1975, 2008) has discovered a common experiential state that he refers to as flow. Flow is "the state in which people are so involved in an activity that nothing else seems to matter; the experience itself is so enjoyable that people will do it even at great cost, for the sheer sake of doing it" (2008, p. 4). The most typical kind of flow experience is play. Csikszentmihalyi (1975) explains,

> It is the state in which action follows upon action according to an internal logic which seems to need no conscious intervention on our part. We experience it as a unified flowing from one moment to the next, in which we feel in control of our actions, and in which there is little distinction between self and environment; between stimulus and response; or between past, present and future. (p. 43)

Flow is experienced when there is a match between a child's capabilities and the tasks that they are performing. A person in flow is in control of their actions and their environment: "A sense of control is definitely one of the most important components of the flow experience" (p. 52). When children are in the experiential state of flow, I believe they are optimally self-regulated. "A flow activity allows people to concentrate their actions and ignore distractions. As a result, they feel in potential control of the environment … people performing it can temporarily forget their identity and its problems" (p. 55). During flow, children find the process intrinsically rewarding and therefore need no external goals or rewards.

Curiosity, exuberance, and receptivity are elements that connect play and self-regulation in the social domain. When play emerges from children's interests, it helps them to stay focused, consider other perspectives, and figure out their own thinking. When play is self-initiated and authentic, children are highly motivated to generate strategies to sustain the play. In other words, children have an incentive to self-regulate to sustain the play. Being sensitive towards others encourages them to continue playing. Understanding social cues is important for developing the ability to play cooperatively with others. It demands perspective taking, as a child has to figure out what others think. It encourages communication about what one wants and what others want. If teachers or other adults intervene, this intervention can take away from the benefit play has for helping children develop problem-solving and logical thinking strategies as well as the sense of self-worth and confidence that comes from independent self-regulation (Shanker, 2013b).

Pelletier (2014a) found that play and small group time were the classroom contexts that were most likely to promote self-regulation and engagement (see also Hawes et al., 2012; Timmons et al., 2016). Pelletier (2014b) added further that class observations showed that the children were more self-regulated and engaged during play as compared to sitting in a whole group, suggesting that children need play opportunities where they feel engaged and can regulate their behaviour. Hawes et al. (2012) claim that the research findings indicate that play drives children's learning and development in kindergarten. When children are playing, they are highly engaged and demonstrate self-regulation. Pelletier (2014a) claimed that the children in full-day kindergarten were much more able to inhibit responses, focus their attention, and regulate their behaviour. This strongly indicates that an important benefit of full-day kindergarten is that there is more opportunity for play.

SELF-REGULATION IN THE PRIMARY CLASSROOM

Research on self-regulation in schools has emphasized the role of teachers and classroom environments in scaffolding children's learning. Jerome Bruner (2004) introduced the concept of *scaffolding*, which he defines as "a process of 'setting up' the situation to make the child's entry easy and successful and then gradually pulling back and handing the role to the child as he becomes skilled enough to manage it" (p. 60). For example, the influential research-based curriculum Tools of the Mind is grounded in the Vygotskian theory of development where teachers scaffold children's learning in order to improve executive functions with the aim of improving academic learning (Blair et al., 2011). Both Diamond et al. (2007) and Bodrova and Leong (2007, 2008) argue that the executive functions associated with self-regulation develop as children engage in interpersonal actions using external aids to facilitate attention and memory, self-regulatory private speech, and dramatic play. External aids can help skills become automatic. For example, symbols of ears and lips help children remember when it is their turn to listen or their turn to read. Teachers can model the use of private speech and encourage children's use of private speech. In order for children to develop self-regulation skills they need to have many opportunities to experience and practice them with adults and more capable peers.

Diamond et al. (2007), in their landmark study on self-regulation, divided pre-kindergarten children from public schools into two programs, Tools of the Mind and Literacy in a Balanced Way. Tools of the Mind includes techniques for scaffolding, training, and challenging executive functions by interweaving them in all class activities. Literacy in a Balanced Way is a literacy program that includes a combination of reading, writing, and listening activities in the context of thematic units. Children in both groups were given a series of tests at five years of age. They found that markedly better executive function performance was found in at-risk children after one or two years of the Tools of the Mind classroom, showing that executive functions can be improved in young children. The children were attentive and focused on their work in these classrooms, and the behaviour problems observed in the Literacy in a Balanced Way classrooms were absent. They concluded that play challenges children to exercise their executive functions and should be a component of all early childhood programs.

Bodrova and Leong (2008) identify four strategies that teachers can use to promote the development of children's self-regulation skills. First, they believe that teachers should teach self-regulation to all children, not just the ones that appear to have problems. Second, teachers should create opportunities for children to follow, make, and apply rules in new situations to move from co-regulation to self-regulation. Third, teachers should provide children with visual and tangible reminders when learning to self-regulate to support their memory and attention. The fourth strategy that teachers should use is to let children be involved in play and games where they set, negotiate, and follow the rules. Self-regulation is the underlying skill that makes learning possible, so instruction in self-regulation needs the same, if not more, attention than academic subjects. Significantly, Forgas et al. (2009) report that there is little evidence that children suffer from being overly capable of self-regulating their attention and behaviour.

Rimm-Kaufman and Wanless (2012) report that classrooms vary widely in how they support and challenge children's self-regulatory abilities. They believe that self-regulatory skills create opportunities for positive engagement, although stimulating environments need to exist so that these opportunities translate into academic and social learning. Young children are exposed to culturally specific values and expectations, social interactions, and a variety of experiences that contribute to the emergence of their self-regulatory and academic skills. When kindergarten children enter school, they display self-regulatory behaviours in reaction to the new environment that reflect their disposition and early learning experiences. This new context provides children with the opportunity to practice their self-regulatory abilities, and in turn the context socializes children in ways that enhance or diminish their self-regulatory abilities. Effective teachers support the development of self-regulation by organizing their classrooms in a way that proactively guides children's behaviour, using instructional strategies that are interesting and engaging as well as cultivating emotionally supportive relationships. Teachers use different strategies to down-regulate and direct the attention of children who are misbehaving and being loud, and up-regulate and connect to children who are withdrawn and not getting involved. Teacher language is also a strategy that supports children's self-regulatory skills and engagement. When teachers verbally model problem-solving situations, children use these verbal dialogues in their own private speech when attempting to regulate themselves.

Shanker (2013b) also identifies many strategies for adapting classroom environments in order to enhance children's self-regulation. These strategies include reducing visual and auditory stimuli to avoid sensory overload; providing fidget toys and disc chairs for children with attention or sensory-integration issues; introducing yoga, tai chi, breathing exercises, or meditation; having a predictable schedule so children can anticipate transitions; planning specific activities and transitions that help children self-regulate; playing games that enhance children's ability to pay attention; providing children with collaborative learning experiences; and helping children identify their own arousal state. Children are more likely to be optimally self-regulated when teachers give children choice and ownership over their own learning, so they have a sense of control and are fully engaged with their learning.

Similarly, Sonia Mastrangelo (2012) argues that teachers play a pivotal role in the acquisition of learning strategies that help students become competent and resilient learners, despite the challenges they face and the stressors they encounter. She emphasizes that "students may be able to acquire the strategies, but it is the teacher who plays a key role in facilitating and scaffolding experiences that allow for every child to reach an optimal level of self-regulation" (p. 9). Ida Florez (2011) further explains that teachers use a variety of strategies to scaffold children's development of self-regulation, such as using hints or cues and modelling optimal self-regulation. For example, they use simple directions, gestures, and touch to provide children with cues about how to regulate their emotions, attention, and behaviour. Teachers demonstrate appropriate behaviour by modelling important language and social skills. Teachers co-regulate and gradually withdraw their support, intervening only when necessary, as children learn to regulate their thoughts, feelings, and behaviour.

Shanker's (2016) *Self-Reg* five-step method also provides guidance for teachers to enhance the development of children's self-regulation skills. This method requires recognizing when a child is overstressed, identifying the child's stressors, reducing the child's stressors, helping the child be aware of when they need to reduce stressors, and helping the child develop self-regulation strategies. Teachers should learn how to recognize a child's signs and understand the meaning behind the child's behaviour. Once teachers are aware that a child's difficult behaviors are caused by too much stress, they start to see the child in a new light and reframe their perception of the child's behaviours. When teachers recognize the difference between stress behaviour and misbehavior, they are more likely to pause and think about what is causing the stress rather than reacting quickly and adding to the child's stress. Instead, the teacher should help the child to calm and recover. Stress behaviour is physiologically based, and the child has neither deliberately chosen their actions nor are they aware of what they are doing. The child is behaving poorly because their nervous system has sensed danger and is in fight, flight, or freeze mode (Porges, 2011). When a teacher is dismissive of a child's fears and sense of danger, it increases the child's anxiety as the child now feels ashamed because of the teacher's response. Once a teacher has identified and reduced a child's stressors, they need to help the child learn how to recognize when they are overstressed and how to reduce those stressors. Teachers should empower their students to be self-aware, manage their own stress levels, and use self-regulation strategies so they can meet everyday challenges that cause stress.

CANADIAN EDUCATION POLICY

Education policy differs across Canada because schooling is a provincial/territorial responsibility rather than a responsibility of the national government. In many provinces and territories—including Alberta, Manitoba, New Brunswick, Newfoundland and Labrador, Northwest Territories, Nova Scotia, Nunavut, Prince Edward Island, Quebec, and Saskatchewan—SEL is central to current education policy. Recall that SEL is encapsulated by the emotional, social, and prosocial domains of self-regulation. Two of the provinces, British Columbia and Ontario, embrace both SEL and self-regulation more generally. Yukon follows the British Columbia curriculum.

The five core competencies of SEL—self-awareness, self-management, social awareness, relationship skills, and responsible decision-making—introduced by CASEL are at the heart of the movement. Alberta, Manitoba, New Brunswick, and Nova Scotia all adopt the CASEL framework (CASEL, 2022b). For example, the Government of Alberta believes that SEL requires a long-term whole school approach that embraces families as well as community partners. It is fundamental to building positive social behaviour, health and well-being, moral development and citizenship, motivation, and academic learning. Socio-emotional skills need to be taught in the classroom. The government's vision is for elementary teachers to work together to include SEL in their programs through activities like read-aloud stories, guided discussion, dramatic role-play, as well as demonstrate their learning through a variety of media. Students are encouraged to take home socio-emotional materials to reinforce the learning with families, and school events introduce ideas for using SEL skills across different contexts. The K–9 Health and Life Skills curriculum directly addresses many aspects of SEL (Government of Alberta, n.d.). Northwest Territories and Nunavut follow the Alberta curriculum.

Similarly, Nova Scotia's curriculum has been renewed and modernized to support learner engagement and well-being (Government of Nova Scotia, 2021). In its *Action Plan for Education* (Government of Nova Scotia, 2015), it committed to designing and implementing curriculum components that embrace SEL across the grades. For example, in its new *Health Education Foundational Outcomes* document there is an emphasis on healthy self and healthy relationships. Healthy self focuses on recognizing signs of anxiety and practicing skills for managing stress. Healthy relationships include being able to identify relationships that promote positive health outcomes and making healthy decisions that demonstrate prosocial behaviours (Government of Nova Scotia, 2020).

In British Columbia, the new curriculum has three core competencies: thinking, communication, and personal and social. SEL and self-regulation are viewed as an essential component of education and are embedded in the personal and social competency strand. In this strand students learn to understand and care about themselves and others. A sub-competency in this strand is personal awareness and responsibility, which involves the dynamic between the facets of well-being, self-regulating, and self-advocating:

> People who are personally aware and responsible demonstrate self-respect, persevere in difficult situations, and exercise responsibility. They understand that there are consequences for their decisions and actions. A personally aware and

responsible individual takes steps to ensure their well-being, sets goals and monitors progress, regulates emotions and manages stress, and recognizes and advocates for their own rights. (Government of British Columbia, 2021)

In British Columbia, self-regulation is integrated throughout the curriculum in the primary grades.

Self-regulation, including SEL, is also an important theme in education policy in Ontario. For example, the new 2020 mathematics curriculum expectations are organized around six distinct but related strands. One of these strands is SEL skills in mathematics and the mathematical processes. SEL skills include identifying and managing emotions, recognizing and managing sources of stress and coping with challenges, maintaining positive motivation and perseverance, building healthy relationships and communicating effectively, developing self-awareness and a sense of identity, and thinking critically and creatively. SEL skills can be developed across all subject areas as they help learners to develop confidence, cope with challenges, and think critically (Ontario Ministry of Education, 2020).

An exemplary illustration of self-regulation in Ontario's curriculum is *The Kindergarten Program* (Ontario Ministry of Education, 2016). In this framework, belonging and contributing on the one hand, and self-regulation and well-being on the other hand, are two foundations or broad areas of learning that occur during children's play and inquiry. Belonging and contributing focuses on relationships that are key to children's personal, social, and emotional development. Authentic relationships help children develop a positive sense of self as well as a sense of belonging and contributing. Teachers nurture emotional development by creating warm and responsive environments for children. Children develop the ability to get along with their peers and be empathetic. They learn to understand their own emotions and express them in respectful ways, manage their impulses, and adapt their responses. Teachers support social development by modelling how to manage conflict and affirm positive choices. They need to be aware of individual differences, including incoming sensory stimulation and cultural differences in expression of emotion. As children develop a sense of belonging and contributing, they begin to learn about their role as a responsible citizen inside and outside the classroom community, as well as in the world around them.

Self-regulation and well-being focus on children's ability to manage their emotions, attention, and behaviour. This allows children to develop habits of mind like persistence, curiosity, and emotional well-being that are essential for learning. When interacting with others, children develop a sense of awareness and a stronger sense of self, monitor and adapt their own behaviour and emotions, and become aware of and learn to accommodate others' feelings and thinking. Teachers need to support children as they learn to self-regulate and step back to make room for children to consolidate their learning. The key to supporting children's emerging self-regulation skills is to provide children with choice in the learning environment. Children learn to choose space and materials that best fit their needs in terms of providing stimulation or a calming effect. Teachers should create learning environments that are healthy, caring, safe, inclusive, and accepting, and in this way, support the development of self-regulation as well as children's mental health, resilience, and overall well-being (Ontario Ministry of Education, 2016). The kindergarten report card is divided between the four frames of the kindergarten program. This means half of the report card is devoted to reporting on belonging and contributing as well as self-regulation and well-being. The province of Ontario is distinctive because the elementary school report card also requires teachers to assess students' self-regulation skills.

CHAPTER SUMMARY

This chapter has focused on self-regulation and aligns with researchers who understand it as arousal regulation. Self-regulation as arousal regulation refers to "a child's ability to deal with stressors effectively and efficiently and then return to a baseline of being calmly focused and alert" (Shanker, 2012b, p. 12). It is a reflective learning process where children become aware of what it feels like to be overstressed, recognize when they need to up-regulate or down-regulate, and develop strategies to reduce their stress and restore their energy. Sources for stress can be biological, cognitive, emotional, social, or prosocial. SEL is encapsulated by the emotional, social, and prosocial domains of self-regulation.

Children learn how to self-regulate by first being regulated by others. When children are between the ages of three and six, the rapid development of oral language plays a pivotal role in their social development. At this age, play enables them to foster the development of their SEL and executive functions, use oral language as a self-regulatory tool, and experience a state of flow. Curiosity, exuberance, and receptivity are elements that connect play and self-regulation.

Research on self-regulation in schools has emphasized the role of teachers and classroom environments in scaffolding children's learning. Teachers should empower their students to be self-aware, manage their own stress levels, and use self-regulation strategies so they can meet everyday challenges that cause stress. Effective teachers support the development of self-regulation by organizing their classrooms in a way that proactively guides children's behaviour, using instructional strategies that are engaging, and cultivating emotionally supportive relationships. Education policy varies across Canada. In many provinces and territories, SEL is the focus, whereas British Columbia, Ontario, and Yukon embrace both SEL and self-regulation more generally.

REFLECTIVE QUESTIONS

1. How does thinking about self-regulation through the lens of arousal regulation change your current understanding of self-regulation?
2. Do you think that young children's ability to self-regulate has been adversely affected by the COVID-19 pandemic? If so, what extra steps will you take to ensure they develop these skills?
3. In what ways have you supported the development of young children's self-regulation skills? What might you do differently in the future?
4. What is the education policy in your province on SEL and self-regulation more generally? Are there other provinces that have developed their policies in more depth and, if so, how might this influence your own understanding?
5. What did you learn about self-regulation that you did not know before? How will you apply this new knowledge in your personal life and/or professional practice?

RECOMMENDED READINGS

Jones, Stephanie, & Kahn, Jennifer. (2017). *The evidence base for how we learn: Supporting students' social, emotional, and academic development.* Aspen, CO: The Aspen Institute.

Shanker, Stuart. (2013). *Calm, alert, and learning: Classroom strategies for self-regulation.* Toronto, ON: Pearson.

Shanker, Stuart, with Barker, Theresa. (2016). *Self-reg: How to help your child (and you) break the stress cycle and successfully engage with life.* Toronto, ON: Viking/Penguin Canada.

Shanker, Stuart. (2020). *Reframed: Self-reg for a just society.* Toronto, ON: University of Toronto Press.

Willey, Kira. (2017). *Breathe like a bear: 30 mindful moments for kids to feel calm and focused anytime, anywhere.* Emmaus, PA: Rodale Kids.

ONLINE RESOURCES

The MEHRIT Centre
https://self-reg.ca

The Collaborative for Academic, Social, and Emotional Learning (CASEL)
https://casel.org/what-is-sel

Supporting Self-Regulation Video Series
http://www.edugains.ca/newsite/Kindergarten/primaryresources/selfregulation.html

Dr. Stuart Shanker: The Foundation of Self-Regulation: Stress Regulation in Infants 0–3
https://youtu.be/0_w-5sXz0sQ

TEDxYMCAAcademy—Dr. Stuart Shanker—Self Regulation and Learning
https://youtu.be/HTbAFmOdImY

The Zones of Regulation
https://zonesofregulation.com/index.html

Why Self-Regulation May Be More Important than Literacy | Alissa Antle
https://youtu.be/5YUddOJfgK8

Jump, Wiggle, Learn? Self-Regulation | Candice Charlton and Heidi DeLazzer |
   TEDxWestVancouverED
https://youtu.be/NSQepSNH-lQ

The Way I Feel by Janan Cain
https://youtu.be/ITPUxVQ6UIk

Listening to My Body by Gabi Garcia
https://youtu.be/-B6Rik-TA-Q

In My Heart: A Book of Feelings
https://youtu.be/xIfLgHBwYx4

Chapter Two

Emergent Curriculum and Inquiry-Based Learning

> Curriculum is what happens in an educational environment—not what is rationally planned to happen, but what actually takes place.
> —Elizabeth Jones & John Nimmo, 1994, p. 12

In the introduction to the book, I noted that emergent curriculum supports inquiry-based learning, which is an approach that encourages active learning and critical thinking through collaborative student-led investigations guided by interesting questions or problems. The term *emergent curriculum* was first coined by Elizabeth Jones in 1970 to describe a particular type of curriculum planning or teaching practice that many educators were pursuing in their classrooms across North America. In an influential early account of emergent curriculum, Copple (1994) explains that "*emergent* emphasizes that planning needs to emerge from the daily life of the children and adults in the program, particularly from the children's own interests.... Yet, as the word *curriculum* conveys, there is also teacher planning" (p. viii). Wien (2008) observes that "the course of this curriculum is not known at the outset. It is emergent" (p. 5). Its path is determined by the connections the children and teachers make as they bring their ideas and theories to the topic under investigation and construct the course to follow. Emergent curriculum focuses on what children are learning, where teachers build on children's interests as they co-construct genuine knowledge and practice empathy and respect for their peers through inquiries (Jones, 2012). In essence, emergent curriculum explains what the children will be learning, while the inquiry-based approach explains how the children will go about it. There is a continuum of inquiry-based learning extending from low-level structured inquiry to high-level open inquiry. Open inquiry involves students formulating and investigating their own questions. Emergent curriculum inquiries, like open inquiries, are sustained investigations built around the children's interests and are co-constructed between the teachers and children as the inquiry unfolds.

FRAMING EMERGENT CURRICULUM

The Reggio Emilia approach to education has had a profound influence on the practice of emergent curriculum in North America as well as my own understanding of it. For Reggio educators, teaching begins with Malaguzzi's powerful image of the child as being "rich in potential, strong, powerful, competent, and most of all connected to adults and other children" (quoted in Moss & Petrie, 2002, p. 22). Emergent curriculum starts when teachers observe, listen, and record the children's ideas as they engage in classroom activities. They reflect on why the children are interested in a particular topic and discover what they already know about that topic. Forman and Fyfe (2012) elaborate:

> Teachers seek to uncover the children's beliefs, assumptions, or theories about the way the physical or social world works. Their study goes beyond simply identifying the children's interest. Their analysis reveals the reasons behind the children's interest—not strictly what is familiar but what paradox or curiosity drives their interest.... Children are encouraged to talk about what they know before they begin their projects. (p. 248)

After the teachers decide that the topic will sustain the children's interest, they brainstorm and record different possibilities about how the inquiry might evolve, the choices the children might make, and where these will lead. The curriculum is co-constructed with the children as the inquiry unfolds and new ideas emerge, which means the direction of the inquiry can change at any time, keeping it fresh and exciting for the children and teachers. This type of curriculum is "child-originated and teacher-framed" (p. 248).

Emergent curriculum is a creative collaboration that can emerge from both the children's and teachers' interests, encounters with materials, or unexpected events. It is generated by the children, the teachers, and the environment itself. In order to develop this curriculum in depth, teachers must listen to children's questions and come up with ways to extend them, document the learning, and reciprocate with more questions to further the children's interests. Teachers who practice emergent curriculum, observes Wien (2006, 2008), build many layers into their program to expand the children's thinking. These layers include focused conversations to find out what children know and think, rich resources that enable children to use different modes of expression, activities that are thoughtfully prepared, expansive time frames, collaborative sharing, and revisiting and studying documentation. In effect, emergent curriculum is about making connections and building relationships through a variety of activities and experiences.

Stacey (2009) provides a useful list of underlying assumptions for emergent curriculum. First, it is a child-initiated curriculum, framed by the teacher, that allows for collaborations and gives everyone a voice. When teachers observe children and notice details about their play, they begin to uncover the children's thinking, intentions, and understandings. The children's interests are validated and respected as they co-construct the direction of the curriculum with the teacher. Second, emergent curriculum is responsive to children because it builds on their interests. Over time, teachers become adept at distinguishing which interests can turn into long-term investigations. Third, the teacher is a facilitator who takes their observations and provides children with opportunities to dig deeper and construct further knowledge. The teacher scaffolds the children's learning by bringing their knowledge and expertise to the situation as they think about how to further their interest, knowledge, and engagement in the topic. Fourth, it is flexible, as curriculum planning is constantly developing, and plans made by teachers may have to be let go in order to address what children are really interested in. Finally, emergent curriculum enables children's and teachers' thinking to be made visible through documentation. When children and teachers revisit documentation, it allows them to reflect upon the work, make sense of it, and plan future directions. It also helps teachers find answers to their own questions about what children are thinking and doing and how they learn.

What makes emergent curriculum inquiries unique is that they contain all four core components of emergent curriculum: inquiry design, design of the environment, documentation, and conversation. These components reflect my adaptation of the distinction made by Forman and Fyfe (2012) and Fraser (2012) in their discussion of design, documentation, and discourse in negotiated curriculum. These four core components are interwoven throughout the process as an inquiry unfolds. Each component affects the others: documentation informs conversation, conversation informs documentation, and design provides the structure for the inquiry to grow. Design represents a prediction or a plan, whereas documentation records the performance during a learning experience. In other words, design instructs, and documentation explains. Each component is reciprocal where design can be used to strengthen documentation, documentation can be revisited to strengthen conversation, and conversation can be documented to influence the next design phase. Design and documentation also focus, maintain, and support conversation during emergent curriculum inquiries.

INQUIRY DESIGN

The inquiry design phase begins when the teachers decide on a topic that will sustain the children's interests. After the teachers have identified possible directions

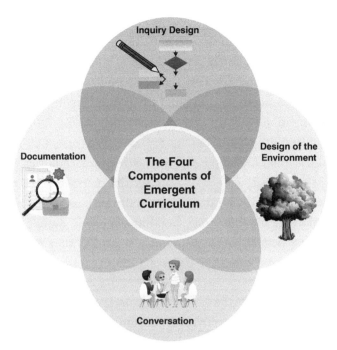

the inquiry might follow, they also list ideas for how to provoke the children to think more deeply about the topic being investigated. Jacobs (2008) explains that "a provocation can be an idea, an event, or an object that captures the children's imagination and desire to learn more" (p. 82). When teachers provide provocations, children engage in new ways of learning and build on their thinking. Fraser (2012) emphasizes that children are intimately involved in the design phase of the inquiry. Design "refers to any activity in which children make records of their plans or intended solutions" (Forman & Fyfe, 2012, p. 249). They are encouraged to discuss and represent their ideas throughout the inquiry so that teachers can reflect on their understanding of the topic. Children share these representations with others and, as the inquiry unfolds, their representations become more detailed and elaborate and are included in the documentation.

During play children have the freedom to choose what they want to do and, as they play, they explore their own interests. Emergent curriculum "places extremely high value on play as a generator for curriculum" (Stacey, 2009, p. 49). Although children's ideas are an important source of the curriculum, teachers need to have a vision for how the inquiry will unfold. Jones and Nimmo (1994) explain, "Emergent curriculum … requires of its practitioners *trust in the power of play*—trust in spontaneous choice making among many possibilities" (p. 1). It is not possible, however, for teachers to pursue all of the children's interests initiated during play. Some ideas are fleeting and, although exciting at the time, not sustainable. They add, "An emergent curriculum is a continuous revision process, an honest response to what is actually happening. Good teachers plan and let go. If you're paying attention to children, an accurate lesson plan can be written only after the fact" (p. 12). Teachers need to determine the potential of any interest for in-depth learning and the possibility of pursuing it through long-term investigations.

Having an inquiry stance is, in my view, an essential feature of all inquiry-based learning, including emergent curriculum inquiries. Teachers and children adopt an inquiry stance or mindset that permeates all thinking and learning in the classroom. Children are naturally curious as they move through the world exploring, manipulating, building, creating, wondering, and asking questions. Teachers also take an inquiry stance, as they express their own thinking and wondering about the children's learning. They observe and reflect on children's interests, listen to children's theories and ideas, watch how the children are engaging with the classroom materials, interact and think about what concepts the children are exploring, document the children's learning, and respond to the children in thoughtful ways through reciprocal actions (Fraser, 2012). Reciprocal actions occur when teachers ask children questions to provoke further thought, provide provocations that scaffold the children's learning, adapt the classroom environment to accommodate these interests, and take the children on outings to enhance their understanding.

An important aspect of inquiry design is that it allows for expansive time frames with few transitions. When the clock does not dictate when activities change, it sends a message to children that their activity is important and allows them to sustain attention. Slowing down time enables teachers to become more alert to the children's activity and thinking (Wien & Stacey, 2014). It provides them with the opportunity to watch carefully and support children's play. These teachers refrain from changing topics, abruptly transitioning to other learning experiences, or creating competing demands for the children's interest. "Unhurried time is ecologically sound in that it respects children's own pace in activity, giving them sufficient time and space to experience satisfaction and permit an organic close to activities" (Wien, 2008, p. 147). Expansive time frames allow children to repeat activities in order to think through their ideas and theories as inquiries require sustained attention, persistence, endurance, hope, and positive energy. They also enable a child to take a break when tired before taking up the task again.

The inquiry design component of emergent curriculum is illustrated here with detailed descriptions of four inquiries—Invisibility, Office, Running Club, and Community—recently undertaken in Canadian primary classrooms.

THE INVISIBILITY INQUIRY

This inquiry started one morning when Steven drew a picture of his mother and said that she was invisible. When Lauren asked Steven how he could show that his mother was invisible, he said that he had to roll the picture up. Deepa was also thinking about invisibility when she was at the Light Table trying to make a jewel invisible because she didn't want anyone to see it. She thought you could make things invisible by covering them up. Lauren then provided an art experience, as a provocation, that challenged the children to draw something or someone that was invisible. Based on these experiences and stories that Lauren read, a group of children started to explain their initial theories and ideas about what invisibility meant.

Lauren conducted two experiments with the children. One experiment involved placing a small glass inside a large glass and then pouring oil into the small glass and letting it overflow until it filled the large glass. Lauren wanted to know if the children thought the small glass was invisible and if it was still there. The children thought that because they couldn't see the small glass it was no longer there. In the second experiment the children were given a variety of materials and asked to see if they could make a gemstone invisible. After using the materials to hide the gemstone, the children explained that when a gemstone is the same colour as the cloth it blends in and is invisible.

Having explored invisibility through sight and touch, the children were next provided with an opportunity to think about sound by banging on a variety of pots and pans with drumsticks. Later, looking at the photographs of the experience, Lauren asked the children what they could see and what they couldn't see. By showing the children the video of the experience, they realized that what was missing in the photographs was movement and sound. Lauren asked the children to represent sound on the photographs with markers. The children then shared how different markings represented different sounds.

Lauren revisited the documentation on the Invisibility Inquiry with the whole class because she wanted the children who had not worked on the inquiry to have a chance to share their thinking. While Lauren shared the documentation, several children spontaneously joined in the retell and she encouraged them to share any new ideas. Lauren then invited a small group of children to draw their theory or idea about invisibility. In their drawings, the children showed that when two things are the same colour, they blend in and become invisible, and that black makes things even more invisible.

Three provocations were shared with the class using the worm jar, Rory's watch, and the snack box. Some children thought the worms were hidden in the dirt, the watch was real and had electricity, and the snack-box sticks could be heard and felt but not seen. When the children were asked what else they might be thinking, the idea of water being invisible surfaced. Lauren set up a water experiment to explore the children's ideas. The children were thinking about questions like: How do you know which jar has water in it? What happens to water when it spills on the table? Where did the water drawings go? What happens when you pour water from the small jar into the vase? Why does the water bend when you blow it?

Lauren showed the children photographs of the water experiment and asked them to explain what was happening. They talked about how water contains air, it is see-through, it changes depending on the angle, it disappears, and it bends when you blow on it. After viewing a video of Samantha talking about invisibility, the children thought about whether invisibility is white or see-through. Rory said invisibility is something you cannot see even if you can still feel it. Three children shared how they had used white paint to draw on white canvas and this led to a discussion about whether the pictures looked invisible. This sparked new thinking about whether invisible beings can see people who are not invisible and what happens when they are both invisible. The children were invited to draw their invisible selves with silver markers on mirrors as they thought about the relationship between invisibility and colour.

THE OFFICE INQUIRY

This inquiry began spontaneously one morning while the children were at Inquiry Centres. Victoria explained that it had all started in the construction area. The children had moved several chairs to the middle of the room and collected other materials like their I Wonder books and pencils. Some of the girls were writing in their books, others were pretending to sleep, and Rachel was the security guard. The space was quite contained, and when the children were asked what they were doing, they responded that they were "working." The next day the girls recreated the office and continued with their play.

Kathryn and Victoria presented the children with the provocation of visiting the junior school office. While at the office they explored all the rooms, asked the office staff questions, and sketched and wrote words in their I Wonder books of all the things they had seen. When they returned to the classroom, the children co-constructed a list of the items they found in the office that included a computer, desk, pencils, paper, books, and decorations. Kathryn and Victoria collected the items on the list, as well as other items, and put them in a pile on the floor of the Drama Centre so that the children could recreate their office themselves. Several girls participated in transforming the Drama Centre into an office space. While exploring the office, the children became interested in creating nametags for all their peers, typing on the typewriter, and using the envelopes and blank paper to write letters to their families.

One morning, Liza and Vicky made an appointment with Ms. Harland in the office so that the JKs could revisit that afternoon. When the JKs went to the junior school office they were looking to see if there was anything else they could add to their classroom office. Upon returning to the classroom the children shared what they had found, and Kathryn recorded their ideas on the whiteboard. They made several items, including a clock, a sand and sparkle tray, some candies, and paintings, and added them to the office. The children also became very interested in creating a security TV. An impromptu outing was organized, and Victoria took several children outside to photograph images of the outside doors. Once the photographs were printed the girls constructed a security TV for their office.

The children's continued interest in security led them to investigate how the school entrance is monitored in the junior school office. The whole class went outside and pretended to visit the school. They announced their arrival through the intercom and Ms. Harland buzzed them in. Then Kathryn, Victoria, and the children met with the head of security for the school, and he answered all the questions they had about security. The children learned that if you work at the school you can use a swipe card to enter the school, so they went outside and came in a different door using a swipe card. When they returned to the classroom, the girls made their own swipe cards and a scanner for their office. The children used the mirror as a swinging door to indicate the swipe card giving access to the classroom office.

Kathryn, Victoria, and the children discussed what it means when we say we are working. The children came up with their own ideas and theories about the different roles of the office staff. To build on their understanding of offices across different contexts, the parents were sent an email that included a list of questions the children wanted to ask their parents about what they do in their offices. Some of the parents sent in photographs and responses to the questions and these were added to the Office Inquiry documentation book that was later shared with the whole class.

THE RUNNING CLUB INQUIRY

This inquiry started one day when a group of children approached Darlene at lunchtime and asked if they could run in the hall. Darlene was busy at that moment and said, "Who wants to run in the hall?… How can you let me know that?" To her relief, Gabriel suggested that they make a list of all the children who wanted to run. When the children returned with the list, Darlene asked, "Well how is this going to work? Do you have a plan?" The children met and came back with a plan where they would take turns running with a partner. When they tried to implement their plan, it quickly became disorganized. Darlene told them that they needed to have another meeting and come back with a better strategy. The new strategy involved having teams. Connor emphasized how they needed to start in a circle and remind each other of the rules before they ran.

After the children ran in the hall, they talked about how running made their body feel. Darlene invited the children to draw a picture of what their body was feeling inside before and after they ran, and she recorded their ideas on the back of their drawing. Then the children started to talk about their different running ideas, so Darlene also invited them to draw their ideas to help clarify what they were thinking. She shared the pictures and photographs of what had happened so far in the inquiry with the children in the Running Club. Surprisingly, Michael said that he thought they should connect each person's running idea and make it into one big idea. Darlene explained that this new focus "led us to places we were not expecting and took us away from our original interest … this is what happens when children take the lead!" The children then shared their pictures and theories about their running ideas with the rest of the class to see if they could help them think about "the big idea."

During a discussion, the children talked about all the materials they needed to show their running idea. Then Darlene provided a provocation: a box with a happy face on the outside and inside a stopwatch, tape, and materials to make tickets. Over the next few weeks, the children took turns sharing their running ideas, which led to new thinking. For example, after Zara's run, the children talked about who was the fastest runner. They thought through how the children with the lowest times recorded were the fastest runners. This later turned into an opportunity for the class to sign a chart about who they thought the fastest runner(s) were. The children continued to build onto or adapt their original idea as they became influenced by previous demonstrations. Interestingly, when the children were in the hall demonstrating their running idea, the stethoscope appeared again and again as the children listened to each other's heartbeat. After each child shared their idea, Darlene asked them to draw a picture of how the run actually went.

Michael was then invited to look at the documentation with Darlene and he began to articulate how he thought all the little running ideas could be made into one big idea. After he shared his thoughts with the rest of the Running Club, Darlene put a large piece of mural paper on the table and explained to the children that the goal was to draw the big idea. The children began to negotiate how to draw it. When it was finished, Michael suggested that the next step was to hang the mural in the hall. He explained, "Yeah then we can remember where we are and then go from there." Michael was looking forward to trying his running idea in the hallway.

THE COMMUNITY INQUIRY

This inquiry began with a larger focus on the City of Toronto. The initial spark was a tiny picture that Omja drew of the CN Tower. After Omja shared the picture with his classmates, they had a discussion about the CN Tower and shared their personal experiences. Then Sharon and the children looked at books about cities and talked about the differences between a country, a city, and a community. The children used classroom materials to create the CN Tower and the city centre and went for a community walk to sketch the cityscape in their inquiry books. One day, Dea asked, "Why do people make cities?" and this led to a knowledge-building circle discussion. Then the children worked collaboratively in small groups to draw large posters of the City of Toronto.

This led to further discussions and recordings of what the children knew about the city. Sharon summarized all the children's ideas on chart paper so the children could revisit their learning.

The children then turned their focus towards the community where they live. They sketched the apartment buildings that surrounded the school and wrote about them. While looking at the sketches, Sharon commented, "That's when we started to realize it wasn't so much the bigger picture of Toronto, that it was they could see the CN Tower from their apartments, and therefore the apartment actually is the core part for them." Sharon showed the children photographs she had taken of the apartment buildings. The children were very excited and many of them pointed to the pictures and said, "That's where I live." Sharon had the children identify which building was theirs and other places where family and friends lived. Esita drew a bird's-eye view of her building that included the details of her apartment layout. After sharing her drawing, the children were curious to see what Sharon's apartment looked like, so she drew it for them. The children then drew their own apartments and showed what features were important to them.

Sharon and the children then went on a community walk to the valley nearby the school to see the river. During a knowledge-building circle, the children shared their ideas about water, including where water comes from. The children then drew pictures and wrote about their visit to the Valley. Sharon shared a photograph of the valley with a small group of children. During the conversation, Mahdi said, "Nature is a friend of the community." Sharon later followed up this idea. She wrote, "What is a friend?" on chart paper. The children brainstormed ideas while Sharon recorded them. One idea was that nature is a "friend" because it helps us. The children then shared their ideas through pictures and words. Sharon felt that when she showed the children the photograph it was a turning point for them. They started to think about community in a different way. The children now saw nature as being a part of the community, whereas when the inquiry had started they only saw the city and the buildings.

When the children were at learning centres, they built the CN Tower out of blocks and other building materials. This turned into a collaborative building project that grew bigger and bigger and included the city, community, and valley. A few children documented the experience by drawing and labelling the structures. Sharon then created a mind map with the children to consolidate all their knowledge about the community. This map helped the children to come up with ideas for the collaborative community collage art piece they were creating with Mikayla. The children all worked together to draw miniature versions of things that you find in the community, like houses, apartment buildings, shops, trees, flowers, people, animals, cars, and a school bus, and then the pieces were assembled to create a collage on black paper.

The children began to focus more on the valley rather than the community itself. While in the valley the children did observational drawings, explored nature, and played in the sunshine. The children documented these experiences in their inquiry books. The children also shared their experiences in knowledge-building circles. They talked about what they liked about the valley, and this helped to generate some initial ideas for the collaborative watercolour paintings of the valley. The children worked together sharing ideas and negotiating who should draw what and where. The children described what was in their paintings as Sharon documented what they said. The paintings represented a consolidation of the children's learning about the valley.

DESIGN OF THE ENVIRONMENT

Children become more engaged in their learning when they help to plan and design the classroom environment. During emergent curriculum inquiries, they are intimately involved in the design process, often working collaboratively with the teacher to create the physical space. When children help to organize the materials and find places to store them for easy access, they can make independent choices as they play and interact in that environment. The arrangement of equipment and materials in the classroom encourages "children to see relationships and develop deeper understanding of a subject" (Fraser 2012, p. 185).

Classroom environments are an essential part of the learning process and, as Taguchi (2010) explains, provide for an "intra-active ecological encounter." This reflects "the performative agency of the materials in the intra-actions of the learning event" (p. 65). Her point is that the learning process includes an encounter with "things, matter, artefacts, materials, furnished environments and architecture" that have agency, which shape and even determine some actions and responses (p. 65). The classroom environment has performative agency that is crucial to our meaning making. Teachers co-create aesthetically pleasing classroom environments with rich, accessible, open-ended materials and tools to support the children's learning. This kind of environment calls children to action, where teachers observe their interests, and the curriculum can begin to grow. Teachers need to think about how their physical environment supports the children's interest in a particular investigation. When teachers provide materials in response to children's ideas, the children might use them in ways that were not envisioned, which provides direction for teachers to think about how to reciprocate the children's interests in the future.

In Reggio Emilia, the environment is described as a "third teacher." This means that there are three teachers in the classroom: adults, peers, and the physical environment. Halls and Wien (2013) explain that, when we speak of the environment as a third teacher,

> the context has been so carefully prepared, organized, and structured that it scaffolds children's engagement, ongoing interest, and multiple interactions. It builds complexity of thinking by its very complex structure so that it is possible for children to make multiple connections in multiple directions. (p. 5)

Gandini (2012a) elaborates further by saying,

> To act as an educator for the child … all the things that surround and are used by the people in the school—the objects, the materials, and the structures—are seen not as passive elements but, on the contrary, as elements that condition and are conditioned by the actions of children and adults who are active in it. (p. 339)

Classroom environments that embrace inquiry-based learning are, in this sense, not one-size-fits-all spaces but rather ones that children and teachers can create together.

When designing a classroom environment for inquiry-based learning, teachers need to think carefully about what they believe about children, adults, and learning. Spaces and materials should communicate respect for children and the teaching and learning process, allowing for children's decision-making and ownership of their activities, and an opportunity to assume responsibility for their actions. The spaces need to be flexible and materials open-ended so that things can be moved around and repurposed. Wien (2008) explains that space and materials can be organized and designed in ways that invite learning without teacher intervention, which promotes the children's autonomy, enabling them to pursue their own interests, represent what is on their minds, build relationships with others, and develop a love of learning. Open-ended materials that have multiple purposes can spark children's imagination and allow them to continually rearrange and combine materials as they explore their learning environment. Curtis and Carter (2003) note that children are fascinated with the physical world and how it works, so it is important to add engaging attractions and discoveries to the environment. Materials that provoke a sense of mystery and wonder ignite children's curiosity about how things work and what can be learned from exploring them.

Natural materials in the environment are important because they engage children's senses. Gandini (2012a) observes that because we develop our senses and cognitive abilities through interaction with our environments, the classroom can be a laboratory for the senses. Young children learn about their world through sensorial explorations. Meaningful sensorial experiences can help children make connections that lead to cognitive discoveries. Materials should create a multi-sensory setting with a variety of textures, chromatic colours, and lights. It is important, however, to avoid overstimulation, so it is best to provide a moderate tone with sensorial possibilities. Sensory-related features from engaging textures to aromas and aspects of the natural world, like tree stumps, pinecones, and rocks, can also fill a classroom with a sense of wonder (Curtis & Carter, 2003). Opportunities to provoke wonder, curiosity, and intellectual engagement make the environment rich.

It is the teacher's role to establish a positive social environment in the classroom. A sense of belonging is at the core of every primary classroom, and without it young children will simply not thrive. Social relationships that are developed in the classroom "are the fabric into which everything else is woven" (Fraser, 2012, p. 12). Children have a strong desire to have relationships and be a member of a group. When planning a space, teachers should consider creating connections to others and a sense of community. A cozy and comfortable environment brings out a strong sense of connection and belonging among the teachers and children. Wien et al. (2014) explain that when an environment is beautiful, caring, and sensitively organized, it helps children feel like they belong, are safe, and have the capacity to be responsible and productive. If an area is set up well, children are respectful of themselves, others, and the materials. The children will create and act purposefully with enthusiasm, and this allows their ideas to flourish.

Authentic relationships are an important part of the design of the environment. Clinton (2013) argues that "we all learn by observing others and we seek connection and relationship" (p. 2). Since children co-construct knowledge during emergent curriculum inquiries, the quality of their relationships with others is critical to the learning process. Loris Malaguzzi had a vision of an "education based on relationships" (Edwards, 2002, p. 6). He believed "there is no possibility of existing without relationship. Relationship is a necessity of life" (Fraser, 2006, p. 72). Relationships, for Malaguzzi, reinforce each child's sense of identity through the recognition of others, so that a child would feel enough of a sense of belonging and self-confidence to want to participate in school activities (Gandini, 2012b). Wien, Jacobs, and Brown (2015) argue that learning always exists within relationality. A relation is a connection that an active agent deliberately chooses to pursue; it is an act of intention. Relationship refers to the reciprocal aspect of relations where there is an ongoing interconnection between two entities. Each entity can respond, adapt, or be changed by the interaction. Reciprocity or "mutual exchange" is a sharing of power that flows in two directions (Wien, 2008). *Relationality* is an umbrella term for all possible relations, and it encompasses both social relationships as well as the broader relations an individual constructs in terms of materials and places. All of these relations can be found in the design of the environment component of emergent curriculum.

The design of the environment component of emergent curriculum was integral to the Invisibility Inquiry. Lauren's classroom space was warm, peaceful, and welcoming. She explained,

> The materials I choose are open-ended enough to be simple or challenging. There are clearly defined learning centers and cozy seating and resting areas. There are lots of plants. Many of the items in the room have been created with the children, such as the alphabet, number line … [and] calm books. The children are usually focused and engaged … talking, sharing ideas, [and] solving problems. They know the routines and expectations but the materials … often suggest the course of their activity.

What stood out was the care and attention put into establishing centres that have a calming, soothing effect on the children. The Calm Centre had a significant presence in the centre of the classroom. Every child had a Calm Book with strategies they could use to help them calm down. The photographs on each page, as well as the repetitive nature of the text, helped the children read their books independently. The centre also had stuffed animals, stress balls, fidget toys, and "calm jars" that contained water and sparkles. The children often chose to go to the Calm Centre independently, or the teacher would sometimes suggest that they visit this centre and choose a strategy from their Calm Book. At the Light Table, the curtains were deliberately closed to make it a little bit darker so that when you turned the light on, it felt more inviting.

Lauren found that quieter children would share what they had made and talk about what they were doing; she explained, "I think it's just that intimacy of the light shining up in a bit of a darker area." The Peace Centre had a similar effect with the sound of the flowing water fountain and small rakes to push the sand and rocks around. Children went there to look at the lava lamp and watch the shapes move up and down.

One of the most significant features of the design of the environment for the Office Inquiry was that there were endless writing materials and tools located throughout the room, which fueled the children's passion for developing their literacy skills. The adaptation of the Drama Centre into an office allowed the children to play imaginatively in their roles as office workers as they created nametags, wrote letters, and explored how the typewriter worked. The girls would often use resources (such as the alphabet on the wall, name cards, and word banks) from the nearby Graphic Communication Centre to support their writing. Kathryn, one of the teachers, said, "It is everywhere … this year they are voracious writers." Victoria added, "Well, magically, somehow … they just want to write. They just want to record everything, don't they? They just gravitate towards writing." The Book Nook was a cozy space in the corner of the classroom with a material arch that was decorated with colourful triangle shapes. The children would often go there to sit quietly and read books. Victoria explained that "We encourage them [the children] to take time out when they need it—not just on our direction—but they'll go and get a blanket and just hide under it for a while." Kathryn said, "The Book Nook really is a space where self-regulation is really built into their day."

The classroom for the Running Club Inquiry stood out because there were many other inquiries also happening at the same time, where the children explored provocations and shared their ideas, questions, and theories with others. In the Science Centre, there were books about how the body works, a large skeleton puzzle, a figure that could be taken apart in pieces to look inside the body, and the running box. This space allowed the children to think about the connection between running and how it makes the body feel. Other children chose to go to the Calm Centre to stare at the lava lamp, make up imaginary stories about the shapes as they changed in the water, and record their thinking on paper. Darlene explained that the children would go there to "do quiet activities, be calm, kind of self-regulate if they needed to." In the Math Centre, the children explored a provocation with little bears and sleds made out of metal lids and strings. They were trying to problem-solve how 31 children could share 3 toboggans and make sure that they all had turns.

What was noticeable about the Community Inquiry environment was the time and energy Sharon put into building strong relationships with the children and their families in her class of predominantly English Language Learners (ELLs). Sharon made every effort to learn about the children's first languages and cultures in order to establish a sense of trust with a vulnerable community. It helped her understand exactly what her learners needed when it came to introducing provocations to further the children's interest in the inquiry. In the Small Block Centre, the materials were set up to encourage the children's interest in building the city centre. At the Light Table, the teacher organized the materials to create a tree with blossoms, grass, and water to inspire the children to think about how to recreate what they saw when they visited the valley nearby the school. Sharon was also talented at facilitating the adaptation of centres as the inquiry evolved. These centres contained a lot of natural materials that enabled the children to have hands-on tactile exploratory experiences. The Valley Centre was set up with two different valley scenes on placemats, and the River Centre had a river scene with blue felt and fish lying on the rocks. These adaptations encouraged the children to think deeply about the inquiry.

CONVERSATION

The third component of emergent curriculum is conversation. Conversation involves interactions that go beyond teachers listening to children during discussions to reflecting on and analyzing what is said and heard. Teachers engage in conversations during emergent curriculum inquiries to co-construct theories with children about topics in which they are all interested. Fraser (2012) explains that teachers should "pay careful attention to the language they hear and speak, to ask questions to uncover the meaning behind the words, and to try to figure out the reasons for the child's comments" (p. 186). Forman and Fyfe (2012) add that, during inquiries, there is a "deep desire to understand each other's words." Conversation involves "a more reflective study of what is being said, a struggle to understand, in which speakers constructively confront each other, experience conflict, and seek footing in a constant shift of perspectives" (p. 249).

During emergent curriculum inquiries, it is important for teachers to take the time to really hear what children are saying and try to see it from their perspective. When children have not developed enough vocabulary to express their ideas clearly, it is important for the teacher to know them well so they can infer what a child is trying to say and help fill in the missing words. Children need many opportunities to engage in conversations that have purpose and are of interest to them. When teachers revisit conversations, they use transcriptions of audiotaped recordings to remind the children of their earlier thoughts and ideas, and this helps extend their understanding of the topic and come up with new or related ideas.

Young children's initial conversations occur in daily interactions between the child and caregiver (Wells, 2011). During ongoing activity, a child learns oral language by using it to the best of their abilities. Babies are innately predisposed to engage in meaningful interactions as well as discover the organizational patterns of the language they are born into. The ease and speed that babies acquire language depends on the number of interactions they have with the caregiver and how the caregiver responds and extends their conversational episodes. This helps the baby feel confident in their ability to contribute to collaborative meaning making. Babies become more knowledgeable about the topics discussed, and the child acquires a larger vocabulary. By two-and-a-half to three years of age, the child's curiosity leads to how and why questions about what is going on around them and, when answered, these questions extend the child's oral language and understanding about the world. Vocabulary size increases with more adult clarification of words. The responses of the caregiver reflect the child's interests and explain the significance of what they see and hear so the child can make sense of it. Caregivers respond in different ways, so some children are not as prepared for how they are expected to use language at school. By kindergarten all children can participate in conversations of shared importance unless they have a language impairment. Biemiller (2013) notes that the size of a child's vocabulary by age four is determined by the total number and diversity of words spoken by the parents. Malaguzzi connects talking and relationships with his observation that

> from birth, children are in continuous relationships. They have this need, this desire, to master interaction: to be a protagonist one time, to be a listener another time.… For children, dialogue opens this game of playing different parts. Children have the great fortune to know how to pull thoughts and meanings from one another's voices. (Kaufman, 1998, p. 287)

When children engage in conversations, it helps them to understand their own thoughts as well as the ideas of others.

A major force driving cognitive development in the classroom is the quality of the conversations between children and teachers, and children being active in their own investigations (Dickinson et al., 2011). Like parents at home, of central importance are teachers' questions and comments, information they share verbally, and how they respond to children's ideas and questions. When teachers model listening with care, it helps establish collaborative contexts where conversations are focused as the group theorizes about a particular topic. Frequently, "we do not know what we think until we create a gap or space in which to examine our thoughts. When we create this gap with others and try out our thoughts, we can see thought develop" (Wien, 2008, p. 153). Teachers relinquish control of the movement of thought and open themselves up to what children have to say as they support children in focusing their thinking. Pacini-Ketchabaw et al. (2015) claim that the teachers' questions are not

> intended to seek "truth," nor are they attempts to categorize what children know as right or wrong. Instead, they are grounded in what the children are saying and doing at that moment; they show a respect for children's fantasies and a curiosity about how children construct theories. They use these moments to create curriculum. (p. 21)

As children invent their own theories about a topic, it motivates them to seek out answers where they learn to distinguish between their interpretation of reality and reality itself (Wien, 2008).

During conversations, teachers scaffold the children's learning. Scaffolding is setting up situations "to make the child's entry easy and successful and then gradually pulling back and handing the role to the child as he becomes skilled enough to manage it" (Bruner, 2004, p. 60). Vygotsky (1978) distinguishes between what a child is capable of doing independently and their sphere of imitation. Imitation is what a child "can be taught or what he can do with direction or cooperation or with the help of leading questions" (p. 202). What the child can do independently reveals their mature capabilities and functions, whereas the sphere of imitation identifies their maturing processes. "The area of immature, but maturing processes, make-up the child's zone of proximal development" (p. 202). This zone is "the distance between the actual developmental level as determined by independent problem solving and the level of potential development as determined through problem solving under adult guidance or in collaboration with more capable peers … what a child can do with assistance today she will be able to do by herself tomorrow" (pp. 86–87). The foundation of the zone of proximal development is a relationship of learning between and among people.

Teachers provide scaffolding during conversations within Vygotsky's zone of proximal development so that the child can perform at a higher level. When just the right amount of assistance is given, by guiding, coaching, or prompting, a child can achieve more than they can do on their own. Bodrova and Leong (2007) explain, "With scaffolding, the task itself is not changed, but what the learner initially does is made easier with assistance. Gradually, the level of assistance decreases as the learner takes more responsibility for performance of the task" (p. 47). Bruner (2006) found that the scaffolding process is most effective when the teacher is first able to get the children interested in the task; the task is simplified and has manageable limits; the teacher keeps the children motivated, willing to take risks, and focused on the task; the teacher accentuates relevant features of the task; the teacher's assistance reduces the children's potential for frustration; and the teacher demonstrates solutions to tasks that children can already do fairly well.

The concept of exploratory talk is useful to understand conversation as a component of emergent curriculum. Exploratory talk, explains Barnes (2008), "is hesitant and incomplete because it enables the speaker to try out ideas, to hear how they sound, to see what others make of them, to arrange information and ideas into different patterns … in exploratory talk the speaker is more concerned with sorting out his or her own thoughts" (p. 5). Mercer and Dawes (2008) add that exploratory talk requires the speaker to "think aloud" and take a risk so that others can comment on and challenge their ideas. The speaker must be brave, so there has to be a sense of trust within the group. Listeners benefit from hearing a speaker's tentative thoughts, and their feedback might require the speaker to elaborate their point of view, reword it for clarity, or change their mind. During these genuine collaborative interactions, children can problem-solve as they share and build onto each other's ideas.

Bruner (2004) is helpful here in distinguishing between communicating in general and talking, which for him is a form of successful communication. Talking requires a child to "master the conventions for making his intentions clear [to others] by language" (p. 39). Forman and Fyfe (2012) argue that "to truly understand the children's talking, we should treat it as … an intelligent pattern of thoughts that is worthy of study." This causes teachers to "look for theories, assumptions, false premises, misapplications, clever analogies, ambiguities, and differences in communicative intent, all of which are pieces to be negotiated into shared meaning by the group" (pp. 246–247). Talk involves at least two people negotiating with a shared understanding of what they are talking about. It is also transactional, which means that the participants are exchanging their intentions.

Critical exploration, like exploratory talk, places value on providing contexts where children are called upon to think and to share what they think

(Duckworth, 2006). Teachers can provide children with opportunities to share wonderful ideas and let them feel good about it. The child explores the subject matter, and the teacher explores the child's thinking. Critical exploration involves developing an inquiry where the questions are open-ended and appealing so the children will share their ideas and continue to think about them. Teachers need to listen attentively to what children say without influencing what they say. The teacher responds with a question or resources to help the children take their own thoughts further.

Similarly, knowledge-building circles are part of inquiry-based learning where children come together to ask questions, share their theories, and revisit and negotiate their ideas. During these productive dialogues, children gain a deeper understanding through exposure to different perspectives and the shared ideas of the class. Children's new or unresolved questions, theories, and ideas serve as new entry points that continue the investigation. Teachers provide a variety of opportunities for children to reflect on their learning experiences and discuss possible solutions to their questions about an inquiry. As children engage in conversations, they sit in a circle to promote respect, attentive listening, communication, and equality, as everyone is a co-learner. This approach is an emergent process that can nurture the children's curiosity about the world that they live in (Chiarotto, 2011).

Gallas (2017) has stressed that, during conversations, young children are able to talk constructively about matters that are important to them. She found that this was especially true when her students engaged in "science talks." One of the most important functions of an inquiry is to generate opportunities for purposeful dialogue. Children co-construct ideas through dialogue, and they have a sense of control over the process of their learning. During science talks, "the reward is the ability to watch and document the natural unfolding of dialogue among children, to see a class of children beginning to think in concert, and to witness the power and deep intelligence they have as individuals and as a group" (pp. 18–19). When teachers listen to their students' conversations without interrupting, they see that the process of collaboration has potential to teach them about what children are thinking. Jacobs (2008) adds that, during this type of conversation, "Children become aware of their own ability to think, aware that they have their own opinions and theories, and understand that through dialogue they continue to build their own knowledge" (p. 82).

Conversation was an important component of all four of the inquiries introduced in this chapter. In the Invisibility Inquiry, for example, Lauren focused on how to ask children questions to get them to think more deeply about their theories and ideas. She explained, "I really am conscious of that and that's something I'm always working on, like the questioning and the trying not to lead." Lauren will ask a question, listen attentively to a child's answer, and then phrase the next question in light of the child's previous response. Her conversation during inquiry aspires to be truly reciprocal. In the Office Inquiry, Kathryn thought that it was her role to be an active listener, to nurture the children's interests and provide provocations to keep the interests going so that "they don't fizzle out." She said, "When a question is posed to a teacher, you can often overhear us replying back with a question: What do you think?"

DOCUMENTATION

The final component of emergent curriculum for discussion is pedagogical documentation, which is a research narrative about the children's and teacher's learning, shifts in their thinking, and their search for meaning. It is generated and made visible to others on posters or panels, or in diaries, books, binders, and portfolios, and studied by inviting collaborative discussion and interpretation as well as thinking about possibilities for next steps. Documentation becomes "pedagogical" when it is studied with children, parents, or colleagues, leading to a deeper analysis of the inquiry.

The documentation phase begins once the teachers have decided on the different forms the documentation will take, such as written observations, audiotaped conversations, work samples, and photographs. Documentation makes visible the process the children and teachers follow as they co-construct the curriculum throughout the inquiry. It is a record of the learning experiences that take place in the classroom and shows the connection between these events. Fraser (2012) states,

> Documentation is like a system of gears that sets the curriculum in motion. Making visible the children's ideas, thinking, and experiences in some form of documentation provides the teachers with a means of revisiting them with children, discussing them with colleagues and parents, and making hypotheses and flexible plans for further action. The teachers and children can discuss the documentation together, reflect on the experiences, and perhaps get an idea of how to proceed further with the topic. (p. 144)

Forman and Fyfe (2012) add that documentation "records the performance during a learning encounter as well as the documenter's interpretation of that performance ... the intent of the documentation is to explain not merely to describe" (p. 250). When teachers document, it nurtures the development of reciprocal relationships and the co-construction of curriculum in the classroom. It also demonstrates that the children's work is valued and their ideas are respected.

Dahlberg et al. (2013) describe pedagogical documentation as "a *process* and an important *content* in that process" (p. 156, emphasis in original). Pedagogical documentation as content is material, including the work of the children, that is a record of what they are saying and doing, as well as how the teacher relates to the children and their work. The material can be generated in many ways and take different forms. The material makes the work of the children and teachers visible and is therefore an important part of the process of pedagogical documentation. The process involves using that material to reflect upon the children's work in a rigorous, methodical, and democratic way. Wien et al. (2011) argue that pedagogical documentation "reflects a disposition of not presuming to know, and of asking how the learning occurs, rather than assuming—as in transmission models of learning—that learning occurred because teaching occurred" (p. 2).

Documentation, explains Rinaldi (2001, 2006), makes the nature of the learning paths and processes, and strategies used by the children visible. It enables analysis, revisiting, and assessment during the experience to take place. Documentation is built on trusting relationships where students feel comfortable sharing their thoughts. When teachers generate documentation and revisit it with the children, it changes the image of the role of the teacher from teaching children to studying and learning with children. As the children reflect on the documentation, they can see the meaning that the teacher has taken from their work, that their work is valued, and that what they say and do is important. When children revisit documentation, it enables them to think about the nature of their own learning process as they co-construct knowledge. Their theories need to be shared and listened to by others. Differences need to be expressed and negotiated and nurtured through the comparison of ideas so that theories are modified and enriched. Documentation is one of the fundamental strategies that teachers use to carry out this kind of listening during emergent curriculum inquiries.

Wien (2008) observes that pedagogical documentation slows down our thinking processes so we can consider topics with care. It lifts thinking out of our lived experiences at school and makes it visible to others. When documentation is revisited, children see that teachers value their thinking, and it leads to new thoughts, connections, and possibilities for future activities. Teachers use documentation as a vehicle for sharing multiple perspectives. Pedagogical documentation offers those who document and those who read the documen-tation an opportunity for reflection and further learning. Wien et al. (2011) ex-plain that

> two important levels of thought are made evident in strong pedagogical doc-umentation. The teacher presents data in ways that show others what children have been thinking, feeling, or valuing. At the same time, the teacher selects material and composes a display that expresses her hypotheses about the chil-dren's experiences and ideas. (p. 12)

It is important to remember that when teachers select and compose documenta-tion, it is a subjective judgement, and they take responsibility for their choices by sharing the documentation with others.

When children revisit, reflect on, and interpret the documentation, it supports their memory; they make comparisons among themselves and discuss differences of opinions (Rinaldi, 2006; Vecchi, 2001). Children learn about themselves by listening to other people's perspectives. Halls and Wien (2013) have noted that documentation holds children's theories in place so that, when they revisit them, they can consider their logic and discuss it with others. Through these kinds of discussions, we can see how children shift their thinking as they begin to absorb and consider other children's theories as well. Revisiting documentation allows children to "reflect on, clarify, and elaborate both their own and others' thoughts and theories" (p. 9). New levels of understanding emerge, which leads to some children testing out more theories and altering their own as they incorporate other people's ideas.

Stacey (2015) shares how documentation has the power to sustain and in-spire children and teachers during inquiry-based learning:

> Documentation at its best is a process that spirals upward to higher forms of listening, thinking, and learning for all the people involved. It begins with the children, then moves to the teachers as we respond to the children's work with interest, questions and careful observation. It moves back again to the chil-dren, as teachers explore with them, looking for meaning and co-constructing knowledge through further conversations or invitations to action. Then the teachers engage in more thinking, as we try to construct visible traces of the work. Then the process moves outward to families or colleagues, as we share the children's and teachers' thinking and actions. (p. 95)

This collaborative process is complex, not simple, as it often continues by moving back to the teachers and children once again.

In the Invisibility Inquiry, Lauren made documenting the children's learning a priority in her classroom every day. She wrote, "The materials, learning experiences and provocations are carefully chosen and crafted by me so the children are engaged, and there will be something to document and also that they will be too engaged to distract [from] the documentation process." Lauren documents the children's learning experiences using her iPad and iPhone to take photographs and videos of the children. She later transcribes what the children have said, matching the dialogue and photos. Lauren keeps all the documentation she has generated and studied in binders and on the walls both inside and outside the classroom. For some inquiries, she produces more polished pieces of documentation on panels and puts them on display. Lauren also has a documentation book for each child. She documents many learning experiences and includes the photographs, questions she asks, the children's responses, and some information to provide context. These documentation books span two years and are a record of the children's learning experiences and what they were thinking at the time.

Lauren believes that the whole point of pedagogical documentation is that it is public. She said, "It's something that you share with the children, with the families, with other colleagues." Lauren shares her documentation with other teachers at her school to hear their perspectives and think about possibilities for next steps. Similar to the Harvard Project Zero Protocol (Project Zero et al., 2003), first the teachers and Early Childhood Educators look at the documentation and have a chance to say what they see, what they wonder, and what they think. Then Lauren briefly responds to their perspectives and explains what she was trying to show in the documentation. She believes that when teachers reflect on how children's thinking changes over time, it transforms their own thinking. Listening to other people's perspectives on her documentation enlightens her own understanding of the work.

Kathryn explained how she saw the process of pedagogical documentation during the Office Inquiry:

> I see inquiry as active listening on the part of the teacher and really listening to the questions and the wonders and the theories of children and allowing that to guide where the content of the program goes. And then, pedagogical documentation, being that vehicle for highlighting and valuing and making visible the thinking and the theories and all of the inquiry that takes place.

Both Kathryn and Victoria collected and organized the data daily. They took many photographs and used a laptop computer to record what the children were saying. They collected a lot of data, recognizing it was a challenge because there were always so many possibilities about what to nurture and explore further. Kathryn explained that "I have to trust that the environment is supporting them [the children] and I don't need to like document or keep data on everything."

Documentation was organized in the classroom in several ways. Each child's portfolio contained documentation of her learning and included descriptions of her experiences, photographs, and work samples, as well as direct quotes of questions, theories, and ideas. At each of the Inquiry Centres there was a clipboard with documentation of the experiences that the children had shared together at that centre. There were also documentation panels that were displayed on the classroom walls. Kathryn met with her colleagues to look at documentation, especially when preparing for special events where they would invite other early years educators to come to their school for coffee and conversation. It was an opportunity to share some of the exciting inquiries that had emerged in their classrooms and engage in meaningful dialogue with other educators in the community.

During the Running Club Inquiry, Darlene and Kerri took turns collecting and organizing the data. They used an iPad to take photographs and videos, recording what the children were saying on paper and then later entering it into the classroom desktop computer. When they had an idea, they would pursue it, and usually there were several things being documented at the same time. Darlene said that some of the documentation on the walls, like the Running Club, was still ongoing and that she would later decide "whether to go more formal" with it. She explained,

> Usually something about it twigs me that I think this is really important for teachers to know, for parents to see. And if that's the case, then I would go into more formal documentation with it as well. Definitely, I'll put a wall up outside in the hall for the parents to see. I think that would be really good.

Darlene and Kerri both felt that sometimes you just have to "throw" the documentation pieces together and put the pieces up because, if not, time passes and then something else interesting happens.

Like Lauren, Darlene and Kerri got together sometimes at school with other teachers and Early Childhood Educators to study documentation. Darlene shared the Running Club documentation with her colleagues. As part of the protocol, Darlene stayed quiet until after the others shared what they saw, what they wondered, and what they thought. Darlene then described how the inquiry started, summarized the children's different running ideas, and explained that the children were working on combining their ideas. She then opened it up to her colleagues to share their thinking about possible next steps in terms of the direction the inquiry might take. Darlene and Kerri found it helpful to hear other interpretations of the documentation and what might be possible in terms of how to move forward.

Sharon's expertise in generating and studying pedagogical documentation throughout the Community Inquiry was quite evident. She and Mikayla both collected the documentation and then Sharon organized it into inquiry binders or posted it on the wall. They used the classroom camera to take photographs of the learning experiences. During knowledge-building circles, they recorded what the children said on a laptop computer. At other times, they made anecdotal notes on paper. In addition to sharing documentation with her colleagues at school, Sharon shared her documentation with the wider community when doing professional development workshops as an institute facilitator for the organization Learning for a Sustainable Future. These workshops are based on inquiries for responsible citizenship and sustainability and are structured around the needs of the participants and where they are in terms of their understanding of the inquiry process.

CHAPTER SUMMARY

This chapter focuses on how emergent curriculum supports inquiry-based learning. Emergent curriculum is a particular type of curriculum planning or teaching practice that many educators are pursuing in their classrooms. Inquiry-based learning encourages active learning and critical thinking through student-led investigations guided by their own questions and problems. An essential feature of all inquiry-based learning is that the teachers and children adopt an inquiry stance or mindset that permeates all thinking and learning in the classroom. Emergent curriculum explains what the children will be learning, while inquiry-based learning explains how the children will go about it. Emergent curriculum inquiries are sustained investigations built around the children's interests and are co-constructed by the teachers, the children, and the environment as the inquiry unfolds.

Emergent curriculum inquiries are unique because they contain all four core components of emergent curriculum—inquiry design, design of the environment, conversation, and documentation—which are interwoven throughout the inquiry as it unfolds. The inquiry design phase begins when the teachers decide on a topic they believe will sustain the children's interests. They identify possible directions the inquiry might follow and list ideas for how to provoke the children to think more deeply about the topic. Children become more engaged in their learning when they help plan and design the classroom environment. Conversations involve interactions that go beyond teachers listening to children during discussions to reflecting on and analyzing what is said and heard. Teachers and children engage in conversations during inquiries to co-construct theories about topics in which they are all interested. Pedagogical documentation is a research narrative about the children's and teacher's learning, shifts in their thinking, and their search for meaning. It makes visible the process the children and teachers followed as they co-constructed the curriculum throughout the inquiry.

REFLECTIVE QUESTIONS

1. How has this chapter helped you to understand the relationship between emergent curriculum and inquiry-based learning?
2. How can emergent curriculum and inquiry-based learning co-exist with a mandated standardized school curriculum?
3. What are the challenges of implementing inquiry-based learning in your role working with young children?
4. Think about an experience you have had with inquiry-based learning. What might you have done differently in light of the information presented in this chapter?
5. In what ways can you support your colleagues who are learning how to implement inquiry-based learning in their classrooms?

RECOMMENDED READINGS

Anderson, Doug, Chiarotto, Lorraine, & Comay, Julie . (2017). Lisa's story. In *Natural curiosity 2nd edition: A resource for educators* (pp. 219–225). Toronto, ON: OISE.

Cavallini, Ilaria, Filippini, Tiziana, Vecchi, Vea, & Trancossi, Lorella (Eds.). (2011). *The wonder of learning: The hundred languages of children*. Reggio Emilia, Italy: Reggio Children.

Fine, Melissa, & Desmond, Lindsey. (2015). Inquiry-based learning: Preparing young learners for the demands of the 21st century. *Educator's Voice, VIII*, 2–11.

Fraser, Susan. (2012). *Authentic childhood* (3rd ed.). Toronto, ON: Nelson Books.

Gandini, Lella. (2015). The amusement park for birds: Emergence and process of a project. In Lella Gandini, Lynn Hill, Louise Cadwell, & Charles Schwall (Eds.), *In the spirit of the studio: Learning from the atelier of Reggio Emilia*. New York: Teachers College Press.

Gerst, Barb, & Fraser, Trish. (2009). Using teacher dialogue to bring nature based learning to kindergarten: The hippo inquiry. *Canadian Children, 34*, 29–36.

Stacey, Susan. (2009). *Emergent curriculum in early childhood settings*. St. Paul, MN: Redleaf Press.

Vecchi, Vea. (2001). The ring-around-the-rosy game. In Project Zero & Reggio Children, *Making learning visible: Children as individual and group learners* (pp. 191–210). Cambridge, MA: Harvard Graduate School of Education.

Wien, Carol Anne. (2014). *The power of emergent curriculum*. Washington, DC: NAEYC.

ONLINE RESOURCES

EduGains

http://www.edugains.ca/newsite/Kindergarten/play_inquiry.html

Sky Inquiry Filming Series Video 5—Impact on Learning

https://youtu.be/qmR_9HVPaYY

Learning is Co-constructed Inquiry: Provoking an Inquiry Stance

https://vimeo.com/104014500

Chapter Three

Self-Regulation and Inquiry Design

> Consider how design helps children. Selected records of the children's assumptions or plans certainly serve the children as they revisit their own ideas to deepen and broaden the application of their concepts. Design helps teachers plan follow-up activities. Design helps parents who want to extend the child's study into the home.
> —George Forman & Brenda Fyfe, 2012, p. 251

In this chapter, I focus on self-regulation and the inquiry design component of emergent curriculum. Inquiry design has five aspects: (1) building the curriculum, (2) engaging in reciprocal actions, (3) taking ownership over the direction of the inquiry, (4) promoting positive emotions such as excitement and curiosity, and (5) encouraging collaboration and inclusivity. When each of the five aspects are considered together, they demonstrate clearly how inquiry design enables children to become self-regulated learners in the primary classroom. The four compelling insights about the relationship between self-regulation and inquiry-based learning outlined in the introduction are interwoven into the discussion of inquiry design.

The inquiry design component begins when teachers, based on their observations and children's conversations, decide on an investigation that will sustain the children's interests. The teachers identify possible directions the inquiry might follow and provocations to encourage the children to think more deeply about the topic. Children are intimately involved in the design component and have opportunities to discuss and represent their ideas throughout the inquiry. They make their ideas and theories about the inquiry visible by using a variety of materials to represent their thinking. The four inquiries introduced in chapter 2 are used here to illustrate concretely the relationship between self-regulation and inquiry design, which is one of the components that supports inquiry-based learning.

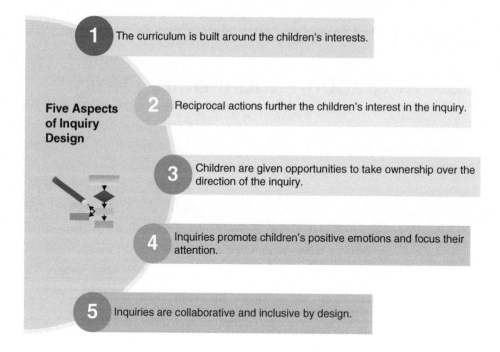

Five Aspects of Inquiry Design

1 — The curriculum is built around the children's interests.

2 — Reciprocal actions further the children's interest in the inquiry.

3 — Children are given opportunities to take ownership over the direction of the inquiry.

4 — Inquiries promote children's positive emotions and focus their attention.

5 — Inquiries are collaborative and inclusive by design.

FIVE ASPECTS OF INQUIRY DESIGN

The Curriculum Is Built around the Children's Interests

One of my compelling insights is that children learn how to self-regulate during inquiry-based learning in the same way they do during play. Inquiries are similar to play because they emerge from the children's interests, they are enjoyable and intrinsically rewarding, and there is a sense of control over the activity. As we saw in chapter 1, existing research clearly shows that children learn how to self-regulate during play (Porges, 2015b; Shanker, 2010, 2013b; Vygotsky, 1978). Play is an especially valuable opportunity to exercise our nervous system in order to foster social and emotional learning (SEL). It is also a major mechanism for developing executive functions and using oral language as a self-regulatory tool. Vygotsky (1978) explains that "play creates a zone of proximal development of the child. In play a child always behaves beyond his average age, above his daily behavior; in play it is as though he were a head taller than himself" (p. 102).

I believe that inquiry is like play because it helps children to stay focused, consider different perspectives, and figure out their own thinking, which are all important mental processes in the cognitive domain. Inquiry is an enjoyable and intrinsically rewarding activity, which is similar to how Csikszentmihalyi (1975) describes play. During inquiry, children have a sense of control over the activity, so they can concentrate and ignore distractions. They can self-regulate because they feel capable to meet the demands that the activity places on them.

This particular aspect of inquiry design highlights the role of children's interests. Children are able to self-regulate during inquiries based on their interests for the same reasons that they can self-regulate during play. The inquiries introduced in chapter 2 arose out of the children's choices in play. The initial idea for the Invisibility Inquiry came from Steven, who had drawn a picture of his mother and said, "My mom is invisible." When Lauren asked Steven how he could show that his mother was invisible, he said that he had to roll the picture up and then you couldn't see her anymore. Lauren said, "Yeah, and that just sort of sparked the whole thing." Then a few days later Deepa was playing at the Light Table and said, "I am going to make this jewel invisible … because I don't want anyone to see it." Deepa made the jewel "invisible" by putting a black ribbon on top of it. She thought it was invisible because you could not see it. Lauren said, "That's what made me think oh, invisibility … I might have something here!"

Photo 3.1: Steven Holding a Picture of His Mother

In Lauren's classroom, the curriculum emerges around the children's interests. Lauren observes the children and finds opportunities to extend their learning by asking them thought-provoking questions. She documents the learning experience by taking photographs and videos and later transcribes the text. Then Lauren shares the documentation with the children in small or large groups. Next, she introduces new provocations to further the children's interest in the inquiry. Lauren explained,

> I find the curriculum is so broad.… I kind of see it everywhere. I see it in every single thing … and the documentation does actually help to uncover a lot of that, I find. I'll be going back through something [documentation] and oh my gosh that was really measurement, so when I go back to speak with that child again or bring something over to their attention, I'm going to make sure it's around that and we can maybe expand that a little bit further.

Lauren believes it is important to keep things as open-ended as possible so the children can discover things for themselves. In essence, the children are uncovering the curriculum based on their interests.

Victoria explained how the children initially became interested in the Office Inquiry:

> Well, it started actually in the Construction area. All of a sudden, there was not a chair in the room.… They [the children] were all in the middle of the room. They had made it sort of box like and they were all in there with their notepads working away, and I thought, what are they doing? "We are at the office—we are working at the office." So that was it. One of them was the security guard … and then they've got all sorts of things. Their phone was going and all sorts. Anyway, so then they did it two days in a row.

The girls' initial interest in the office led to a month-long investigation into what items belong in an office and what it means to be "working" there. Victoria and Kathryn both felt that the curriculum should be uncovered naturally through child-initiated activities.

The origin of the Running Club inquiry was Darlene's realization that running in the hall was important to the children, so she opened the door and let the inquiry flourish because of their enthusiasm. When the children initially approached Darlene during lunch to ask about running in the hall, she could have put the children off by telling them she was busy. Instead, she responded

Photo 3.2: The Children Line Up Chairs to Create an Office

by saying, "Who wants to run in the hall?... How can you let me know that?" Gabriel suggested that they make a list of all the children who wanted to run. Again, when the children returned with the list, instead of shutting it down, Darlene asked, "Well how is this going to work? Do you have a plan?"

Darlene believes that the curriculum in her program is built around the children's interests:

> I feel like, especially in this school ... we can do things the way, how we view them. I think we are educated enough to know what's good for the children and I think we have a pretty good grasp on being able to do things the way that we believe in doing them.

Darlene emphasized the importance of listening to children and how this gives direction to the curriculum in the classroom. She said, "I'm here more to set up learning rather than to dictate how learning will occur. So, I like to listen ... for all the possibilities that may happen, and something that may twig me to maybe extend and keep going."

The Community Inquiry began when Omja shared a picture he drew of the CN Tower. This sparked a lively discussion as the children shared their personal experiences about the CN Tower and the city. After looking at books and having further discussions about cities, Sharon added building materials to the Small Block Centre to encourage the children's interest in building the CN Tower and the City of Toronto. During a community walk, the children noticed the cityscape and made connections to what they were discussing and building at school. This led to another walk where the children sketched the cityscape in their inquiry books. Sharon and Mikayla both believe that the curriculum should be emergent and based on the children's interests. Sharon said, "We talk about it in the way of, instead of, covering the curriculum you are uncovering the curriculum."

Reciprocal Actions Further the Children's Interest in the Inquiry

Teachers engage in reciprocal actions when they ask children questions to provoke further thought, provide provocations that scaffold the children's learning, adapt the classroom environment to accommodate these interests, and take the children on outings to enhance their understanding. Reciprocal actions occur in the children's zone of proximal development. This zone was evident in Lauren's classroom at the beginning of the water experiment. When the children were being challenged and it was not clear in what direction the water experiment was heading, the children were more fidgety and distracted even though they were interested and curious. Although Lauren could have stopped, she explained,

> but then if you wait sometimes, it's just in that waiting, waiting to let something develop. You have to kind of let everything percolate a little bit and it's almost until the kids … sort of start to click and say oh, I better do something here. How can I make this a little more exciting? It kind of puts the onus back on them a little bit.… I better get thinking here. I better get acting and doing something.

Once the ideas started to flow the children were totally focused on the experience. When teachers respond thoughtfully with reciprocal actions that help to propel the inquiry forward, they must find the balance between providing learning experiences that are beyond the children's level and too challenging and providing learning experiences that are not challenging enough. If the experiences are too challenging, the children can become frustrated and distracted from their learning. Reciprocal actions that are challenging, but not overwhelming, support the children's ability to self-regulate because they allow the children to keep their focus on the task at hand.

During the four inquiries the teachers engaged in reciprocal actions by re-sponding to the children's interests. In Lauren's class the children were invited to make invisible drawings and use materials to make gemstones disappear. At the Art Table, for example, Lauren asked them to draw something or someone that is invisible. She gave them a variety of materials, like white and coloured paper, chalk, clear wax crayons, and paint. Steven tried to make his drawing invisible this time by covering it up with his hands. Samantha didn't think it was invisible because she could still see part of it. Then Lauren asked the children if she covered up the picture with her hands whether it would be invisible. Steven said, "No, because I can still see something." Rory explained, "It is invisible because you put something on top." Raina thought, "If you put your hand on top it is still going to be there." Samantha added, "You can't just put your hands on top because people can peek under your hands. If you put paint on top of it, then it really is invisible because you can't peek under paint." While the chil-dren worked on their drawings, they continued to think about what invisibility meant. Graham thought if you hide your hands in your sleeves or your head in your shirt, that makes them invisible. Anna used green chalk on green paper and thought that no one else could see her drawing. Samantha concluded, "It [invis-ibility] means when you can't see something."

Lauren, on another day, provided a group of children with materials that included gemstones, a bottle cap, a clear container, black felt, and green material. She then asked them if they could make the gemstones invisible like Deepa had made her jewel "invisible" at the Light Table. Julian said, "I am closing it all up [in the felt] so you can't see it…. You could see the jewels under the glass. You can't see when they are under the bottle cap." Deepa explained, "I am putting it under the felt so you can't see it…. I put them into the glass container then I put the cap on top then I covered it with the black felt then I folded the green felt on top of it."

Samantha thought,

> To make it the most invisible I put one glass underneath and then I put one glass on top. I put the gem in the glass and green cloth on the bottom and the black cloth on the top…. I can't see it. I can just feel it…. I can hear it.

Daryl added, "If I had the same colour cloth as this gem [blue] then I would put it on the cloth, and nobody would see it anymore … you can't see it because it is blending into something." Later Jian wanted to draw a picture, and when he was finished, he immediately covered it with black felt. He removed the cloth and then coloured over his picture with a black crayon. He said, "This is invisible.… I coloured black on top, that makes it really invisible." When Lauren asked Samantha what invisibility means, this time she said, "It means that there is something there, but you can't see it. Like Santa is invisible."

Reciprocal actions were likewise important to help further the children's interest in the Office Inquiry. Kathryn and Victoria took the girls to visit the school office and invited their parents to share ideas about what it meant to work. After the teachers had observed the children's interest in "working" at the office for two days, they decided to take them to visit the junior school office. While at the office, the girls sketched and wrote in their I Wonder books about all the things they could see. When they returned to the classroom, Kathryn, Victoria, and the children co-constructed a list of the items they found in the office. The teachers gathered the materials from the list and put them in a huge pile in the middle of the Drama Centre, leaving it to the girls to organize the space. Victoria said, "I think, give them the chance to own it totally." Kathryn added, "And if they are owning where the materials all go too, I think that will make it all the more powerful for them." It was up to each child to decide for herself whether she wanted to be part of creating the office. While at "the office" the children enjoyed creating nametags, using the typewriter, and writing letters.

The teachers also reciprocated when the children were interested in sharing their ideas and theories about what it means when we say that someone is "working." To build on their understanding of what working means across different contexts, Victoria recorded the questions that the children wanted to ask their parents about what they do at their office. She then sent an email with the list of questions to the parents. Many parents responded by sending in photographs and responses to the children's questions. Some girls shared what their parents did during a class discussion.

In Darlene's class, the children were invited to draw their running ideas and to use materials from a special box to demonstrate their thinking. After she took the children out in the hall to run, the children talked about how running made their body feel. Darlene then asked the children to draw a picture of what their body was feeling inside before and after they ran, and she recorded their ideas on the back of their picture. Similarly, when the children were all talking about how they had different running ideas, Darlene had them draw their ideas. She said, "So I thought writing it down and drawing it, what they envisioned would help me see into their theory a little bit better. Which they did and it really did help a lot." It also helped the children to understand their own idea better, and as Darlene pointed out, "It changes their thinking, too."

Photo 3.3: The Children Write about What They See in the School Office

Photo 3.4: A Child Draws the Telephone in the School Office

Photo 3.5: A Child Explores a School Office Desk

One day, after the children shared their running ideas with their peers, Darlene reciprocated by putting together a provocation that was a special box with the materials the children had asked for. She said,

> I have a surprise. Come and sit down. So, remember all the things you talked about that you needed for running? So, I put together a running box. This was the best box I could find because a lot of you feel happy when you run.

Darlene then invited Michael to open the box and take out what was inside. After looking at all the materials Gabriel took the stopwatch and was the first child to demonstrate his running idea. By providing this provocation, Darlene was able to further the children's interest in the inquiry.

During the Community Inquiry, the children went on community walks and engaged in knowledge-building circles. After going on one community walk, Sharon observed, "They were really excited to talk about it, their buildings, but it didn't launch them forward … it didn't provoke any questions." She realized that she needed to have photographs of all the apartment buildings, so she followed up by taking the children for another community walk around the entire horseshoe loop of apartment buildings where they lived. While on the walk, the children told Sharon when they saw their building or their friends or their cousins and she took photographs. Sharon asked the children to remember

Photo 3.6: Darlene Shows the Children a Stopwatch

Photo 3.7: Two Children Talk about the Stopwatch

their building number. At the end of the day, Sharon shared the photographs with the children and had them identify their building. She wrote their names on sticky notes and attached them to the photos. Sharon also recorded other connections the children were making, like where their friends or cousins lived. She then put up all the documentation on the whiteboard so the children could see their building and the buildings of their friends.

Another time, Sharon followed up Mahdi's idea that "nature is a friend of the community" during a whole-class knowledge-building circle. Sharon explained,

> I was trying to think about where to go next. There hasn't been a driving question and I think today was a reminder to me of you can't go forward until you hear from the children where they want to go.

She wrote Mahdi's statement on the whiteboard and then showed the children the same photograph of the valley that she had shared with Mahdi's small group. She first asked the children, "What is a community?" Sharon observed, "What was interesting was the parts that came out first were nature this time rather than the buildings ... and finally Adhita added buildings." Then the children talked a bit more about Mahdi's original statement, but it still seemed quite abstract. Sharon followed up once again by writing "What is a friend?" on chart paper. The children brainstormed ideas about what a friend is and she recorded them on the chart. One idea, for instance, was that nature helps us and shares with us. Then in small groups the children shared their ideas about how nature is a friend, and they drew and wrote about it.

Children Are Given Opportunities to Take Ownership over the Direction of the Inquiry

Children's thinking helps initiate and shape the design of emergent curriculum inquiries. For instance, Rory and Daryl's thoughts about water and invisibility led to the water experiments. Rachel's role as the security guard led to making a security TV, swipe cards, and a scanner. Michael's thought about connecting all the little ideas to make one big running idea led to each child wanting to demonstrate their own idea. Esita's bird's-eye view of her apartment fueled her peers' interest in drawing the important features of their own apartment. Play and inquiry are both authentic and can be self-initiated. These types of activities are highly motivating, so children generate new ideas and strategies to sustain them (Brooker, 2011; Copple & Bredekamp, 2009; Howard, 2010; Whitebread, 2010). It is easier for children to maintain their focus when they are highly engaged in their learning. Howard (2010) explains, "The fact that the boundaries in play are set, regulated and modified by children themselves, means that play promotes and protects self-esteem and maintains children's attention" (p. 154).

Inquiry-based learning is also like play in that it is voluntary and the children are given a choice about whether they want to participate or not. When children have the choices that inquiry provides, they have an incentive to self-regulate to sustain the inquiry and keep it moving forward. A key to supporting children's emerging self-regulation skills is to offer them choice in their learning, which is what enables the children to take ownership of the inquiry. Shanker (2013b) states that activities

> can be delivered in ways that enhance self-regulation—by providing a choice of engaging activities and a degree of student ownership of their learning. The more students are engaged in an activity, and have a sense of control over their learning, the more likely they are to achieve a state of optimal self-regulation. (p. 19)

Play and inquiry are similar activities as they enable children to become self-regulated learners.

Lauren seized opportunities for the children to take ownership over the direction of the Invisibility Inquiry. For example, one day Lauren opened up a discussion to see what else the children were thinking about invisibility.

Lauren: Rory, do you want to say something else about invisibility?

Rory: If you don't shake the water bottle and there is water in there, but you might think there isn't.

Lauren: Oh … because you can't see inside your water bottle. Is, that right? Hmm interesting …

Daryl: People sometimes don't see their water, cause, it is see-through …

Lauren: That's a very interesting idea that Daryl just brought up. Sometimes people don't see the water in their water bottle because the water is see-through. Does that make water invisible, Daryl?

Daryl: Yes.

Lauren: Yes, you think so or very hard to see?

Rory: If water is inside your water bottle … actually water is invisible.

Lauren: Water is invisible?

Rory: Cause the water it could be the same colour inside your cup.

After Rory and Daryl explained their thoughts about water and invisibility, Lauren and the children created a water experiment that helped the group expand their thinking about whether water is invisible.

During the water experiment, Rory came up with the idea of pouring the water from the small jar into the vase, and this led to a lot of excitement and new ideas. As Lauren and the children took turns pouring water into the vase, everyone anticipated that the water would overflow.

Lauren: So, what would happen if I poured this in?

Samantha: It would go higher.

Daryl: So, we know water's in there.

Lauren: Okay let's try it.… Watch if I shake the vase, what happens?

Samantha: The water shakes.

Rory: So, you can see it inside … I can see like kind of a pool underneath. It looks still like a pool …

Samantha: Yeah, it looks like the … round thing on the bottom. On the top, it looks like a swimming pool.

Raina: It's the sun coming from here, that's why it looks like a pool ...

Lauren: Okay are we ready for this?

Group: Yeah ... do all of it ...

Lauren: Don't touch the table, let it go really still and watch it ... carefully.... What do you see right now?

Daryl: ... I'm seeing air in it every time, I see some air inside it ... the air is very small ...

Rory: You can't see the pool anymore.

To everyone's delight, the water did flow over the top of the vase.

Once the water overflowed, the children spontaneously decided to cover the entire table with water. Then they bent over and started to blow the water. This action led to a whole new set of ideas related to how blowing with our mouths can move the water on the table.

Rory: What if you blow it?

Lauren: Try blowing it. What happens if you blow it?

Samantha: The water goes fast.... It also makes this little pool thingy ...

Daryl: If you blow the water bends. Look the water is bending.

It was the children's ideas and excitement that propelled the water exploration.

The children's ongoing interest in security enabled them to propel the Office Inquiry forward. In the Construction Centre, for example, Rachel took on the role of the security guard. Then, after a visit to the junior school office, Nikki said, "I know what we need for our office. We need a TV to check if some people are coming or not." The girls decided that they wanted to make a security TV for their classroom office. Victoria responded by taking several children outside to photograph images of the school doors. Kathryn commented, "Victoria was like, come on, everybody come along.... Victoria is so good with stuff like that." Once the photographs were printed the children constructed the security TV. Then the girls wanted to know how the school entrance was monitored by the junior school office. Kathryn and Victoria decided to take all the children outside and they pretended to visit the school. First, they announced their arrival through the intercom and were buzzed in. Then they went back outside and entered the building through a different door using Victoria's swipe card. When the children returned to the classroom, they made their own swipe cards and a scanner. The girls decided to use the mirror as a swinging door to indicate the swipe card giving them access to the classroom office.

Photo 3.8: The Children Begin the Water Experiment

Photo 3.9: A Child Pours Water into the Vase

Photo 3.10: The Children Watch the Water Rise in the Vase

The children took ownership over the direction of the Running Club Inquiry from the outset. As Darlene put it, "We don't own what's going on here at all. They own this whole entire project. They designed it. They led it. They are doing it themselves and so it's their responsibility. And I think they feel that." For example, one morning the Running Club was invited into the Cubby to look at all the documentation that had been generated so far. There were photographs of children running in the hall, a list of children's names, and Cole's drawing of the planning circle. There were also work samples showing how the children felt before and after they ran as well as their different running ideas. Darlene sat back and waited to hear what the children had to say about all the work they had done. Michael's thinking completely surprised everyone and led the inquiry in a new direction.

Darlene: I want to hear what you have to say about the work you've done …
Michael: Maybe if we could connect all our ideas and make a huge big one it would all work.
Darlene: A huge big what?
Michael: Idea.
Darlene: How can we do that? How can we connect all our ideas?
Michael: We could take a little bit of our ideas and then … make a big idea out of those little pieces of ideas.
Darlene: Okay so give me an example of that. A little idea …
Michael: So, my idea was … run with this one person. Connor what was your idea?
Connor: We gather up in a big circle for plans.
Michael: Okay … so for example if me and Connor were the only ones here, we would make a big circle and run with one person at a time …

The inquiry became focused on sharing everyone's thinking to create one big running idea.

Darlene reflected on Michael's leadership that day and said, "He did an incredible, articulate, beautiful job.… He just ran the whole show. We just sat back and watched.… It was amazing." He was really in control of the situation. Kerri said, "I've seen him do that. He's able to collaborate with the children and bring them together. It's amazing how he can do that." We discussed how Michael was clearly the leader when it came to articulating ideas and how Gabriel was the leader when it came to running in the hall. Darlene explained,

Photo 3.11: A Child Shares His Idea

But if you knew them really well, you would see that Michael is the articulate speaker in the classroom and he wows his group all the time. So that's his strength ... and Gabriel knows that that is Michael's strength. When they are in the hall, though, and they start doing something physical, Michael knows that's Gabriel's forte.

Kerri commented, "So it's good that they know that, you know, each other's strengths and they can be leaders in their own right and that they are recognizing their own strengths."

Darlene later explained how the leadership roles in her classroom really stood out to her during the Running Club Inquiry. She said,

Quiet individuals began to take risks and take on leadership roles. They would discuss, argue and work together with little support from the adults. The role was shared dependent on each other's strengths. Even the children began to recognize where their peers lead best and would encourage them. They developed trust within the group, which allowed us to stand back as teachers and let things happen.

When children were given opportunities to take ownership over the direction of the inquiry, it enabled them to take on leadership roles.

The children were provided many opportunities to take ownership over their own learning in the Community Inquiry. For example, one day some children started to draw pictures of the City of Toronto completely on their own initiative. When the teachers offered the children large poster paper, several groups started to work on creating the city posters collaboratively. Through these illustrations, the children were able to share what they knew about the City of Toronto and then they were ready to move on and focus more closely on the local community.

After Esita drew a bird's-eye view of her building that included the details of her apartment layout, the family car, and aspects of nature like the sun and flowers, the children asked Sharon what her apartment looked like and could she draw it. Sharon drew her apartment layout and the contents and she labelled them. The children worked for a long period of time drawing their own apartments, adding and layering details as they thought about their living spaces. They drew features of their apartment that were important to them. Some children drew themselves, their family and friends, and their toys, furniture, computers, and TVs. Others added apartment numbers on their doors, hallways, and balconies. A few children also talked about what they could see or hear from their balconies.

Photo 3.12: The Children Work Collaboratively on the City Poster

Photo 3.13: The City Poster Is Finished

Photo 3.14: Bird's-Eye View of Esita's Apartment

On a different day, the children built the CN Tower and the community, including the valley, out of blocks and other building materials. After visiting the valley a number of times on walks, the children had started to think about the valley as being part of the community. During the collaborative building project, it was almost like the children were taking everything they had talked about and learned since the beginning of the inquiry and were using that knowledge to inform their thinking around how to build their structure. When later reflecting on this experience Sharon said, "It was like ... we had reached the pinnacle moment of so much information.... I feel like this was really one of the richest tasks and it was completely derived from them." The children had transferred all that rich knowledge about the community into their creation.

Inquiries Promote Children's Positive Emotions and Focus Their Attention

As explained in the introduction, one of the four compelling insights about the relationship between self-regulation and inquiry-based learning is that inquiries promote positive emotions. SEL is a process of acquiring and applying knowledge and skills that enable us to recognize and manage our emotions, developing empathy for others, making informed decisions, establishing authentic relationships, and being resilient when facing challenges. The research field of SEL has found that negative emotions make it difficult for students to concentrate and pay attention (Jones & Kahn, 2017). Positive emotions such as inspiration, curiosity, excitement, enthusiasm, interest, confidence, pride, and happiness strengthen children's ability to learn. Children communicate their emotions through affect signals such as tone of voice, gestures, and facial expressions. Inquiry is connected to self-regulation in the cognitive domain through positive emotions like elation, inspiration, pride, and curiosity.

The positive emotions generated by inquiry-based learning remind me of Wien's windhorse effect. Wien (2008) explains, "The term *windhorse* ... refers to raising positive energy, the life force that whirls through us ... the animation by emotion that occurs in emergent curriculum" (p. 15, emphasis in original). During the four inquiries, rising positive energy drew in the children, teachers, and visitors and also spun out into the community through the sharing of documentation. I felt this windhorse effect during the water experiment, the demonstration of running ideas, and visits to the office and valley. The positive energy that arose out of the children's emotions also fueled further learning and fostered their ability to self-regulate. The windhorse effect was evident when Lauren was working with the children on the Invisibility Inquiry. She wanted the children to stay so she didn't lose their great ideas about sound and invisibility:

> The way the kids were at the table, to me that was true self-regulation because they were starving … [and] they still were focused on what we were talking about.… So that to me is like an even more impressive example [of self-regulation] because the conditions were not ideal.… So for them to just all hold it together and keep contributing, that was kind of amazing.

It was like the children could sense that what they were doing was important. When Iliana thought of movement and Samantha thought of sound, everyone was quite euphoric about the breakthrough, which generated a lot of positive emotion and enthusiasm to think about how to make sound visible. These positive emotions were evident in each of the inquiries.

Many of the children were excited and curious as they participated in the Invisibility Inquiry. During the water experiment, the water in the vase got higher and higher and the children anticipated that it would overflow. Daryl held the little jar carefully and concentrated on what he was doing. He was looking at the bubbles that were being created in the vase as he poured the water. Lauren said, "This means something to him. Like, he's so deliberate and focused and he's really trying to make sure that he's doing it in the exact way he wants it done." Similarly, Steven had a plan, as he dipped his fingers in the water and drew his robot on the table. He drew a line and then dipped his fingers again and drew another line. Later, he was so excited to discover that his robot became invisible when he poured water on top of it. Lauren commented that usually Steven likes to be on the move, and for him to be so quiet and focused "really meant something." Cassie was curious about the inquiry and she wanted to be part of it. One morning, after sharing the documentation with the children, Lauren invited a small group of them to draw their idea of invisibility. Cassie was inspired by the documentation and volunteered to draw a picture. Lauren said, "I have to say … that's the first thing Cassie's ever voluntarily participated in, in the classroom, the very first thing."

Even when an inquiry generates positive emotions, some children still become distracted and disengaged. For example, Henry, who generally found it difficult to maintain and shift his attention, initially joined the water experiment but struggled to stay on task even when he was interested and curious. He shared his ideas and theories about invisibility with his peers and one-on-one with adults but found it hard to remain focused and take turns during group activities when the other children were sharing their thinking. He went off to a centre to play and later rejoined the group briefly once he heard how excited the children were.

Positive emotions were readily evident during the Office Inquiry. Liza was especially interested in visiting the junior school office the second time. She was very excited as she walked down the hall smiling and skipping along. When she and Vicky stepped inside the office to see Ms. Harland, Liza asked, "Can we have an appointment for this afternoon?" Kathryn explained that Ms. Harland printed out a confirmation for them, so it made it official. After setting up the appointment, the confirmation slip disappeared. Later that day when the class visited the office, Liza pulled out the confirmation when Ms. Winters asked for it and said, "Here it is." Kathryn and Victoria were so surprised. Liza had been enthusiastic about the Office Inquiry right from the very beginning, so she had, on her own, taken complete responsibility for the confirmation slip and kept it in a safe place because she knew it was important.

Once the children had finished creating an office space in the Construction Centre, they focused their attention on role-playing office workers. There was only one entrance, and it was pretty small. Victoria explained, "I don't think they wanted us in there. Well, every time I went over there to talk to them, they'd say 'we're busy, we're working' … it was definitely like 'could you leave us alone, please.'" Later the girls were very enthusiastic about setting up their own classroom office in the Drama Centre. They thought very carefully about where they should put all the materials the teachers had gathered for them. They spent a lot of time creating nametags, typing and rolling paper through the typewriter, and writing letters.

One morning, the Running Club was so inspired by their inquiry they disappeared into the Cubby Area and had a meeting. When the children came out, they were very excited. Darlene asked, "Where have you been?" The response was, "We were meeting! We were in the meeting room." Gabriel explained that during the meeting they made some teams, "So all this side are on a team and me and Rose and Evan and Connor and Zara are on a team.… So Michael are you the captain of your team?" Michael responded, "Yeah." Gabriel said, "Okay, I'm the captain of my team. So, Michael you get to make your team okay. And you get to make the name for your team. And I get to make the name for my team." Darlene asked, "And is that okay that Gabriel is making all these decisions, or does anyone have a different idea?" Gabriel said, "I have been sort of the leader of the whole running group.… Who agrees with me raise your hand?" Almost all the children raised their hands.

Photo 3.15: The Children Create Running Teams

Evan, who was the youngest child in the Running Club and saw Gabriel as a role model, took risks and gained so much confidence because the other children were accepting of his thoughts and ideas. When it was his turn to share his running idea, he was just jumping with excitement because he was so proud that it was his turn to share. Positive feedback from his peers encouraged Evan to stay focused on the inquiry and take more risks. As the inquiry progressed, his voice became much louder, his body language showed confidence, and he became a big part of the group because the other children accepted him as an equal.

Visits to the valley during the Community Inquiry fuelled positive emotions in the children. While walking to the valley, Sharon pointed out interesting things in the environment for the children to look at and think about. The children listened attentively while she talked about different trees, flowers, birds, buildings, bridges, and the GO train. Sharon said, "I feel that they don't have the vocabulary … you have to open it up and point things out to them because … they don't have enough time and experience out there." As the children looked over the bridge to see the river, they were very excited and recalled how when they were there the last time, they walked along the river, listened to different sounds, and watched the water bubble when it was moving. In the valley, the children were very curious, and many of them chose to use the nature cups and magnifying glasses to go on a nature hunt. Others laughed and played in the

Photo 3.16: A Child Looking through a Magnifying Glass

sunshine with their friends, while others chose to use the clipboards and paper to do observational drawings of the trees. For instance, Amina focused for a long time and kept rotating her observational drawing of the tree as she attempted to draw it from different angles. Sharon said, "I love to see this because I want them to feel more, like for sketching … trying it out and experimenting and not wanting it to be perfect, and not meaning it to be perfect." After the children returned to school, Mahdi shared his idea about the butterflies in the valley. Sharon said, "So when you went to the valley … what did nature share with you on that day?" Mahdi responded, "Butterflies." Sharon asked, "How did that make you feel when nature shared butterflies?" and Mahdi replied, "Happy." Mahdi's response was not unusual as the children all seemed to enjoy their time in the valley.

Inquiries Are Collaborative and Inclusive by Design

The collaborative and inclusive nature of inquiry-based learning makes me think of the experiential state described in Csikszentmihalyi's (1975, 2008) seminal work on flow theory, introduced in chapter 1. Flow is a sensation we experience when we are totally involved in an activity. Csikszentmihalyi emphasizes that "there is a common experiential state which is present in various forms of play, and also under certain conditions in other activities [like inquiry] which are not normally thought of as play" (1975, p. 43). He refers to this experiential state as *flow* and describes it as a sensation that is present when we are totally involved in an activity. During inquiries, I believe an experiential state of flow develops for those working collaboratively and inclusively on an activity that requires working out creative ideas. Like Vygotsky's zone of proximal development, flow is experienced when there is a match to our capabilities (Csikszentmihalyi, 2008). It is also in flow that positive emotions surge, much like the windhorse effect (Wien, 2008). During the unified flowing from one moment to the next in an inquiry, children feel in control of their actions and able to ignore distractions, which are both important aspects of the flow experience. When teachers engage in collaborative and inclusive inquiries in the experiential state of flow, this supports the children's ability to self-regulate.

Belonging and understanding social cues are important for collaborative and inclusive inquiries, just as they are for play. During inquiries there is a sense of connectedness with others, of being valued, and of forming authentic relationships where ideas and theories are co-constructed. Secure relationships that are positive, caring, and respectful contribute to children's emotional well-being (Clinton, 2013). Inquiry-based learning demands perspective taking, as a child has to figure out what others have in mind. It encourages communication about what one wants and what others want. Being sensitive towards others encourages children to stay immersed in the inquiry. Children demonstrate a sense of belonging by taking action to assist others. When working collaboratively and inclusively with others, children engage in behaviours that are positive and helpful, and promote social acceptance, friendship, and empathy. The Ontario Ministry of Education (2016) notes that when teachers create a kind, caring, collaborative environment, this helps to develop children's social and prosocial self-regulation. Learning environments that are healthy, caring, safe, inclusive, and accepting support the development of the five domains of self-regulation.

Collaboration and inclusivity were an important part of the Invisibility Inquiry. Lauren believed the children worked so well together and were inclusive with one another "because they are totally engaged in the actual inquiry itself. The material is interesting to them, fascinating really, to them." For instance, while working together during the water experiment, the children shared their ideas about what they might do next with the water. They took turns and were very respectful towards one another after they decided to pour the water from the small jar into the vase. They wanted to make sure that everyone had a turn. Similarly,

Photo 3.17: Dipping Fingers in the Water

when the children decided to pour the water on the table, they took turns dipping their fingers into the jars to get their fingers wet. The children worked together to smear the water around and cover the entire surface of the table.

On another occasion, when the children were drawing their invisible selves on the mirrors, Lauren realized that having a small mirror was a novelty for the children and that they first needed to play with looking at themselves in the mirror. While the children explored their different facial expressions, they shared their discoveries with one another and respected each other's space. They didn't bother anybody else or interrupt anyone else's experience. The children shared the metallic markers to ensure that everyone had an opportunity to complete their drawing because there were not quite enough markers. As they created their "invisible selves" they talked with one another about what they were drawing.

When Kathryn shared the Office Inquiry book with the children, they all sat together on the carpet and listened attentively to each other as they took turns sharing their thoughts and ideas. For example, the girls shared their thinking about why the school doors were locked and talked about what their parents did at their offices. They also read parts of the text aloud, counted the squares on the intercom, and role-played scenarios. For example, Rayana and Vivian demonstrated how to use their swipe cards to gain access to the classroom office by swinging the mirror open. After Kathryn shared the book, she then explained

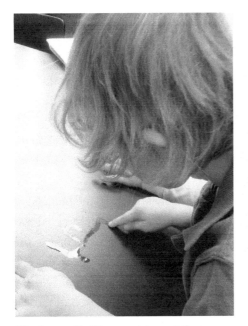

Photo 3.18: Steven Uses His Finger to Draw on the Table

Photo 3.19: Samantha Makes a Funny Face in the Mirror

that she was going to put out a pack of sticky notes and pencils with the book so they could add their new ideas and thinking. She encouraged the children to put the sticky notes on the book wherever they wanted to and that later they could share their thinking with the class. Victoria added that it would be nice to look at the book with a friend and that they could have a chat about what they did. As the children took turns looking at the book in the Drama Centre, they were very collaborative and inclusive with one another, sharing their ideas, recording them on sticky notes, and attaching them to the book.

The Running Club Inquiry was very inclusive as it allowed for fluidity in its membership. Some children in the group were regulars and others weaved in and out. Some children only wanted to be in the hall to do the running, while others wanted to be involved in the discussion and planning next steps. Darlene observed, "So that again, tells you about the differences between children and how they learn, how they learn best, what they know is best for themselves and what they can handle and what they can't handle." The children could choose when they wanted to participate in different aspects of the inquiry. Darlene also made sure to include the rest of the class by having the seven core members of the Running Club present their drawings to their peers and explain their thinking. This gave those children an opportunity to think more deeply about their running idea as they shared it with others. It also gave the other children in the class an opportunity to add their ideas and say how their body feels when they run. Another time, the teacher shared a chart with the whole class that showed the Running Club members' racing times. Darlene asked, "Who thinks that Connor, Gabriel, and Zara were the fastest runners?" Some of the children's hands went up. She then had the children go up to the chart one at a time and sign their name in the column under the name(s) of the children they thought were the fastest runners. Darlene asked the children to share their thinking about why they chose that particular column.

One day, the Running Club worked collaboratively after Darlene put a large piece of mural paper on the table and explained to the children that the goal was to draw the big idea. Michael said they should start with a planning circle so the children could plan what exercises and run they were going to do. Darlene suggested drawing a line down the middle of the paper. As Darlene began to draw the line, Adele realized right away that the paper represented the hall. Adele

Photo 3.20: The Running Club Shares Their Theories

was excited to draw the tape to indicate the starting positions. The children negotiated where to put the tape. Connor decided where to draw the children in their planning circle. Michael decided where they should draw the children doing their exercises. Zara and Gabriel volunteered to draw children doing exercises and Gabriel also drew a picture of himself holding the stopwatch. Michael thought we should show "high fives" with a girl and boy, so Connor drew a girl on one side and a boy on the other. The children took turns drawing themselves at the starting line. The children then negotiated where to write and how to spell the words STOP and GO. In the end, it was decided that one side of the hall was for competitive racing and the other side was for running and slapping high five in the middle.

The children were collaborative and inclusive during the Community Inquiry when they drew the posters of the city. They were free to come and go as they planned and worked together on different posters. The children shared the materials and negotiated what and where to draw on the paper. Interestingly, after the city posters were finished, a new boy joined the class and Bihar found a way to include him by explaining his poster to Ahlam in his home language. Bihar reached up and pointed to the poster as he was labelling the parts for him.

Photo 3.21: Working on the
Running Mural

Photo 3.22: Making Watercolour Paintings of the Valley

Photo 3.23: A Watercolour Painting of the Valley

By referring to the documentation, Bihar could revisit the experience with Ahlam so he knew what had happened in the Community Inquiry before he arrived.

Similar inclusiveness occurred when the children collaborated on paintings of the valley. First the children shared what they enjoyed about going to the valley. Anima commented, "When I saw the river and it was so fast and sometimes on top it's slow but under the water is fast." Dea said, "I like the tree because it was growing really tall." Esita said, "Sliding down the grass mountain." Raem added, "I like the frog my mom found." Sharon explained how initially the children created smaller individual paintings of the valley and then poster size collaborative paintings on watercolour paper. She said,

> We asked them initially to draw their valley and we realized that … it really wasn't showing as much as we knew they understood about the valley.… It was too small for that because the valley is so big. So, we realized that the children needed to collaborate together on a larger piece of paper and it would allow for that larger sense of the valley.

When creating the paintings, the children used permanent black markers to draw different features of the valley in the morning and then in the afternoon they used watercolour paint to paint them. Children would add to the artwork, leave, then perhaps come back and work on a different picture of the valley. This way the paintings belonged to everyone. The children shared their ideas about what they had seen in the valley and negotiated who would draw what and where.

CHAPTER SUMMARY

This chapter has focused on self-regulation and inquiry design. I have argued that inquiries support the children's ability to self-regulate in the same way as play because they emerge from the children's interests. Recall that all four examples of inquiries I provided arose out of the children's choices in play. This helps children to stay focused, consider different perspectives, and figure out their own thinking, which are all important mental processes in the cognitive domain. Inquiry-based learning that arises out of children's play is enjoyable and intrinsically rewarding, and there is a sense of control over the activity. Children are able to concentrate and feel capable of meeting the demands that the inquiry places on them.

Children's thinking shapes the design of the inquiry as it unfolds. When investigations are self-initiated and authentic, children are highly motivated to generate new ideas and strategies to sustain them. The more students are engaged in an activity and have a sense of control over their learning, the more likely they are to be self-regulated. Teachers who engage in reciprocal actions that are challenging, but not overwhelming, support self-regulation because they enable the children to feel more confident and stay focused on the investigation. Inquiries promote positive emotions like elation, inspiration, pride, and curiosity that generate energy, which improve children's concentration and strengthen their ability to self-regulate in the cognitive domain. SEL was evident in each of the inquiries. The collaborative and inclusive nature of inquiry-based learning enables children to be in a state of experiential flow and ignore distractions. The inquiry design component in each of the four inquiries clearly illustrates how inquiry-based learning supports children becoming self-regulated learners in the primary classroom.

REFLECTIVE QUESTIONS

1. Is inquiry-based learning reliant on play-based environments? If not, why not?
2. What are some examples of reciprocal actions you have undertaken during inquiries that have supported the children's ability to self-regulate?
3. Why might it be difficult to let children have control over the direction of an inquiry?
4. In what ways have you supported children's social and emotional learning during an inquiry?
5. How does the collaborative and inclusive nature of inquiry-based learning support all learners in your classroom environment?

RECOMMENDED READINGS

Anderson, Doug, Chiarotto, Lorraine, & Comay, Julie. (2017). Stephanie's story. In *Natural curiosity 2nd edition: A resource for educators* (pp. 142–149). Toronto, ON: OISE.

Chiarotto, Lorraine. (2011). Carol's story. In *Natural curiosity: A resource for teachers* (pp. 63–73). Toronto, ON: OISE.

Chiarotto, Lorraine. (2011). Susanna's story. In *Natural curiosity: A resource for teachers* (pp. 134–140). Toronto, ON: OISE.

Wien, Carol Anne, & Halls, Deborah. (2018). "Is there a chick in there?" Kindergartners' changing thoughts on life in an egg. *Young Children, 73*, 6–15.

ONLINE RESOURCES

It's About Inquiry: Planning for Inquiry
https://vimeo.com/91973564

It's About Inquiry: Types of Inquiry
https://vimeo.com/91973477

Sky Inquiry Filming Series Video 1—Provoking the Thinking
https://youtu.be/g13t50DJZPw

Sky Inquiry Filming Series Video 2—Planning for Intentional Learning
https://youtu.be/0CiV8ppZyT4

What Does It Look Like and Sound Like to Co-construct Inquiry with the Children?
http://www.edugains.ca/resourcesKIN/Video/Inquiry/mp4/Inquiry(06).mp4

Chapter Four

Self-Regulation and the Design of the Environment

We value space because of its power to organize and promote pleasant relationships among people of different ages, create a handsome environment, provide changes, promote choices and activity, and its potential for sparking all kinds of social, affective, and cognitive learning. All of this contributes to a sense of well-being and security in children. We also think as it has been said that the space has to be a sort of aquarium that mirrors the ideas, values, attitudes, and cultures of the people who live within it.

 —Loris Malaguzzi in Gandini, 2012a, p. 339

This chapter focuses on self-regulation and the design of the environment, another component of emergent curriculum that supports inquiry-based learning. This design component has six aspects: (1) organizing the classroom space and materials, (2) keeping the environment uncluttered and neutral, (3) adapting and extending beyond the classroom, (4) developing daily routines, (5) using expansive time frames, and (6) building authentic relationships. When each of the six aspects are considered together, they show how the design of the environment enables children to become self-regulated learners in the primary classroom. The four compelling insights about the relationship between self-regulation and inquiry-based learning outlined in the introduction are also interwoven into the discussion of the design of the environment.

 I rely here on an expanded notion of the learning environment that comprises not only the physical space and materials inside and outside the classroom, daily routines, and schedules but also the socio-cultural context that includes the relationships among the teachers and children and between them and the materials. These organic and dynamic learning environments are co-constructed between the teachers and the children. The design of the environment begins when teachers consider the role of the environment as they brainstorm possible directions the inquiry might follow and provocations to encourage the children to engage in the topic being investigated. Children are intimately involved in this design component,

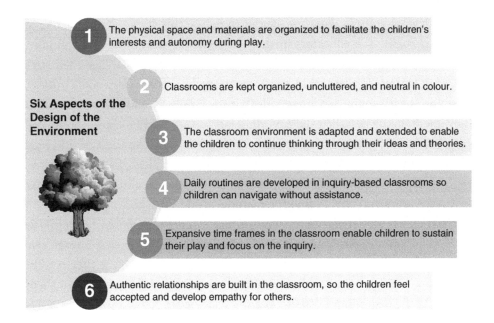

Six Aspects of the Design of the Environment

1   The physical space and materials are organized to facilitate the children's interests and autonomy during play.

2   Classrooms are kept organized, uncluttered, and neutral in colour.

3   The classroom environment is adapted and extended to enable the children to continue thinking through their ideas and theories.

4   Daily routines are developed in inquiry-based classrooms so children can navigate without assistance.

5   Expansive time frames in the classroom enable children to sustain their play and focus on the inquiry.

6   Authentic relationships are built in the classroom, so the children feel accepted and develop empathy for others.

which enables them to make connections and develop a deeper understanding of the inquiry. As in chapter 3, the four inquiries are used to illustrate concretely the relationship between self-regulation and the design of the environment.

SIX ASPECTS OF THE DESIGN OF THE ENVIRONMENT

The Physical Space and Materials Are Organized to Facilitate the Children's Interests and Autonomy during Play

Inquiries based on children's interests that arise out of their choices in play support their ability to self-regulate because, as I argued in the previous chapter, the children are able to stay focused, consider other perspectives, and figure out their own thinking, which are all important mental processes in the cognitive domain. Classroom environments that facilitate children's interests and autonomy likewise support their ability to self-regulate. Heroman and Copple (2006) remind us that when we organize materials logically, this enables children to find them on their own and return them to their proper place when finished. When children help to organize the materials and find places to store them for easy access, they can make independent choices as they play and interact in the classroom environment. An important dimension of Shanker's approach is the emphasis it places on teachers helping children learn to recognize when and what is causing them to be overstressed in the classroom environment and how to develop self-regulation strategies to reduce this stress (2016; Shanker & Hopkins, 2020). The educators in the four inquiries worked with the children in their class to help them understand when they needed to alleviate their stress and what strategies they could use to achieve this. Their classrooms afforded possibilities with centres and materials that could help the children self-regulate. They intentionally designed the environments so the children could choose centres where they could go to up-regulate or down-regulate on their own in order to return to a calm and alert state.

In Lauren's classroom the space was organized so the children knew where the centres were and how to find the materials and return them. She put a lot of time and effort into setting up the physical space in her classroom so the children could be as autonomous as possible when exploring their interests. Lauren said, "I think it's really important that children are as independent as they possibly can be. So, I really try not to do anything for a child that they can do for themselves." At the beginning of the school year, she began to organize the space by first reflecting on what happened the previous year and why she made specific changes. Then she thought about how to organize the classroom and divide it up so the children would know exactly where the centres are located, how to find the materials, and how to put them back. Lauren also considered the purpose of each centre, what the centre would look like, and what materials should go there.

When the children began school, Lauren introduced the materials slowly as the children were getting used to their new environment. At the Light Table, for example, she put out different coloured gemstones and then later added more variety by including different sizes. She also changes the materials by introducing watercolour paints or other design materials like ribbons. Lauren said,

> So, I'm kind of constantly looking at ... how they could use the materials in an interesting way. And the trick is you need the materials to be open-ended enough, but also that lend themselves sort of naturally to the kind of learning experiences you want the children to have.

As the year progressed, Lauren would co-construct the environment with the children as their inquiries unfolded.

When Kathryn and Victoria set up Inquiry Centres they think about the children's interests. Kathryn explained,

> I think that because it's a space that reflects them [the children] and their interests and because they are engaged at their Inquiry Centres for the morning ...

we position ourselves in the classroom and are listening to their interests, observing their interests, and then we create that space based on those interests.
So, for example, the Drama Centre is becoming an office.

The children were given lots of opportunities to be intimately involved in the
design of the environment as the classroom space and materials evolved to reflect
their interests and support authentic and meaningful learning.

Kathryn and Victoria kept the classroom materials at the centres in clear
bins or open baskets so the children could choose the materials independently.
Kathryn said,

> We were intentional with the amount of clear bins in the classroom as a part of
> the environment because it allows them to kind of be empowered to self-select
> the materials that they need rather than constantly coming and asking us for
> materials. So, there's a lot of clear bins around the classroom which kind of
> supports them in getting what they need and having that independence.

The children were resourceful and could usually find the materials they needed
quite independently, and if not, they helped each other. For example, one day
Susan wanted to write Victoria's last name and three other girls took her around
the classroom to show her the possibilities. They didn't do it for her, but they
helped her to complete the task successfully. At the beginning of the year Kathryn
would have helped Susan, but now the children took the initiative to find the
resources on their own and model this behaviour for others. The girls were also
free to move the classroom materials among the different Inquiry Centres. For
instance, the Office Inquiry began in the Construction Centre as the children
gathered and collected materials from all over the classroom, including their I
Wonder books, pencils, and a large number of chairs. When the teachers introduced new materials into the environment, such as putting sorting trays and
buttons in the Hands On Thinking Centre and the children decided to use other
materials to measure, the teachers were fine with this. Kathryn explained, "They
are not tied to the provocation. They don't have to do that." In fact, Kathryn and
Victoria then nurtured the new interest by adding other measurement materials.

Victoria and Kathryn talked about having a balance of activities available
at the Inquiry Centres for the children to choose from. Kathryn explained, "So
there's some that are a little quieter, some that maybe require a bit more energy."
Victoria commented, "They [the children] seem to know what they need." The
girls will choose quieter, calmer activities when they need to down-regulate.

Kathryn said, "They definitely each kind of have their place where they want to go to bring that energy level down." The children also chose more active, busier learning areas when they needed to up-regulate, which indicates that the girls knew what they needed to manage their own energy levels and the environment offered them ways they could do this.

Darlene and Kerri wanted the classroom space organized so the children could be autonomous and pursue their interests. Darlene explained,

> I feel that our classroom environment is a work in progress. It moves and changes along with the children. As children grow, show interest in specific areas of the curriculum, then we develop/change/adapt the environment accordingly. We have noisy areas where children design, create and imagine and we have quiet areas where children listen, read and discover.

Her classroom space was constantly evolving. At times she organized the classroom so that the quiet centres like the Calm Centre and the Book Centre were at the front of the room, the Art Centre and the Writing Centre are in the middle of the room, and the noisy centres like the Blocks, Sand, and Water centres were at the back. When she felt that wasn't working anymore, she moved the blocks back to the middle of the room so the children could have more space to build. This meant that she could move the large paint easel to the back of the room: "It gives you a better view to have it out of the way like that too. So, you can see better. It doesn't chop the class up as much … it feels kind of open."

Later Darlene combined the Calm Centre and the Science Centre so she could use the entire corner for Math and Science. I asked Darlene if she felt she was losing anything by taking the Calm Centre out. She answered, "No. Science is pretty calm and hands on and pretty tactile." Darlene also moved the Reading Centre over beside the Writing Centre, and it was a lot cozier. This way the two centres could share the materials: "I feel that it's working really well now." This particular classroom set-up enabled the children to be even more autonomous. For example, when sharing the materials from the Book Centre and Writing Centre the children no longer had to walk across the classroom because now the centres were side by side. It also made it easier for the children to put the materials back in the right spot when they were tidying up.

Sharon and Mikayla also sought to give the children as much autonomy as possible in the classroom. Sharon said, "You have to change your environment to fit the needs of the kids that are there." She explained that at the beginning of the year her classroom looks like a hospital room because the walls are bare and only a few materials are out. She wanted the space to be very calm when the children arrived: "If they came in and they were overwhelmed by everything all over the walls it's like visual harassment." The classroom environment was built up with the children as the year progressed. Sharon said,

> My classroom looks different from September to June. It changes based on the learning needs of my students, and as I get to know their interests and person-alities, the room reflects them. In September, I start with a very neutral starting point (i.e., bare walls). The learning areas are set up with materials that require little to no adult support to access or engage with. In the first week, even the first day, I … put student drawings/work up right away. This is for them to have ownership of the classroom.… My ultimate goal [is] to invite the students into a classroom that is calm and caring.… As the year progresses, the classroom learning areas change to meet the student's areas of interest.

Her classroom was a reflection of the children currently living in that space.

The educators placed a lot of emphasis on building the classroom environ-ment collaboratively with the children, so it truly reflected their needs and in-terests. Sharon said the children "contribute to the discussion about the design of the classroom. If something isn't working at the Drama Centre, if there is not enough space, I encourage the students to problem solve with me." Sharon and Mikayla did not limit how many children can be in one learning area, although it was evident in some cases because of the number of chairs. It was fine for the children to move chairs from the snack table over to the Art Studio, but in the Drama Centre this was not possible because there was not enough room. They tried to leave these decisions to the children because they had their own under-standing of space limitations.

Mikayla explained the connection between the children's autonomy, the materials being accessible, and how this facilitates relationship building in the classroom:

> A big, big deal for us is for the children to have ownership of their own space. So that, to me anyway, means the materials are accessible. They have a choice of materials. And while we do put out provocations and invitations to play, they also know that they have a great deal of freedom to use the materials in ways they want. And depending on the materials, I would say 90 percent of the time, they are able to take them to other centres and use them in other ways. So, be-cause they have that freedom and that accessibility, they just can build on their

own ideas. They are not limited in terms of what we, our vision for the materials are for the different learning areas. So, because of that … the imaginative play that we see just builds and builds and builds.… And the relationships, again, it also facilitates the relationship building because they are not … focused on their limitations.… So they have the freedom to focus on their ideas and their interactions with each other.

Sharon added that they also looked at the complexity of the learning areas and materials and how they change and grow throughout the year. Both of the teachers believed that the children respected the materials and that they in turn could trust the children to take care of everything in the room because they had such a strong sense of ownership over their environment.

Sharon felt that when children were able to self-regulate, they knew what they needed at that moment and why. So, if a child needed to be moving around a little bit more, being active and moving their body, they knew the place in the room where they could do that and, if they needed to be in a calmer, quieter place, they also knew where they could go. Sharon also explained the role of defined spaces in her classroom:

We also have it designed in a way that can limit the interruptions because there are twenty-eight bodies in here normally. You need to have those quieter zones, the spaces, the learning areas that are not going to be distracted.… If you look along that spread [Books, Small Blocks, Discovery, Drama], this I would consider a calmer zone, louder, calmer, louder.… I think when we make our learning areas, we try not to put something necessarily beside something else, like two loud areas … or an area that might encourage louder.

This helps to avoid it being loud and chaotic in one part of the room because there is a buffering zone in between. Mikayla believes that children need to be able to choose a centre where they can "soothe themselves … calm their bodies down … [and] lower [their] anxiety." She often saw children, who are at a heightened level of anxiety or at an activity where they are getting overly worked up, choosing to go to the snack table to eat and drink some water. Having something to eat or drink helps them to soothe and calm their body down.

Classrooms Are Kept Organized, Uncluttered, and Neutral in Colour

Educational programs focused on inquiry-based learning such as Reggio Emilia have long emphasized that children are able to concentrate better in an environment with a reduced number of visual distractors. There are an increasing number of children today who are easily overwhelmed by visual stimuli in the classroom. Shanker's approach to self-regulation is designed in part to help teachers learn to recognize when a child is overstressed, and to identify and reduce the child's stressors in the environment. Patricia Tarr (2004) highlights the importance of painting classroom walls white or in light pastels because these colours reduce visual overload and have a calming effect. Visual clutter can be distracting so there should also be a reduced amount of material on the walls. She observed that feelings caused by visual chaos and clutter occur when there is no empty space on the walls "to allow the eyes to rest" (p. 92). For these reasons, I believe that classroom environments that are organized, uncluttered, and neutral in colour support the children's ability to self-regulate during inquiries.

As the teachers in the four inquiries were Reggio-inspired, it is not surprising to me that they were cognizant of keeping their classrooms uncluttered and neutral in colour. The educators all felt that it was important for the classroom space and materials to have a calming effect on the children. They were aware of how visual clutter can lead to sensory overload for some children, so they created classroom environments with a reduced number of visual distractions. Shanker (2016) notes that teachers also need to be able to identify and reduce their own stressors so that they can stay calm and attentive when interacting with their students. In my view, when classroom environments enable both the teachers and children to feel calm, this helps everyone remain optimally self-regulated.

Lauren's classroom was Reggio-inspired and felt tranquil. She thought that the appearance of her classroom was important:

> My classroom looks clean, organized, and uncluttered. There is nothing in the room that is not being used. Materials that are no longer used leave and new materials are brought in as the children's thinking, understanding and interests evolve. There are no commercial bulletin board products, no primary coloured "junk." I use as many natural products as possible.

Over the years, Lauren had removed all commercial type visual materials from the wall because they were too visually jarring. The colours on the wall were neutral; even the number line was made out of little cork squares. She deliberately left parts of the bulletin boards empty because this helped the children to avoid becoming overloaded by sensory input, which would hinder their learning.

Lauren recalled a time when there was a school district review and all the children's writing samples had to be up on the wall. She said, "It changed the whole look of the room and it changed the way the children responded in this

Photo 4.1: Lauren's Classroom

space, I felt. They [the children] were a little bit jittery because it was so busy and so frantic looking." She found that the children were distracted by the walls. Lauren added, "So I'm always trying to be conscious of not having too many things up on the wall, and anything that is there is actually used and needed."

Kathryn described her classroom environment as a natural, calming space for the children. The walls were painted white and only displayed documentation panels and things made collaboratively with the children like the alphabet and numbers one to ten. The furniture and cupboards were all made of natural birch wood, and the materials were kept in clear bins and baskets. Materials that the children were currently not using were stored in a large closet between the classrooms. By using neutral colours, the environment was not visually distracting. In addition, the glass windows and doors let in a lot of natural light at the children's eye level, which avoided having them feel overwhelmed by fluorescent lighting. Also, most of the floor was carpeted, which helped with noise reduction. Kathryn and Victoria explained that the environment made them feel calmer as well. Kathryn said, "The trees do a lot in there. I love the branches, the trees. I think that's what I notice the most." Victoria added, "So many people come in and say oh, this is my favourite room in the school.... It kind of hugs you when you walk in."

Photo 4.2: The Tree in Kathryn's Classroom

In Darlene's classroom, the colours in the environment were neutral, the walls were painted white, and many of the materials were made from natural products. Two walls contained large white bulletin boards and a whiteboard that the educators used to display their documentation. All the documentation for the Running Club Inquiry was on either a white or black background. The large windows had white blinds and most furniture pieces were made of natural birch wood. At the front of the classroom there was a large beige carpet with a white couch where the children met to talk with Darlene about the day's activities and reflect on their learning. The classroom environment went through a number of changes in an effort to become tidier, more organized, and less cluttered. These changes were time-consuming as the classroom was quite large and spacious.

Sharon's classroom had a natural, authentic, Reggio-inspired appearance. The school was only a few years old, and the way the space was designed made the classroom look organized and uncluttered. There was a large, spacious cubby area for the children to store all their belongings. One side of the cubby had a wall that was connected to the hallway and the other side had a long open shelf unit that acted as a natural divider between the cubby area and the rest of the classroom. This shelf was large and held a lot of materials, including the art supplies. Also, one wall in the classroom had a teacher workspace to help keep

Photo 4.3: The Nature Centre in Sharon's Classroom

teaching materials organized and lots of cupboards for classroom materials that were currently not in use. In addition, every shelf and bin had been arranged so that it was accessible to the children and they knew where to return the materials at tidy-up time. The colours in the classroom were neutral. The storage cupboards and furniture, except for the tables and chairs, were all made of birch wood. The walls were painted white and there were whiteboards and corkboards used for display. Even the blinds on the windows were white. The materials were kept in wicker or clear plastic bins. The environment was visually appealing, and everything in the classroom looked meticulous.

The Classroom Environment Is Adapted and Extended to Enable the Children to Continue Thinking through Their Ideas and Theories

Another insight of this book is that teachers use scaffolding strategies, such as planning provocations that adapt and extend the environment during inquiry-based learning, to enable children to become self-regulated learners. Provocations capture the children's imagination and their desire to learn more. Research on self-regulation in schools has emphasized the role of teachers and classroom environments in scaffolding children's learning. Recall that Bruner (2004) defines scaffolding as a process where teachers set up situations so that a child can easily enter and then gradually extend the scope of the child's role as they become skilled enough to handle it. Scaffolding is an effective process that strengthens the executive functions that are important for self-regulation. Gandini (2012a) explains that a classroom environment needs to be flexible: "It must undergo frequent modification by the children and the teachers to remain up-to-date and responsive to their needs to be protagonists in constructing their knowledge" (p. 339). Heroman and Copple (2006) note that when children express their interests through their theories and ideas, a dynamic social space evolves that is fluid and inclusive. The classroom environments during inquiries become collaborative creations that reflect and extend children's learning. In my view, planning specific provocations during inquiries that adapt and extend the classroom environment can enhance children's self-regulation. The four inquiries all provide examples of these kinds of provocations.

In the Invisibility Inquiry, Lauren thought about new ways she could change the classroom environment to further the children's thinking about the inquiry. For example, she decided to add a large worm jar to the Nature Centre. One morning, Henry and Andrew were at the Nature Centre and they started to share their thinking about invisibility.

> *Henry*: They're invisible because the dirt is covering them.
> *Andrew*: Yeah.
> *Lauren*: Is it because the dirt's covering them?
> *Andrew*: Yeah, and the dirt is brown and they're both brown …
> *Lauren*: The worms are brown, and the dirt is brown. Ah.

From this brief exchange, we can see the boys were thinking about how, when we hide things, they become invisible. Then Lauren asked the children a question, and this extended their thinking to how the dirt and worms blend together because they are both brown. The children started to talk about invisibility quite spontaneously because something was intentionally added to their environment to provoke such thinking.

Lauren also thought carefully about how to extend the inquiry outdoors. One morning, she carried out a variety of pots, pans, and drumsticks and arranged them on a long bench. Lauren commented,

> I don't know if it's because of the way I had things laid out, because I did, sort of, have a pot and a drumstick beside each one. It's not like they took the pots and started clashing them together. They sort of knew exactly what I was hoping they would do.

Photo 4.4: Children Experimenting with the Pots and Pans

This outdoor provocation gave the children an opportunity to explore in greater depth how sound is invisible. Tagwen was the first to approach the pots and pans and immediately start tapping in different ways to explore the sounds she could make. Then Tagwen encouraged other children to join, and she shared her experience of tapping with them.

Kathryn and Victoria adapted the Drama Centre, during the Office Inquiry, so that the children would have a space to continue thinking through their ideas and theories about what it means to be "working" in an office. When the Drama Centre was changed to an office, it originally had a table with a typewriter, lamp, and two chairs. The girls would type on the typewriter, make nametags by writing the names of their friends on sticky notes, and write letters to their families. Next to the table there was a shelf that acted as a separate writing surface for the children to write messages on paper and then roll them through the typewriter. On the shelf there was paper, envelopes, clipboards, and pencils. Other materials from the Graphic Communication Centre also found their way to the office, such as plastic letters, name cards, and books. A cozy chair sat next to the mirror. The mirror later had the security camera on one side and a scanner on the other. The children used their swipe cards and moved the mirror to gain access to the office. The girls later added other items to the office, like a clock, a tray with sand and sparkles, candy

Photo 4.5: A Co-constructed List of Items for the Classroom Office

Photo 4.6: Making a Clock

Photo 4.7: A Clock for the Office

and lollipops, and artwork for the walls. The office continued to evolve throughout the inquiry as the children came up with new ideas and theories.

Darlene adapted the environment in numerous ways to scaffold the children's thinking. For instance, the Running Club met in the "cubby" room that was shared between two classrooms. In the centre of the cubby, four tables had been joined together to make one large table. This meeting place was significant for a variety of reasons. It helped the children in the Running Club focus when sharing their ideas and theories. It also helped other children in the classroom not be distracted while exploring at the centres. Having this space also symbolized for the children that there was important work going on here as they led the inquiry forward towards "the big idea." Darlene also extended the inquiry outside the classroom into the hall. It became a space that felt intimate as the children spent so much time there. Luckily the hallway was very wide and long, so it was spacious and a perfect place for the children to try out their running ideas. In the hall was a hexagonal table that the children used to record the children's names and running times.

Photo 4.8: The Children Doing Warm-Up Exercises

Photo 4.9: The Children Doing a High Five While Running in the Hall

Photo 4.10: Illustration of Children Running in the Hall

There was a Science Centre inside the classroom with a table and chairs. Here Darlene was providing a space for the children to explore the connection between running and how it makes the body feel. On the table, there were books about how the body works, a large skeleton puzzle, a figure that could be taken apart in pieces to look inside the body, and the running box that contained materials like stopwatches, masking tape, paper, and stickers. On the wall behind the table was the documentation of the children's pictures and theories about how they feel before and after they run.

Sharon was always thinking about creative ways to extend the classroom environment outdoors to provoke further thought about the inquiry and see if the children could consolidate their learning. During community walks the children found their own apartment buildings, sketched the cityscape and trees, played in the sunshine, and explored the river in the valley. Sharon also took the children out onto the school grounds on a few occasions. It was here that the children sketched the apartment buildings and first started to wonder about where water comes from. These excursions helped the children to think through their ideas and theories and make connections between the city, community, and valley.

Photo 4.11: Children Sketching the Apartment Buildings

Photo 4.12: The Apartment Buildings

When Sharon decided that she wanted to bring the valley into the classroom learning areas, she asked, "How can I use the materials in the classroom for you [the children] to re-enact and revisit your understanding and ideas of an experience outside?" Sharon decided to create two new centres with the help of the children. The River Centre was set up at the Discovery Centre table with blue felt, glass fish, different sizes of rocks, wood pieces, and small green and blue shapes. As a provocation, Sharon organized the materials to look like a river scene by using the blue felt and adding lots of details, like having fish lying on the rocks. The Valley Centre was initially set up at the Playdough Centre with blue and green playdough, miniature plastic plants, wood stumps and branches, rocks, and animals. There was also documentation on the wall behind the table with photographs of the valley. Sharon later added two pieces of grey felt that looked like placemats, wooden people, green and blue square lids, and gemstones. She set up two different valley scenes on the grey felt. The Light Table was also later adapted and set up with new materials including small coloured stones, blue, green, and brown transparent shapes, and coloured lids for the children to recreate the valley. Behind the Light Table there was documentation of the inquiry, including the collaborative valley paintings and photographs of the

Photo 4.13: The Valley Centre

Photo 4.14: Recreating the Valley at the Light Table

valley. Sharon organized the materials to create a tree with blossoms, grass, and water to get the children's ideas flowing. She was always using materials as provocations to extend the children's learning.

Daily Routines Are Developed in Inquiry-Based Classrooms So Children Can Navigate without Assistance

Heroman and Copple (2006) explain that when teachers plan and organize the day in a thoughtful and intentional way, young children feel more secure because they know what happens next. Daily predictable routines help children anticipate transitions throughout the day, which enables them to up- or down-regulate as they prepare to meet the demands of an activity (Shanker, 2013b). These routines allow children to self-regulate with little or no external input from the teachers. When children help to create flexible daily schedules that are visually displayed, this process is further enhanced. Daily predictable routines, I believe, make children feel more secure and develop their self-confidence and sense of responsibility as they learn to navigate in the classroom on their own.

Daily routines are an integral part of inquiry-based classrooms. The educators in the four inquiries all established daily routines that were predictable so the children would know what activity to expect next. Lauren made it a priority each year to think about the clarity of movement and the flow of the room so that the children can function on their own. Lauren explained,

> From the time the children walk into the building, [I think] what do I want them to do. What routines do I want them to follow…. I'm thinking okay, I want them to be able to do this or work in this way. I want them to be able to enter this [room] and put their things here and then know that they're going to go to their table or go to the carpet, whichever that happens to be. So that's kind of how I start. I don't look at the physical set-up of the room until I've sort of gotten the flow of the day in my mind and I think of the routines I want to start.

Lauren put a great deal of thought into the children's daily routines even before she started to set up her classroom space.

While observing Lauren's classroom, I could see that the children understood the class routines. In the morning when they entered the classroom, after outdoor play, they knew exactly what to do. After they hung up their belongings and put on their shoes, they went to their table and wrote their name on the sign-in sheet. Then they took out their folder of books and read quietly on their own or with a friend. The music played to signal that reading time was over, so the children put away their folders and went to sit quietly on the carpet. A child from each of the table groups would give Lauren their sign-in sheet for the attendance. At one point, Lauren read a book and connected it to how they had been talking about feelings in the classroom. Then she introduced new activities the children might like to explore. Lauren explained that, as the year progressed, her support and guidance around daily routines was less necessary. These daily routines helped the children navigate through the day themselves because they knew what to expect.

In Kathryn's classroom, the children understood the daily routines and could follow them without assistance. When they first entered the classroom, they hung up their belongings in the cubby and put on their shoes. After attendance was taken, the girls would have a quiet start with morning prayers or DEAR (Drop Everything and Read) time. Kathryn would then use the peaceful sound of the rain stick to signal the girls to come to the carpet. Here the children might share their news, look at some documentation, or be introduced to a new provocation. Then they would choose an Inquiry Centre.

Photo 4.15: Participating in Daily Routines

One afternoon, after going to a specialty teacher for dance, the children went to Inquiry Centres. When it was time to tidy up, Kathryn gathered the girls on the carpet. While waiting for all the children to arrive, Kathryn kept the children who were ready engaged by playing simple games like counting backwards and deliberately making mistakes to see if they would notice. Once everyone arrived, she asked, "Who would like to make the Light Table look fabulous?" The girls then volunteered to clean different Inquiry Centres. As the children worked together, Kathryn made comments like, "I'll count to 10. Construction really needs help." Then other girls would go and help in order to get the job done more quickly. Kathryn said, "Thank you Nikki. Before you arrive [back] at the carpet you can bring a piece of learning with you." Then several children were given an opportunity to share their learning. The girls exhibited confidence because the daily routines were predictable, and they could complete them on their own.

Darlene and Kerri developed daily routines so the children could manage them without help from others. In the morning, after outdoor play in the kindergarten playground, the children signed in by writing their first and last name and then sat down quietly with a book. When the books had been tidied, they went and sat on the carpet with Darlene or Kerri. Some of the children would then pursue current inquiries, like the Running Club, and other children would explore at the centres. At the end of the morning, Darlene would gather the children once again on the carpet to reflect on their activities. During one of my visits, Darlene looked at the large piece of white paper on the painting easel and said, "It made me feel like spring when I saw your picture." She invited three girls to come up to the front of the carpet and explain what it was like to work together. Zara said, "Nina and Faith were painting, and I asked if I could help." Faith explained, "We were trying to figure out what to paint and we decided on this." Nina added, "We had ideas to make flowers and Faith had the idea of a sun and Zara had the idea to make the splatters and the names." Zara said, "We made the rainstorm by splattering the paint." Darlene commented on how well the girls collaborated with one another and listened to each other's ideas.

On a different occasion, when the children came back from their daily outdoor play in the afternoon, they lay down on the carpet, exhausted. Darlene commented, "It looks like Faith is asleep. Evan is asleep." Darlene waited for it to be quiet and then put on a taped story. The children lay still, listening and relaxing, and then they began to imitate the animal sounds in the story. Then Darlene talked to the children about how they had just been playing outside with the parachute. Rose said, "I like outside because I have more space to run around, and you need that space." Caleb added, "You go outside and get fresh air." Darlene commented, "The sun felt good, and we all had a little nap and now we are ready to learn." Darlene read a story about how the body works and connected it to how our bodies feel when we can't go outside.

Daily routines in Sharon's classroom were an important part of the program because most of the children in the class were English Language Learners (ELLs). In the morning when the children first arrived at school, they took their name card off the table, placed it in the pocket chart, and changed their borrowed books. They also signed their name on chart paper where Sharon either wrote a statement or had a question for them to answer. The children then chose a book to read on their own or with a friend. When reading time was over, the children gathered on the carpet. The teachers would take attendance by singing the children's names, and the children responded back singing, "Here I am." Then everyone would sing songs and stand for "O Canada." The Helper of the Day chose a question to answer from the question box. She clapped the syllables in her name and then chose a friend to take the attendance to the office. The other children would then decide what centre to go to. Sharon then explained the visual schedule using pictures displayed on the cupboard so the children could anticipate transitions throughout the day.

At the end of the morning, Sharon and the children sang lots of songs, like "Octopus's Garden," "Yellow Submarine," "Tiny Tim," "Little Green Frog," and "You Are My Sunshine." Sharon used lots of intonation, expression, and actions to bring the words to life. This helped the children learn new vocabulary and stay focused and on task. The children were enthusiastic participators and enjoyed this time with Sharon. As Sharon prepared to read a story, she used verbal reminders, such as "One, two, eyes on you. One, two, three, eyes on me," to ensure that the children were settled and ready to listen before they headed off to lunch. Such daily routines helped all the children feel more secure and confident as they went about their day.

Expansive Time Frames in the Classroom Enable Children to Sustain Their Play and Focus on the Inquiry

Children are eager to make choices about where they can play and for how long. Expansive time frames provide them with enough time to move between learning centres as well as to sustain their play and concentrate on the inquiries. They also enable children to take breaks when tired and to relax so they can restore their energy before pursuing the activity once again (Wien, 2008). I have emphasized the insight that children learn how to self-regulate during both play and inquiry. When children are at learning centres, they develop skills in the multiple domains of self-regulation. They learn how to be independent, be resourceful, take risks, persevere, problem-solve, show initiative, and be creative. Like with play, I believe that these skills are also practiced and applied during inquiries. Expansive time frames allow children to make choices to pursue inquiries, which help them feel successful at school. When children feel successful, they try harder, and it is easier for them to learn when they feel more confident (Heroman & Copple, 2006). The children in all four primary classrooms enjoyed expansive time frames where they were given a choice about where they wanted to play and whether they wanted to participate in one of the inquiries.

In the Invisibility Inquiry, the children enjoyed expansive time frames in the morning, during an uninterrupted block of up to two hours, when they explored the various learning centres and engaged in inquiries. This gave the children an opportunity to continue their play and think through their ideas and theories as they focused on the inquiry. Lauren explained, "Time is key, and I try to have large blocks of time for an unhurried feel so the children can think deeply and use the materials in a meaningful way." During these expansive time frames, Lauren asked the children to commit to a learning centre during Stay Exploration. For example, she wrote Computer, Blocks, Light, and Art on the whiteboard and invited the children to choose the centre they would like to go to. As the children chose a centre, Lauren recorded their name on the whiteboard under the name of the centre. When a child suggested a centre that was not on the whiteboard, Lauren added it. She thought that not having too many centres listed on the board initially avoided the children feeling overwhelmed. This way of choosing centres helped her to control who was going where because, if not, some children would choose the same centre every day.

Lauren explained, "They [the children] can still choose where they want to go, but they have to stay … at the centre until the Stay Exploration time is over." She used this strategy because she was finding that, if not, the children would just move from one activity to the next, and Lauren wanted the children to persevere at their centre for longer periods of time. For example, Graham built a rocket and played with it for a while until he was tired of it. Because he was staying at that centre, he then extended his play by using the blocks to build a space station to go with the rocket. Normally he would have just moved on to another centre. Having expansive time frames and an expectation that the child is committed to a centre encourages the children to persist and think more deeply about their play. Although Lauren set limits during Stay Exploration, like monitoring who chose which centre and expecting the children to stay at the centre they chose, the children were not restricted during the one-hour Free Exploration in the afternoon.

Kathryn and Victoria used expansive time frames in the morning and afternoon that lasted at least 1 hour and 40 minutes, which gave the children in their primary classroom plenty of opportunity to sustain their play and concentrate on an inquiry. During these expansive time frames, the girls would choose which Inquiry Centre they wanted to go to. For example, one day Kathryn put out photographs of the Inquiry Centres that were open on the magnetic board. She waited to see which of the girls were ready to choose their Inquiry Centre. Alia chose to go to the Production Centre. Kathryn asked, "Alia what is your plan?" Alia explained that she was going to make sparkly sand. Angie chose the Production Centre. Kathryn asked, "Are you going to collaborate with Alia?" Angie replied, "Yes." Kristina chose the Production Centre so she could make a clock, and Vicky chose Drama so she could use the typewriter. After the children made their initial choices, Kathryn had them think about what they would do at the centre, so they had a plan in mind when they arrived. The teachers were quite flexible when the children were involved in important, purposeful work. For example, when the girls showed an interest in role-playing office workers, there were seven of them in Construction, even though that centre wasn't supposed to be open. The teachers realized this, but they just let it go because, as Kathryn said, "They were so into Office … it was like what's the point of squashing that." Having expansive time frames enabled the children to maintain their play and persevere for long periods of time on the Office Inquiry.

During an expansive time frame in Darlene's classroom, the children explored the various learning centres for purposeful play and pursued working on the Running Club Inquiry for an uninterrupted block of time of up to an hour and a half. Darlene explained how the children go about choosing a centre to explore:

> I hold their name card up and they choose what centre they want to go to every single day.… We may encourage some kids, you know, if they are just doing the same thing every day, to try and get them to go somewhere else and try something new.

When a centre was full, Darlene would say, "That is it for Drama, Drama is closed." This signaled to the children that they needed to choose an alternative place to play. Free exploration gave the children an opportunity to extend their play and persist when completing tasks.

In the morning in Sharon's classroom, the children enjoyed expansive time frames where they could sustain their play and engage in the Community Inquiry for up to two hours. The children had both Choice Learning and Free Choice Learning. For Choice Learning, Sharon put up picture symbols of different centres on the whiteboard and the children selected a learning area where they were expected to stay 20 to 25 minutes. Sharon said that this helped her determine if there was enough complexity at that centre for sustained learning:

> In that time, they [the children] are not interrupting each other because they are not moving around. We want to give them both. We want to give them freedom to move around and take materials from different learning areas and explore but we also want to give them that focused intentional time.

Because the morning allowed for expansive time frames, the children also had Free Choice time where they could move around and explore a number of centres.

Mikayla shared what she thought about the connection between building social relationships and expansive time frames. She said, "There's so much time for them to negotiate and navigate their social relationships." For example, one morning during the Community Inquiry, Alma and Umairi were in the Small Block Centre creating an apartment building. The structure they built was very organized, with a car park on the lower level, a family sleeping in their apartment, and a garden on the balcony. As the play unfolded, Alma and Umairi were very gentle when adding or removing the materials. Sharon commented,

> You can tell that they've certainly put a lot of effort and time and energy into this, and I think that's why you get the carefulness. They don't want to break it because they have worked very hard to create this together.

While the children played, they were very cooperative, taking turns and negotiating their roles. Sharon noted, "She's [Alma] quite verbal and ... he [Umairi] is not very verbal and doesn't have a lot to communicate, so they would have had to communicate a lot through their physical actions." Sometimes, Alma had to work quite hard to figure out what Umairi was thinking so that the play could continue. Expansive time frames allow children time to settle, and this is when real learning happens during inquiries.

Photo 4.16: Using the Small Blocks to Create an Apartment Building

Authentic Relationships Are Built in the Classroom, So the Children Feel Accepted and Develop Empathy for Others

One of the four compelling insights about the relationship between self-regulation and inquiry-based learning, as explained in the introduction, is that inquiries promote positive emotions, which improve children's ability to self-regulate. Social and emotional learning (SEL) is a process of acquiring and applying knowledge and skills that enable us to, among other things, develop empathy for others and establish authentic relationships. At the heart of empathy is emotional connectedness, a sense of belonging. Authentic relationships enable children to feel accepted and learn to develop empathy for others. Wien (2014) believes that "the foundational element in educators' capacity to create emergent curriculum is the stance of … aesthetic responsiveness" (p. 6). This stance or disposition integrates the qualities of authenticity, attentiveness, appreciation, and empathy. Empathy, explains Wien (2014), is "an integrative feeling that brings people into partnership" (p. 7).

The prosocial domain of self-regulation, as I noted earlier, refers to positive behaviours that are helpful and promote social acceptance and friendship. Children with optimal prosocial regulation have a heightened ability to stay calm when experiencing stress in the other domains. Social interactions that are successful occur when one child connects with and cares about what another child is feeling. One of the key attributes of the prosocial domain of self-regulation is empathy, which is the capacity to care about other people's feelings and to help them deal with their emotions. Shanker (2013b) stresses that when we think about empathy simply as "putting ourselves in someone else's shoes" and feeling what that person is feeling, we miss the following three critical aspects of empathy: (1) caring about someone else's emotions; (2) trying to help other people deal with their emotions; and (3) understanding the difference between your own and someone else's emotions. Empathy is developed further in authentic relationships when two children resonate positively with each other emotionally, co-regulate, and turn to each other for support. Authentic relationships thrive during emergent curriculum inquiries where children feel accepted and show empathy towards their peers.

Lauren developed authentic relationships with the children; she was very caring and took the time to listen to their ideas and theories. The children respected Lauren, and even when they were busy at centres, if she said quietly, "Everybody listen," the children would reply, "Right now." Lauren would put her hands out to the side and the children copied her. The room would go still in seconds. Lauren's tone of voice and body language had a very calming effect on the children, so her interactions with them were very positive. Vanessa observed that, when Lauren called a child over to her table, "It's like intriguing, right. Come with me, magical ... it creates something special ... with kids."

When building authentic relationships with their peers, the children learned how to use different strategies to resolve conflicts and be empathetic. For example, Jian was crying at the snack table because Henry grabbed his food and ate it. When Jian went to the Calm Centre, Kaitlyn and Cassie followed him. They were very caring and tried different strategies to help Jian recover. They talked with him quietly, gave him hugs, and offered him stuffed animals and squeeze toys to hold. When Jian started to calm down, Kaitlyn and Cassie went and sat on the carpet to listen to a story about invisibility. Jian remained at the Calm Centre for a few more minutes and then joined the girls on the carpet. Lauren asked the children if they thought the people in the story would forgive the bear. Jian turned to Henry and said, "You know, it's a good thing I don't have to forgive you, because it was actually the invisible ghost that ate my chips. It wasn't you, Henry." Jian was laughing about it as he skipped away to get his lunch from his cubby. The children had such strong relationships that they seemed to know how to help their peers when they became upset, providing one another with just the right amount of support. Lauren commented that when a child was upset, she didn't go to the child right away to comfort him. Her absence opened up a space for the children to intervene. She explained, "So then that became more the norm of 'Let's go help our friends,' instead of, 'Oh, the teacher is taking care of it.'" Lauren or Vanessa would step in when conflicts escalated and help guide the children towards a peaceful resolution.

Kathryn and Victoria built authentic relationships with the children in a variety of ways. For example, when the girls were working in the Studio, Kathryn asked Nikki what she could see in the prism and Nikki responded, "I can see a rainbow." Kathryn replied, "Great Nikki. Thanks for your great learning." She also encouraged the children to persist and focus on their work. During class meetings, Kathryn was very positive with the children and made comments such as, "You collaborated well together." Victoria pointed out, "I think the relationship between the two teachers is important for the kids to see.... They see us interacting positively all the time.... We're relaxed with each other and respectful." Kathryn and Victoria modelled how to speak and behave in a respectful way when they were talking to each other and with the children. The closeness of the relationships in the classroom were quite striking. Kathryn said, "Yeah, they love us. We love them. This group is truly wonderful."

Photo 4.17: The Calm Centre

Photo 4.18: The Children Are Empathetic towards Their Peers

Kathryn explained that, when it comes to fostering authentic relationships, it was just like all other areas of the program: she and Victoria wanted the girls to "own it." They wanted the children to own their learning and their thinking as well as the process of resolving conflicts with others. For example, when the girls were looking through the prisms and recording what they saw, there was lots of excitement in the children's voices as they found the colours in the prism that were the same colours as pencil crayons. Nikki said, "I need red." Anna responds, "I am sorry I am using the red right now and then I will give it to you." Angie said, "Who can give me a blue?" Nikki replied, "I can." When the children worked together, there was a strong sense of community in which everyone felt like they belonged.

While building authentic relationships with their peers, the children learned how to co-regulate and turn to one another for support. For example, Vicky and Sally were at the Light Table during tidy-up time. Vicky put her nametag sticker over her mouth and said in a whispering voice, "I am putting this on my mouth because I want to be quiet." Sally seemed to understand that Vicky needed quiet time, so she spoke to her softly and used hand gestures to help convey what she wanted to say. When she realized that Vicky was not picking up and had zoned out, she said, "You have to put these in there." Vicky responded by putting the pink cubes with the rest. Sally and Vicky quietly tidied up the Light Table together. The teachers explained that Vicky often complains of high noise levels in the environment, so she has learned how to use different strategies to calm herself down. Sally is sensitive to Vicky's needs and displays empathy towards her.

Darlene thought that it was important to build authentic relationships with the children so that they felt accepted and part of the community:

> They're not going to take risks and talk about their feelings and talk about their thoughts at all if they don't feel safe with the person they're with. And I believe that relationships are the most important thing when it comes to being with kids. They need to feel safe. They need to trust you. You need to care for them, so they take risks in their thought process, for sure.

Photo 4.19: Co-regulation at the Light Table

For example, Darlene recalled how Lola used to get scared very easily. She said, "Lola would get very, very upset. She'd have to sit with us. She would cry." Over time, Lola learned to just take Darlene or Kerri's hand and stay close to them, or at other times she would just make eye contact with Darlene, who would nod her head to let Lola know that everything was okay. Darlene explained that "Just from getting that reassurance, it's helping her to self-regulate and get back down to a calm state ... she's learning much better how to handle it and how to deal with things."

Darlene and Kerri promoted positive social interactions among the children, and the closeness of the children's relationships was quite evident during the Running Club Inquiry. For example, after a run when Adele was listening to Connor's heartbeat, Adele held the end of the stethoscope up to Connor's chest as she gently rested the other hand on his shoulder. Connor stood very still and quiet as he looked at Adele intently. Darlene said,

> He's trusting her. Like he's got that trust in his eyes. It's like what do you hear?... And she looks so caring. Her eyes are right at him.... He's ready for her to say something to him. Her hands on his shoulder there.... She's very gentle. She's portraying that in her gestures.

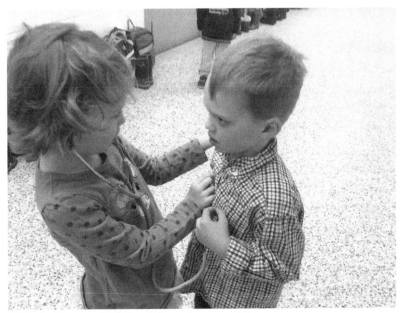

Photo 4.20: Adele Listens to Connor's Heartbeat

Adele and Connor seemed to be able to communicate without words. Connor knew he had to be quiet so that Adele could concentrate and listen to his heartbeat.

One day, Darlene and the children had a rich discussion about empathy after Gabriel became very competitive when running in the hall. Darlene wondered why racing made Gabriel so excited.

Gabriel: Because I just race because I really want to win.
Darlene: And what does winning make your body feel like?
Gabriel: ... happy.
Darlene: Happy. Zara ... what do you have to say about Gabriel feeling so happy when he wins against children that don't win?
Zara: Sad.... Because I don't win ...
Gabriel: But it's not, well it's not actually a real race where you get medals and stuff.
Michael: Well, it is not about winning, it is about having fun.
Whole group: Yeah.
Darlene: But Gabriel seems to have lots of fun when he wins.
Michael: Well, what if you lost Gabriel, would you still have fun?
Adele: ... I need to tell you something. Whenever my Mom goes for a race she just says it's just for fun ...
Michael: I like losing races ... and not winning.... I think it makes me feel too sad when like, when I win and other people don't, so I always like ...
Gabriel: Try to lose.
Michael: Yeah ...
Rose: I have something to say.... If I lost, I would still be proud of myself.... Because usually I lose but I am still proud of myself ... for running.

Although Gabriel sometimes found it hard to be empathetic, the rest of the children in the Running Club were so empathetic towards one another that they would sacrifice winning a race in order to avoid hurting their friend's feelings.

Sharon and Mikayla promoted authentic relationships through their knowledge-building circles where the children shared their questions, wonderings, ideas, and theories about the inquiry they were working on. There was an established protocol where the children were required to listen attentively when other people were speaking and take turns. Sometimes Sharon reviewed the protocol expectations, "In our KBC [knowledge-building circle] we listen to the ideas of our friends, we can build onto our friend's ideas, [and] we can bring new ideas to the KBC. But the most important thing ... is that we are listening to our friends."

Knowledge-building circles provided opportunities for the children to learn about empathy. Sharon explained, "I'm trying to get them to understand … to recognize the feelings of another and understand why that person feels that way."

During one knowledge-building circle, the children were asked to share their thinking about their visit to the valley. At the end of the discussion, Adhita wanted to share the picture she had sketched of the tree she was sitting on:

> When we went down to the valley … I looked how the bark looked like and I said how it would look and I looked behind and I looked around and then I got down but it was not safe to climb around the tree because it bends around…. Then I went back on the tree and sat on the top of the tree. Then I was sitting, then Ehsan sat with me and he was showing me all the buildings and…. No one is clapping for me.

Adhita was upset that her friends didn't clap after she shared her picture. Amina was concerned about Adhita, so she tried to distract her by asking about her picture, which helped to calm Adhita down. This shows how Amina was able to co-regulate Adhita and support her friend.

Photo 4.21: A Child Sitting on a Tree, Drawing

The teachers found that they had to do a lot of modelling when it came to helping the children resolve issues with their peers. Sharon said,

> We dramatize it quite often. We'll be together and I'll … be holding a marker and I'll pretend I'm drawing with my marker and Mikayla … will say I want the marker and she will try and grab it. And then we'll literally role-play these challenges so that the children who aren't speaking English yet … might not understand our words but by the physicality of how we are doing it, they still can get it as well and understand it.

Sharon and Mikayla often role-played issues that came up in class in front of the whole group. They re-enacted challenges that had already been resolved with the small group of children who were initially involved. It reaffirmed for those children that they knew what to do and they could share their ideas with the whole group. The children were learning to be empathetic and think about other people's feelings so that everyone felt like they were part of the community.

CHAPTER SUMMARY

This chapter has focused on self-regulation and the importance of the design of the environment. I have argued that the organization of physical space and materials for the purpose of facilitating children's interests and autonomy during inquiries enables them to stay focused, consider other perspectives, and figure out their own thinking, which are all important mental processes in the cognitive domain. The classroom environments in the four inquiries evolved to reflect the children's interests and afforded possibilities like choice of centres and materials that helped the children self-regulate. Teachers adapted and extended their classroom environments to enhance children's self-regulation by planning provocations to prompt further thought and action.

The design of the environment for inquiry-based learning also includes daily routines, expansive time frames, and authentic relationships, which are important for supporting children as they become self-regulated learners. Predictable daily routines help children become more independent as they can then anticipate transitions that enable them to up- or down-regulate knowing what activity is coming next. During expansive time frames, children have more time to develop skills such as independence, resourcefulness, risk-taking, perseverance, problem-solving, initiative, and creativity in the multiple domains of self-regulation.

Expansive time frames in the classroom give children enough time to sustain their play and concentrate on an inquiry. Authentic relationships that create a sense of belonging and the capacity for empathy promote positive behaviours in the prosocial domain. Social and emotional learning (SEL) is evident when children show empathy towards their peers, which means caring about other people's feelings and helping them deal with their emotions.

REFLECTIVE QUESTIONS

1. How do the physical space and materials in your environment help children learn how to self-regulate?
2. When implementing inquiries, how might you adapt and extend the environment?
3. What daily predictable routines in your classroom have been most helpful so that children can prepare for transitions?
4. What are some of the challenges that exist around scheduling expansive time frames?
5. What strategies might you use in your classroom environment to ensure that children develop authentic relationships and feel like they belong?

RECOMMENDED READINGS

Barnett, Vanessa, & Halls, Deborah. (2008). Wire bicycles: A journey with Galimoto. In Carol Anne Wien (Ed.), *Emergent curriculum in the primary classroom: Interpreting the Reggio Emilia approach in schools* (pp. 52–63). New York: Teachers College Press.

Branzi, Andrea, Bruner, Jerome, Rinaldi, Carla, Vecchi, Vea, et al. (2011). *Children, spaces, relationships*. Reggio Emilia, IT: Reggio Children.

Curtis, Deb, & Carter, Margie. (2003). *Designs for living and learning: Transforming early childhood environments*. St. Paul, MN: Redleaf Press.

Heinrichs, Jennifer. (2016). The co-creation of a "kinder garden." *Canadian Children, 41,* 16–23.

Pineda, Monica. (2018). Mama spider. *Journal of Childhood Studies, 43,* 73–80.

Reggio Children. (2008). *Children, art, artists: The expressive languages of children, the artistic language of Alberto Burri.* Reggio Emilia, IT: Reggio Children.

Taylor, Affrica, & Pacini-Ketchabaw, Veronica. (2015). Learning with children, ants, and worms in the Anthropocene: Towards a common world pedagogy of multispecies vulnerability. *Pedagogy, Culture, & Society, 23,* 507–529.

Topal, Cathy, & Gandini, Lella. (1999). *Beautiful stuff! Learning with found materials.* Worcester, MA: Davis Publishers.

ONLINE RESOURCES

Piazza_Piazze
https://youtu.be/g65ZO7zbVKI

Sky Inquiry Filming Series Video 4—The Environment as 3rd Teacher
https://youtu.be/6iGZ-qrN3Lg

Brain Development in the Early Years—Impact of Positive, Quality Interactions with Children
https://youtu.be/mx10YkEgxpA

Denmark's Forest Kindergartens
https://youtu.be/Jkiij9dJfcw

Chapter Five

Self-Regulation and Conversation

A pedagogy of listening means listening to thought—the ideas and theories, questions and answers of children and adults; it means treating thought seriously and with respect; it means struggling to make meaning from what is said, without preconceived ideas of what is correct or appropriate. A pedagogy of listening treats knowledge as constructed, perspectival and provisional, not the transmission of a body of knowledge which makes the Other into the same.
—Carlina Rinaldi, 2006, p. 15

In this chapter, I focus on self-regulation and the conversation component of emergent curriculum. This component has four aspects: (1) encouraging children to participate; (2) expressing their different ideas and theories; (3) nurturing their reasoning and problem-solving capabilities; and (4) supporting their awareness of how to regulate their emotions. When each of the four aspects are considered together, they illustrate that conversation enables children to become self-regulated learners in the primary classroom. As explained in the introduction to the book, one compelling insight about the relationship between self-regulation and inquiry-based learning is that children use oral language as a self-regulatory tool to help them regulate their own emotions and behaviours. This insight is evident and interwoven throughout this chapter.

Conversation during inquiry-based learning involves sharing multiple perspectives, making sense of what is being said, and constructively confronting differences. Teachers and children use oral language during Reggio-inspired emergent curriculum inquiries to co-construct ideas and theories about topics that they are investigating. The children have opportunities to engage in exploratory talk that has purpose and is of interest to them. Conversation during inquiries involves interactions that go beyond teachers merely listening to children to teachers reflecting on and trying to understand what is said and heard. The four inquiries provide concrete illustrations of the relationship between

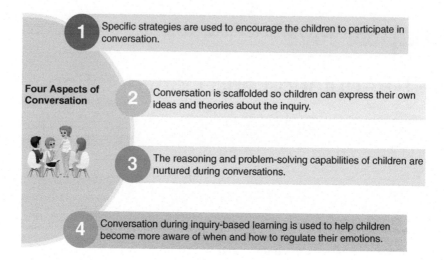

Four Aspects of Conversation

1 Specific strategies are used to encourage the children to participate in conversation.

2 Conversation is scaffolded so children can express their own ideas and theories about the inquiry.

3 The reasoning and problem-solving capabilities of children are nurtured during conversations.

4 Conversation during inquiry-based learning is used to help children become more aware of when and how to regulate their emotions.

self-regulation and conversation, which is one of the components of emergent curriculum that support inquiry-based learning. The examples involving English Language Learners (ELLs) are especially powerful.

FOUR ASPECTS OF CONVERSATION

Specific Strategies Are Used to Encourage the Children to Participate in Conversation

The origins of the importance of conversation can be traced back to Vygotsky (1978), who believed that oral language is fundamental to learning how to self-regulate. He believed that language is an actual mechanism for thinking, a mental tool. Language makes thinking more abstract and flexible and allows the child to imagine, manipulate, create new ideas, and share their ideas and theories with others. Language enables children to solve difficult tasks and manage impulsive behaviour. Bodrova and Leong (2007) distinguish two roles that language performs: it is part of cognitive processing and instrumental to the development of cognition. Listening and talking occur during conversations where children share their thinking in order to understand others. Greenspan and Shanker (2004) point out that children engage in back-and-forth emotional gesturing, such as tone of voice, body posture, or facial expressions, during longer conversations. It is the continuous flow of emotional gesturing that organizes and maintains these high-level symbolic exchanges and provides a constant source of new emotions that stir up the next sequence of ideas or words. Dickinson et al. (2013) explain further how the development of language and self-regulation are linked.

Between ages three and six, the rapid development of language plays a pivotal role in the linguistic cognitive-affective systems of literacy development as well as social development. When children learn to use oral language, this helps them to intentionally regulate their own emotions and behaviours. I think that when children are encouraged to participate in conversations during inquiries, this provides opportunities for them to use oral language as a self-regulatory tool.

The four inquiries provide numerous examples of vivid conversations that are scaffolded by the teachers. For example, Lauren focused, in particular, on how she asked children questions:

> I really try to think about the questions that I'm asking and how I'm asking the questions because so many times, just the way you phrase a question will either [open up] the learning or shut if off completely. So, you have to really make sure that the questions that you're asking are appropriate and that you are aware of the kinds of responses you are getting from the questions. Like, I've really worked hard, even writing down my questions and then say, how can I say that better. How can I keep that a little more open, or how could I spark a child's interest with a question?

When Lauren was working on the Invisibility Inquiry with the children, the dialogue was reciprocal, like a game of Ping-Pong. She would ask a child a question, listen attentively to their answer, and then phrase the next question in light of the child's previous response. Her questions nudged them to think more deeply about their own ideas, questions, and theories.

A conversation between Lauren and Iliana about the different sounds Iliana had drawn on top of a piece of acetate illustrates how the teacher uses different strategies to encourage children to participate in conversations.

> *Iliana*: I am drawing the noise … coming from the pot …
> *Lauren*: What does it sound like?
> *Iliana*: A banging noise.
> *Lauren*: Can you make the banging noise? [Iliana bangs her hand on the table.] I see, and what about these here?
> *Iliana*: Those are the noise coming from the other pot …
> *Lauren*: And so, what do those sound like?
> *Iliana*: They sound like markers banging.
> *Lauren*: Okay … will you show me? [Iliana bangs the markers on the table.] …
> Oh, interesting Iliana, wow.

Photo 5.1: Drawing the Sounds That the Pot Makes

Photo 5.2: A Photo with Sound Markings

By the end of the conversation, Lauren had asked Iliana to describe and demonstrate all the different sounds she had created.

In a different example, Lauren held up a small glass jar that she had filled with water and a small glass jar that was empty.

Lauren: Okay is there water in this one?

Group: No.

Lauren: Is there water in this one?

Group: Yes.

Lauren: How do you know? Daryl?

Daryl: Cause that one I can see there's air in it. I can see air in that one.... It's in the water …

Lauren: Raina, what do you think? Which one has water in it?

Raina: That one.... It's more darker …

Lauren: Henry … how can you tell which one has water and which one does not have water?

Henry: Cause that one I can see through … and that one I can't really see …

Lauren: Daryl, what do you think?…

Daryl: I can see the water in there.... Cause where it stops at the top, where there's no water.

Samantha: If you look at the top you can see ... the water moving.

Here, Lauren asked each child to participate and share their theory about which jar had water in it. These questions led to reciprocal dialogue and deeper thinking.

The teachers in the Office Inquiry also encouraged the children to participate in conversations. For example, Victoria asked the girls if they could remember how the inquiry started.

Rachel: It started with chairs.... Cause, I wanted to let nobody in ... only the people who wanted to play.... And I was the guard.

Victoria: I remember trying to visit the office and you said you were busy working and you really didn't want me in there.... Can you remember what happened next?

Alia: Drama in the office.

Victoria: We changed it to Drama so we could leave it up every night.... We wanted a permanent office. But what did we do next we went on a visit ...

Liza: To the office.

Victoria: That's right what did you find out? What did you learn at the office? Did you see anything that surprised you in the office?

Alia: A button.

Victoria: You saw a button ... a button that you press to come into the school?... And we found out about that a bit later on, didn't we. That was exciting.... What's in the office that you like to use?

Girls: The printer ... the candy ... and the sand too.

Victoria: Why do you think they have those in the office?

Rachel: To keep them busy.

Victoria asked the children thought-provoking questions, listened attentively to their responses, and acknowledged what they had said by adding on to their ideas.

Darlene used specific strategies to help the children learn how to engage in conversation, such as repeating what they said. For example, Darlene had Michael explain his drawing of how his body felt before and after he ran.

Michael: My heart was running really really fast because I was excited.

Darlene: Your heart was going fast because you were excited. I can see that and tell me about this part here [pointing to the drawing].

Michael: Those are my ribs …

Darlene: Those are your ribs, wow … now can you show me something about how it looked after you ran.… And maybe how your heart was feeling …

Michael: This one is before when my heart was beating really really fast and this one my heart was beating slowly. It was beating fast because I was so tired.

Darlene: Because you were so tired. What feeling did you like better? Slow or fast?

Michael: Slow.… Maybe if we were really quiet, we could actually hear our heart.

Darlene: Can we hear our hearts if we are quiet? Do you know, I have a stethoscope inside [the classroom]. We can listen to our hearts.

Darlene said that although she didn't like to repeat what the children said too much, she thought it helped to slow down the conversation. She explained, "It makes me think about what they are saying." It gave her time to think about how she was going to respond back to the children. The children also had an opportunity to think about what they said and whether that was what they meant. If not, the children could rephrase what they were thinking. In this conversation, we can also see how Darlene asked thought-provoking questions to further Michael's thinking about how running made him feel.

Photo 5.3: Michael Draws How He Feels Before and After He Runs

Another strategy Darlene used was to revisit the children's work and give them an opportunity to expand their thinking. For example, when Gabriel first explained how his body felt before and after he ran, he emphasized how running depleted his energy level. The second time, he tries to describe internal reactions in his body.

Gabriel: When I couldn't run, it felt like my heart was melting.

Darlene: How does it feel when your heart is melting? What does it feel like inside of you?

Gabriel: Really hot.

Darlene: You said here ... when I run my heart is beating fast. And what kind of feeling is your heart beating fast for you?

Gabriel: It just feels really good.... When your heart beats slow and then you might die if you can't get your heart beating.

Similarly, Michael originally emphasized the internal changes in his body, and the second time he expanded his idea by including the lungs.

Michael: My body felt before, it felt excited. It was beating slow and after it was beating high.

Darlene: So, you drew a picture of before and after ... talk about your heart expanding. Remember that?...

Michael: It's like a sponge because it gets full of air and then it breathes out and then it gets full of air again.

Adele: Like a sponge gets full of water.

Darlene: So, my heart expands when I run because it is getting more air in it?

Michael: Yeah.

Darlene: So that is why it is like a sponge?

Michael: And the lungs also do that too.

Darlene: So, they expand in and out as well.

By responding to Darlene's questions, Gabriel and Michael were able to extend their original theories.

As most of the children in Sharon and Mikayla's class were English Language Learners, the teachers created a lot of visual support and used simpler language to teach the children how to take part in conversations. Sharon explained that they used sign language for words like *stand*, *sit*, *play*, *music*, *no*, and *finished* to help students understand what they were talking about. They also used tone of voice and body language like gesturing to help the children understand their message. Mikayla said, "I'm very aware of like, what my face is saying, even if they don't understand the words." The teachers provided intensive support, modelling simpler language, especially at the beginning of the school year. Sharon explained, "I play with them and I label what I'm doing.... Here you go. My turn. Your turn. Pass me the block." She would also describe a lot of actions, orally labelling materials in the room and being very specific. For example, "Can you hand me the marker?" rather than "Can you hand me that?" When a child was ready, Sharon would get her to expand a bit on what she said. For example, when a child said, "Look me," she would respond, "You are standing on the rock ... say 'I am on rock.'" The child would add, "I'm rock."

During the Community Inquiry, Sharon engaged in conversation with the children to get them to think more deeply about a particular idea, question, or theory. One day, Sharon and Alma had a discussion about what she could see and hear from her balcony.

Alma: This is the window and that's behind my building and this is the balcony ...

Sharon: Do you go out on the balcony?

Alma: Sometimes I go on my balcony. Sometimes.

Sharon: Who do you go out on the balcony with?

Alma: Sometimes I go with my daddy. Sometimes I go by myself. Sometimes I go with my sister. But my Mommy does not want to go out there ...

Sharon: What do you see when you go on the balcony?

Alma: Just some cars. Some garbage beside the garbage bins ...

Sharon: What do you hear on your balcony?

Alma: I can hear some cars ... and sometimes I can see some people.

Sharon focused on asking Alma questions in order to encourage her to say more about her observations of where she lives.

When the children engage in conversations during knowledge-building circles, Sharon prefers to summarize what the children have said at the end.

I try not to summarize every time someone has said something.... I find that sometimes if I summarize too much then they ... won't attentively listen necessarily to each other. I prefer to bring it back to or summarize at the end ... I usually print out the discussion and I highlight, and I go through and I pull out the information and I take that, condense it, and I would revisit it with them in another way, which is a different way to consolidate than summarize. If you are summarizing after every single student, are you respecting listening?

Sharon thought it was okay to repeat what the children said sometimes because it gave them a chance to listen to what they said, and then if it was not what they meant, they could go back and rephrase their idea. It also gave her a chance to think about what a child had said and ask a question that pushed their thinking further.

Sharon also encouraged the children to explain their ideas in more depth and to build on each other's ideas. After a trip to the valley nearby the school, Sharon thought the children probably had lots of things they would like to share. She wondered what they saw, heard, or even smelled.

> *Sadi*: The snail, the snail was gone when we picked it up, it was already gone. Then we found more of snails, then Raem found one, then I found one and then Mustanjid found one …
>
> *Saami*: You know, when I was in the valley, Raem's mom find two snails' shells.
>
> *Raem*: When we go to the valley, I told my mom I found a bug.
>
> *Sharon*: Can you tell me more about the bug?
>
> *Raem*: Yes, and then my mom found a leaf and then the bug come on the leaf.
>
> *Sharon*: For the people that didn't see the bug can you tell us what it looked like.… Does someone else want to help Raem talk about it?
>
> *Mustanjid*: Yes, Raem and Raem's mom and Sadi and Saami and me, we saw the bug was like first a circle then you have to draw other circle for his face and then you have to draw legs.

This discussion shows how, during inquiry-based learning, children acquire the vocabulary they need to participate in conversations and express their ideas more clearly.

Conversation Is Scaffolded So Children Can Express Their Own Ideas and Theories about the Inquiry

A key insight of this book is that teachers use scaffolding strategies during inquiry-based learning, which enables children to become self-regulated learners. During conversations, educators make the child's entry easy and successful and then gradually pull back as the child becomes skilled enough to manage it. Scaffolding conversation in this way is an effective process that strengthens the executive functions that are so important for self-regulation. Language plays a central role in cognitive development, and children use language to help them think and perform tasks. Vygotsky believed that

> Children become [more] capable of thinking as they talk. The child can think aloud.… He argues that in some cases, our external speech helps us form ideas

that may exist only vaguely.... When children become capable of thinking as they talk, speech actually becomes a tool for understanding, clarifying, and focusing what is in their minds. (Bodrova & Leong, 2007, p. 68)

Oral language helps us to think logically and acquire new knowledge that is socially constructed within a particular context, such as a classroom. When children express their theories and ideas during inquiries, it supports their ability to self-regulate in the cognitive domain.

Scaffolding conversations during inquiry-based learning begins with the image of the child as competent, curious, and capable of complex thinking. Fraser (2012) emphasizes that listening attentively to what children say and following up with questions that reveal the child's understanding are essential elements of conversation:

When teachers expect children to say interesting things and to contribute ideas, they will be much more likely to pay attention to what children have to say. When children know that their ideas are appreciated, they will be more willing to share them. Slowing down and taking the time to really hear what the child is saying and then trying to see it from the child's perspective is important. Reflecting on the child's responses to questions also helps a teacher learn what kind of questions are most effective. (Fraser, 2012, pp. 187–188)

Effective questions are reflective and encourage more elaborate responses. The child's response in turn provides the teacher and other children with unexpected insight into what the child is thinking and feeling.

On numerous occasions, Lauren facilitated conversation so the children could share their ideas and theories about invisibility. She emphasized that children "always have to be free to really express what it is that they are thinking." Lauren also thought it was important that the children knew their ideas and theories were valued and that there is no right or wrong answer. She said,

You can never make them [the children] feel that (a) there is one right answer and (b) that they're not giving you the right answer.... That you are going to accept whatever it is that they say because that's where the value for them comes in because it's not oh, I have 100 different things going on in my head and I have to pick the one right thing or it's going to be a disaster.... Everyone genuinely wants to know what it is that they [the children] are thinking, what are their ideas and so they have to be willing and able to share, but also to understand their ideas are going to be valued no matter what or how outrageous they might seem to someone else and they're not going to be mocked. I'm not going to say wrong, that's the wrong answer. So, they are very comfortable.

Because Lauren set this emotional tone in the classroom, the children felt it was a safe space to share their thinking.

One day, Lauren showed the children the worm jar from the Nature Centre to provoke their thinking about things in the classroom that might be invisible or have some aspect of invisibility to them.

Lauren: Can you always see the worms in here?

Daryl: No, cause they're under the dirt sometimes …

Lauren: So, does that mean that they're invisible?

Daryl: Yes …

Lauren: Then are the worms actually still in there if you can't see them …

Alison: Yes …

Lauren: Can you see the worms in here?

Shannon: No.

Lauren: So, does that make them invisible? Are the worms still in here? How do you know?

Shannon: Because she put the worms in there …

Rory: If the worms go under the dirt and you can't see the worms then you can probably still see their hole they make and where they went …

Lauren: So then if you can't see the worms are the worms still in there?

Rory: Um hum.

Lauren: And maybe the worm holes that they make can help you see where they've been. Help you know that they are there.

Daryl: You can still see the worms because sometimes they make spaces, and you can see them in the corner where there's no dirt.

During this conversation, the children were able to think about things being invisible and things being hidden. They certainly thought that the worms were still in the jar even when they could not see them.

A little while later, Lauren asked the children if there was anything else they wanted to say about invisibility. A few children were still thinking about the worms in the jar.

Zara: Worms blend into the dirt …

Lauren: You can't see them … how do you know they are still there?

> *Zara*: Because they're just underground …
> *Tagwen*: You can't see the worms. If you feel it inside, then you can feel them.
> *Lauren*: Aw, so even if you can't see the worms in the dirt what you can do is you can feel inside the dirt and you … can feel the worms and you know the worms are in there …
> *Rory*: If the worms blend into the hole then you can still stick your hand in and then if you feel something and then you pull it up and you look at it, it is a worm.

Lauren realized the children were still interested in the worms and had new ideas and theories to share.

Kathryn and Victoria scaffolded conversations so the children could share their thinking about the Office Inquiry. In the following discussion, Victoria is trying to determine if the girls know what their parents do at their office.

> *Victoria*: Who's got a mom or dad that goes to an office? What do you think they do in the office?…
> *Olive*: My mommy she types stuff on her computer …
> *Zola*: Mommy has her own computer … and she types lots of things.
> *Victoria*: Oh okay. Alright, Nikki? Does Mommy work in an office?
> *Nikki*: Actually, my Dad does…. He works…. He does homework.

It was clear that the children were not really sure what their parents did at the office. So, Victoria had them brainstorm some questions for their parents about their jobs. She asked the girls if anyone could come up with a good question.

> *Nikki*: I think they write.
> *Victoria*: Is this a question or a comment?
> *Nikki*: A question…. I think what he does is just writes numbers…. I could ask him if he writes, if he reads.
> *Victoria*: If he reads. That's a great question. You could say, "Daddy, when you're at the office, do you have to read?"
> *Evelyn*: My Dad types names…. Daddy, why do you type names?…
> *Susan*: I have only been to my Mommy's work, not my Daddy's.
> *Victoria*: Okay, so what could you ask your Daddy to do so that you know what his office looks like?
> *Susan*: Daddy, can I come to your office?

Victoria: Yeah, you can ask Daddy if you can come to the office but if you can't go to the office what could Daddy do so that you know what it looks like? Any ideas? Evelyn?

Evelyn: Take a picture.

Victoria: That's another question we could ask them [the parents] isn't it? Can we have a picture of your office?

Later that day, Victoria sent the parents an email that included the children's questions.

Darlene often facilitated conversation so the children could express their ideas, questions, and theories during the Running Club Inquiry. She felt that during conversations the children were able to extend their thinking:

They're truly interested. They want to hear ... from each other. And they grew their ideas from each other. It wasn't just like I'm thinking of the next thing I'm going to say. They actually grew their ideas through each other's thoughts.

For example, after Adele shared her running idea in the hall, the children continued to think about how to make the big running idea work.

Adele: Exercises help you not get hurt, that's what I know.

Darlene: So, do you think that maybe that it could be part of the whole big idea that Michael was talking about that everybody does a little bit of warming up before?

Adele: Yeah.... So, I think the next time we do this in the hall, Gabriel should hold up one of these clocks ...

Darlene: Along with your idea you mean?... [Adele nods.]

Zara: How about we have two persons holding the clock and then see on each side how long they took.

Darlene: So, then we would have one, two ideas. And you know what the boys were going on one side and the girls were going on the other. So that was part of Evan's idea about the girls, so we'll actually have three ideas going at once.

Darlene could see how the children were starting to expand their own ideas and incorporate other running ideas into them. She commented, "So Michael's idea of building, taking a bunch of little ideas and making it into one huge idea has almost happened naturally."

When Darlene later reflected on how the inquiry had progressed to this point where the children were starting to come up with the big idea for running, she said,

> So, I think it is building trust amongst us as a whole group. I think that's huge too. To allow them to take risks, to be able to change their thinking, to feel safe in sharing their ideas in the beginning and have other children sort of help them change that thought process.... Like it is just a back and forth. It is that respect, it's that relationship that they have together as well. And that trust they have for each other.

The children in the Running Club were very comfortable sharing their thinking with each other.

Darlene also thought it was important that the children knew their thinking was valued when they engaged in conversations. For example, the children in the inquiry all sat on the couch with a microphone, ready to present their running ideas to their peers. Darlene put all the children's pictures of their running ideas on the whiteboard to help prompt the children, if needed.

> *Darlene*: Michael had a very important question the other day when we were working together.
>
> *Michael*: You guys, if we put a little bit of our ideas and put them altogether [to make one big idea] …
>
> *Darlene*: Do you remember your idea, Evan? It was about the boys and girls, wasn't it?…
>
> *Evan*: The girls were on one side and the boys were on the other side. And then one person runs and then the other person runs.
>
> *Darlene*: Great. Adele?…
>
> *Adele*: One person would go on one side of the hall and one end of the hall and one person would go on the other end of the hall and they would both run at the same time and try to clap hands …
>
> *Rose*: So, I was thinking you could put a piece of tape in the middle and like one team could go on this side and one team could go on this side …
>
> *Darlene*: Some people didn't want to race so is that how your idea came about Rose? Did you want to race or not race?
>
> *Rose*: I wanted to race. And one team could go on this side and one team could go on this side and they could see the line and like they could come back to their side of the team …

Gabriel: I was thinking that there could be one line and one person would go and get through their turn but if they got 15 and then after their other turn they got 10 then they would beat their time ... you would use a clock and you would try to beat your score ...

Connor: My idea was like we could make a circle and tell each other our ideas and we would hold hands and we would do all of our ideas together and make a big one.

Then Darlene invited the other children to share their thinking about what the Running Club was working on. She said, "Anybody else have a question or an idea?" So, for example, Faith said, "If you win you can get another turn. And if the other person wins, they can get another turn." By engaging in conversation, Darlene showed the children that she valued their ideas and theories. The children's ease of expression reveals that they were accustomed to such opportunities to share their thinking.

The children engaged in conversation and expressed their thinking throughout the Community Inquiry. For instance, Sharon followed up an earlier conversation she had with the children when they disagreed with the statement "The CN Tower is the tallest building in Toronto."

Sharon: Zahir, can you tell us what you're thinking ... what did you want to disagree with?

Zahir: There's another CN Tower that's more bigger.... I mean two more that are bigger.

Sharon: Where?

Zahir: I don't know.

Sharon: You don't know. Who told you?

Zahir: My Dad.

Sharon: Do you think that you could bring some information to school to share with us about that if you talk to your Daddy about it? Or ... maybe he can ... get a picture off the computer ... [or] maybe your Daddy could come and tell us.

Zahir: Yeah.

Zahir was remembering that there are buildings taller than the CN Tower elsewhere, but he didn't realize that their focus was on buildings in Toronto.

Sharon then asked Amina if she would like to build on Zahir's thinking. Amina recalled that the CN Tower was very tall, that there was an elevator that goes up, and that people can lie down inside it. Then Adhita followed up on Zahir's idea.

> *Adhita*: There are other different kinds of towers that are bigger than the CN Tower and one tower is bigger than the CN Tower.
> *Zahir*: There were two.
> *Adhita*: Two towers. One tower had fire on it and it is smaller than the CN Tower and the other tower is taller than the CN Tower and … the two towers were in New York …

Adhita was recalling what she knew about the World Trade Center (Twin Towers) in New York. It was not clear whether the children were both thinking about the same two towers. It was also not clear whether she agreed with the original statement or not, because the Twin Towers were shorter than the CN Tower. Sharon then asked Sadi if he would like to add more information.

> *Sadi*: There is a tower in Paris. This one is taller than, the Paris is taller than the CN Tower. It is bigger than the CN Tower.
> *Sharon*: Do you know what the name of it is Sadi? You said it was in Paris.
> *Sadi*: Eiffel Tower.

Photo 5.4: The CN Tower

Sadi believed that the Eiffel Tower is taller than the CN Tower. Other children then joined in the conversation and shared their ideas, questions, and theories about the CN Tower.

Sharon felt that during conversations it was important for every child to be given a chance to speak and their ideas were just as important as everyone else's. She wrote, "I want students to feel that they are valued, respected, and active participants in their learning." Sharon said that knowledge-building circles modelled what happens in the real world. The children learned how to listen to other people's ideas, build onto them, adjust their own theories, and disagree respectfully. When English Language Learners listen to their peers share their ideas, they have heard enough vocabulary that they often feel brave enough to share their own thinking by the end. Sharon said, "It might be a repetition of what someone else has said but they feel the value that they've been included."

The Reasoning and Problem-Solving Capabilities of Children Are Nurtured during Conversations

Children use oral language as a self-regulatory tool during conversations to help them understand, clarify, and focus their thoughts. They share their ideas and theories in a logical, sensible way and find solutions to problems during the investigations. Shanker (2013b) explains that executive functions like reasoning and problem-solving are important for self-regulated learning. He argues that when

> a [teacher] responds to what a child is thinking and trying to communicate by deliberately repeating, recasting, or expanding on the child's utterance … more than language is being learned in such a process: the child's ability to focus attention is also being enhanced. (p. 51)

Oral language is also fundamental to learning how to solve more complex problems (Vygotsky, 1978). In fact, complex ideas and processes such as learning how to solve social conflicts, which is important for self-regulation in the social domain, can only be learned using language (Bodrova & Leong, 2007). When children have trouble understanding something, it is especially helpful for them to explain their thinking to someone else. To think while talking to their peers helps to clarify their understanding of complex concepts. By talking with others, children actually understand their own thoughts better, including how to regulate their emotions and behaviours. This also helps to explain, in my view, why conversations that nurture the children's reasoning and problem-solving capabilities during inquiries enable them to become self-regulated learners.

Lauren often used conversation to foster the children's reasoning and problem-solving skills. On one occasion, Samantha noticed that the spill of water on the table had disappeared, and this led to an interesting discussion about where it went.

> *Samantha*: It went away …
> *Raina*: It evaporated …
> *Lauren*: It disappeared so where did it go?
> *Samantha*: It went all in the table.
> *Raina*: It went between the tables …
> *Samantha*: I don't see any water on the floor.… I know so when the water drops and it goes to the crack it went into the table …
> *Lauren*: So, what do you think Kaitlyn?
> *Kaitlyn*: When the water spills then the water is blue …
> *Samantha*: Nope, nope it isn't blue, it is still the same colour. The water is still the same colour. When you put the water on the table then it just makes the table lighter.

As Samantha and Raina tried to make sense of what happened to the water, the focus of Samantha's thought process shifted to the colour of water. After the children dipped their fingers in the water and made some marks on the table, Samantha changed her mind about how the water makes the table lighter.

> *Rory*: The water is actually blue.
> *Daryl*: No, it's not. You can't see the water because it is see-through. It is camouflaged with the table …
> *Lauren*: What do you think is true, girls?
> *Samantha*: Because the water is all the same colour, it's just see-through. Remember when I told you when you put water on the table it makes it lighter.… It made it a little darker. So, it's still there. I know it's still there because I can feel it and I know the water is not blue.

Through further experimentation, Samantha was able to use her reasoning and problem-solving skills to think about how water made the table darker.

At one point during the Invisibility Inquiry, Lauren followed up the children's thinking about how some colours make things more invisible. She gave the children little silver mirrors and silver metallic markers. They made funny faces and sounds like hiccups. Lauren thought aloud about how it might be tricky for the children to draw something invisible or invisibility on the mirror when they could see their own reflection.

Zara: Yeah, you could copy yourself …

Lauren: Zara just gave me such a great idea. What if you actually drew your own self … made yourself invisible?

Rory: I got it. So, you look at yourself on the mirror and you draw [yourself] …

Lauren: Draw your invisible selves … you are going to draw what you see in the mirror …

Rory: It's invisible. I can't see it.

After the children had drawn their invisible selves on the mirrors, they shared why they thought their pictures were invisible.

Lauren: So, what's making your pictures invisible …

Samantha: Well, I don't really know. Cause I can still see it lots …

Daryl: You can't see my eyeballs inside …

Zara: The clear marker is making everything invisible …

Raina: I made everything invisible … because it is kind of the same colour, but it is not exactly the same colour …

Kaitlyn: The marker you draw and then you colour your face and then you can't see the eyes because the marker is white.

Photo 5.5: Daryl Drawing on a Mirror with a Marker

Photo 5.6: Daryl's Drawing of His Invisible Self

The children were trying to reason and problem-solve what was making the pictures hard to see. Interestingly, Raina was the only child who drew out the connection that both the marker and mirror are silver.

Kathryn supported the children's reasoning and problem-solving capabilities through conversation. For example, she placed a typewriter in the centre of the circle, and a discussion unfolded about how it works.

> *Kathryn*: What do you notice about the typewriter?
>
> *Susan*: I know that something rolls.
>
> *Kathryn*: Susan can you point to the part that rolls? [Susan then points to the roller.] Now Zola, I'd like you to explain … what you think it's [the roller] for?…
>
> *Zola*: I think this is a big knob. You can remember what your paper is for. You can try a number for this, if people are five or four.
>
> *Kathryn*: Okay so if people are five or four you can type that. Do you see numbers?
>
> *Zola*: Yeah, and you can give it to people.
>
> *Kathryn*: Okay, so what's this roll part for?
>
> *Zola*: Printing the paper.

Kathryn then summarized what the children were thinking so far: "So I am hearing girls say that it has a keyboard like a computer and it almost has its

Photo 5.7: Angie Is Typing in the Office

Photo 5.8: The Children Are Working in the Office

own printer because when you type on it, that can come out." She then invited the children to share any other thinking they had about how the typewriter worked.

> *Sally*: This was like where you put your page in.... Then the letters would come out. So, if you put a paper in between this, it will stay …
>
> *Nikki*: If you push the buttons, if it was a real printer and you pressed the letters then it would come out and go on the paper. When you finish writing you can take it out …
>
> *Sally*: You can take it out and read it if you want to.

Here the children were interacting with the physical object to help them think logically as they tried to figure out how the typewriter works.

On a different occasion, Kathryn wondered if the children had any further thoughts about what the people in the office were doing.

> *Kathryn*: What did you notice?
>
> *Sally*: Working …
>
> *Kathryn*: What do you mean they were working? What were they doing?
>
> *Sally*: They were writing on pieces of paper.
>
> *Kathryn*: So, when people are writing on pieces of paper does that mean that they are working?…
>
> *Nikki*: Maybe they might sign some things.... One time when we came inside the office Ms. Harland told me that she was working …
>
> *Kathryn*: I wonder what she meant by that.... Ms. Dixon and I are at work right now. This is our job. Are we doing the same kind of work as Ms. Harland?
>
> *Girls*: No.
>
> *Kathryn*: How is our job different …
>
> *Laura*: Because they are the office girls, and you are a teacher …
>
> *Nikki*: The office girls, they work on what is the day today.
>
> *Anna*: I know. Get a checkmark on each day.
>
> *Kathryn*: Put checkmarks on all the things that they have to do.... What do you think are some things they will put on that list of things they have to do?…
>
> *Laura*: Check people who are sick.
>
> *Nikki*: They might give a message to everybody's Mom and Dad …
>
> *Kathryn*: These are some really fabulous ideas and it got me really thinking about what their job is in the office and what is work.

During this conversation, the children were thinking in a logical, sensible way when they articulated that teachers and office girls have different jobs. They also tried to figure out what exactly the people in the office do when they are working.

Conversations in Darlene's classroom were valuable opportunities to solve problems. For example, Darlene wanted to find out more about the connection the children were making in terms of shorter and longer running times and who was the fastest runner. She showed Michael the sheet on which Connor recorded all the times and how they were the same as the numbers on the oval shapes on the table.

> *Darlene*: What does it tell us about who is the fastest runner?
>
> *Michael*: Let's see who has the biggest number.... That she [Adele] is the fastest. Wait do I have the lowest number?... I think we should race again because I don't think that's right ... if we have a race between Gabriel and Adele we can see who is faster.... I think Gabriel's faster than Adele.
>
> *Gabriel*: But Michael I think that if you have the highest number you are going slowest because if you have 17 you are running faster than 28 seconds.
>
> *Adele*: Well 28 is actually a higher number than 17.
>
> *Gabriel*: Yeah, but if Connor was behind me, so pretend he got 19 and I got 17. So, Connor run behind me and I would touch, and he would touch after so he would have a higher score. So, the lowest one ... would ... win.... Let's see who has the lowest, me or Adele?
>
> *Adele*: Ah, we already seen who has the lowest.
>
> *Darlene*: Who was the fastest?
>
> *Zara*: Gabriel.
>
> *Gabriel*: And Connor and you [Zara]. We all have 17.
>
> *Darlene*: Rose who's the fastest runner there? What do you think? Adele has 28 and Gabriel has 17 and Connor and Zara have 17. Who is the fastest? 28 or 17.
>
> *Rose*: Well 17.... Because it's lower and they were running faster than me and not stopping.

Here the children were trying to make sense of the numbers and problem-solve why the children with the shortest running times were the fastest. It is difficult for children at this age to understand that the shorter the time it takes to run the race, the faster the runner.

Photo 5.9: Connor Recorded the Running Times

Photo 5:10: Who Is the Fastest Runner?

In a different example, the children were trying to problem-solve how to sort the competitive runners who wanted to race from the runners who just wanted to run for fun.

> *Rose*: Okay so I was thinking we could put like a piece of tape or something on the line. Then one person, like the people that don't want to run could go on one side and the people that want to race they could go on the other side …
>
> *Gabriel*: I think I know, so there was tape, the people that wanted to race are on the other side and the people that didn't want to race on this side and that's how many tapes there was.
>
> *Rose*: There's only one tape, Gabriel …
>
> *Adele*: I think she means a long piece of tape against a line.
>
> *Rose*: Yes, that's right.… So say this was the piece of tape, then one person went on this side and one person went on this side.… And then they ran …
>
> *Gabriel*: There should be three lines. Okay there's two people racing.
>
> *Rose*: I know that I just want to put one line, piece of tape, just one long piece of tape.

As Michael listened to this discussion between his peers, he suggested that each child should be in charge when it was their turn to demonstrate their running idea.

One morning, after Michael and Gabriel had just crashed in the hall during a race, Darlene scaffolded the conversation as the boys tried to problem-solve what happened.

Darlene: What happened to you in the middle when you ran that one time?...

Michael: I fell down ... because Gabriel didn't think ... and he hit me ...

Darlene: So, try it right here right now. How would it work in slow motion? Gabriel, try it in slow motion.

Michael: He was wiggling because I was trying to dodge him, and he was wiggling trying to hit me.

Gabriel: No.

Darlene: So, if you were like a car on the road which side would you stay on?

Michael: I would stay and try and avoid Gabriel and if I didn't, I would just put my lights on.

Darlene: Try it in slow motion. Somebody should be.... You know on the road the cars always have to be on the right side so this is right side and on your side over there you're on the right side too. So, if you stayed in your lane and went, then it would work, see that? Alright.

Gabriel: Cause, we were at the same side and I tried to get on the other side before ...

Darlene: So, you crossed lanes. You would have had a head-on collision if you were a car.

With Darlene's support and the analogy of the car, the boys were able to think through running into each other so it would not happen again.

During a small group knowledge-building circle, Sharon showed the children some photographs of the apartment buildings that surrounded the school and soon realized that not all the apartment buildings were in the photographs, so she asked the children how they could solve that problem.

Sharon: Did everybody see their building?

Saami: No.

Sharon: Your building wasn't in my pictures? What should we do ... Saami?

Saami: We can go outside again and take more pictures.

Sharon: Yeah, I think so. I think it would be nice if we could have large photographs of all of our friends' [buildings] ...

Amina: Maybe we could print them off of the computer.

Sharon took advantage of this opportunity to let the children find a solution to the problem. She followed up on Saami's idea by taking the children for another walk so she could take more photographs.

On a different occasion, Omja found a caterpillar in the valley and this led to a discussion about stewardship.

Mahdi: When the caterpillar will eat his leaf again and again and again then he'll turn into a butterfly …

Amina: He can't … because when it was in the leaf he was trying to go to sleep, then someone stepped on it and now he's died. He fell on the floor. Now he is not going to turn into a butterfly because he died.

Mahdi: Really?

Amina: Yes, it was Muhid. It was a good creature but Muhid stepped on it and it died. Now it's died and he can't be a butterfly …

Sharon: So, what can we say about that … why don't we want someone to step on a caterpillar?

Saami: Because if you step on it they will die. We don't want them to die. We want them to stay alive.

Sharon: Why?

Mahdi: Because we respect them.… Then our community and our nature will not be beautiful.

Amina: Nature helps us because he gives us the sun, he gives us the sky for breathing. So, we can't step on butterflies or anything.

The children were trying to make sense of the repercussions of stepping on a caterpillar and why it is important to respect nature and protect it.

Conversation during Inquiry-Based Learning Is Used to Help Children Become More Aware of When and How to Regulate Their Emotions

As explained in earlier chapters, self-regulation is a reflective learning process where children become aware of what it feels like to be overstressed, recognize when they need to up-regulate or down-regulate, and develop strategies to reduce their stress. It is important for teachers to help children become aware of when they need to reduce their stress and to develop strategies to regulate their emotions. Emotions help children to explore and navigate their world as well as to understand and create relations. Cognitive abilities are dependent on how a

Photo 5.11: A Child Looking at a Caterpillar

child is functioning emotionally. It is important to remember that, based on SEL research, excessive negative emotions can damage a child's overall mental health and well-being and impede their ability to learn. Rinaldi (2006) observes that children are not afraid to express their feelings of anger, love, sadness, passion, fear, trust, dread, joy, or disappointment. Children's emotions can be intense and strong, which can make teachers uncomfortable, so they sometimes try to evade or downplay these emotions. Teachers need to be open to emotions, especially difficult emotions. Rinaldi explains that if teachers "listen to these feelings, if we legitimate them, then children will talk about them, narrate them, share them, in order to give them a shape and accept them" (p. 95). Conversations during the four emergent curriculum inquiries provided many opportunities for children to share their emotions.

Lauren, who is very calm and soft-spoken, used conversations to foster the children's recognition of how to regulate their emotions. For instance, after Andrew had a conflict with Henry, Lauren took Andrew aside to speak with him, asking, "What do you need to do?" Andrew responded, "Tell Henry I am sorry." Lauren said, "That's a start." She called Henry over and said, "Andrew has something he needs to tell you." Andrew then said, "I am sorry, Henry. I won't do that again." Lauren reminded Andrew to look at Henry when he was speaking. Then she gave Andrew a fist bump. When Andrew indicated that he wanted to return to the blocks, Lauren said, "I'm worried you're not ready to go back." Andrew sat with Lauren a little while longer until he was completely calm and ready to return to his play. Similarly, after Andrew had a conflict with Daryl, he sat with Lauren for a while and made some interesting observations about the other children. Lauren said, "So who is doing what they should be doing?" Andrew gave her a few examples, like the children playing at the dollhouse, and then said, "He's not listening very well." Lauren asked, "How do you know that?" Andrew explained his reasons. She said, "So you know what it looks like and what it sounds like." By engaging in this conversation, the teacher helped Andrew become more aware of how others were behaving without actually telling him that he could be more empathetic and caring.

On a different occasion, Lauren offered Samantha some guidance after she jumped on some girls who were sitting on the carpet. She gently called her over and said,

> Samantha, you are having a hard time to calm your body.... I see your cheeks are really pink and that shows me that you're really excited.... I'm watching your eyes and your eyes are going really fast looking at things quickly.... Put your hand over here and feel your heart.... I bet your heart is beating really fast, isn't it?

Samantha replied, "Yeah it is." Lauren explained, "Well you're going to need to calm everything down. Calm your cheeks down, calm your eyeballs down ... calm it all down." She then suggested she go to the Calm Centre: "Choose two or three different strategies ... try them all and see what makes you feel the most calm." Samantha frowned as she walked to the Calm Centre.

Kathryn and Victoria used conversations to help the children become aware of how to recognize and manage their emotions. For instance, during a class meeting Angie and Evelyn were not listening while other children were sharing their learning. Kathryn asked them to go to the Book Nook. She said, "Go read a book until your body is ready to sit and listen." After the two girls went to the Book Nook, Kathryn said to the rest of the children, "They will join us when their bodies are ready." Kathryn wanted Evelyn and Angie to honour and respect what the other children were saying. The girls knew that they were welcome to come back to the carpet at any time when they were ready to be calm. A few minutes later Kathryn asked them, "Is your body ready to be respectful? Great, come over and join us."

On a different occasion, Susan and Liza had a conflict. Susan came to tell Victoria that Liza pinched her. Victoria asked Liza to come and talk with her. Victoria took the children to a quiet spot in the classroom and asked them to tell her what happened. After the girls explained the situation, Victoria said, "Can you come up with a plan, Liza? Can you tell Susan what the plan is? Look at Susan when you say it." Liza told Susan that she was not going to pinch her again. Similarly, Angie and Olive had a conflict in the classroom office. Angie tried to roll the sticky notes through the roller and Olive said, "Only big papers work." Olive waited and then pushed Angie's hand out of the way and said, "I can do mine. No, stop doing that and now you ripped it." Olive told Kathryn, "She ripped it." Kathryn responded, "Can we move forward?" Sometimes when the children were having difficulties, Kathryn asked them if they were ready to move forward in an effort to make them more aware of how to manage their emotions.

After a spontaneous run with the teams that Gabriel and Michael created, Darlene saw that Leigh was quite upset. Leigh said, "Gabriel said we didn't get any gold." Darlene brought Gabriel and Leigh together and waited. She commented, "They're solving it together … they have the tools to know how to work things out." When it was apparent that the situation had not been completely resolved, Darlene said,

> You know what I noticed, Gabriel, is that you were picking all the children that run fast.… Gabriel you are a year older. Come on, think about that. What sounds more fair? You need to pick people that are high, medium, and low like on your soccer team.

Gabriel smiled at Darlene, aware that she realized that he had stacked his team deliberately. Darlene reminded Gabriel how he felt when someone beat him. She then turned her attention to Leigh.

Leigh: He said that we didn't get any gold.
Darlene: Why would you [Gabriel] say that?
Gabriel: Maybe he misheard me, but I said all of us got gold.
Leigh: Well, I didn't hear it.
Darlene: Well maybe you need to be clear with him now.
Gabriel: Maybe you didn't hear.… I said we all got gold.
Darlene: Tell him, don't tell me.
Gabriel: Your whole team got gold.… I knew it wouldn't be fair if the people wouldn't get gold, right.… So, you did get gold.

Darlene coached Gabriel as he tried to explain to Leigh what he meant by winning "the gold." Leigh was visibly calming down even though he didn't really believe what Gabriel was now telling him. Under other circumstances Darlene would have just told Gabriel to go and sort the situation out with Leigh because "we don't want our friends to be sad." In this instance, she thought that Gabriel needed to be reminded about his feelings when he lost so that he could relate to how Leigh felt as well.

On a different occasion, the children were in the hall trying to organize themselves so they could start to race. Gabriel had taken the lead, saying, "Guys come on, line up here.... Raise your hand if you want to race.... Rose you are on my side.... When he has crossed the line you can go." Connor commented, "This is not really working." Adele was trying to be the starter and Michael was trying to organize his team of runners. Gabriel persisted as he tried once again to get the runners organized. He said, "Whoever is racing come here.... You are the first ones to go.... We need one more player." Adele decided to join in the racing and Tara took over as the starter. Then Gabriel started to get upset and his voice got louder and louder because he felt like no one was listening to him. Darlene supported Gabriel by encouraging the children to listen to his instructions. Gabriel eventually managed to get all the children to sit down and look at him while he explained what to do. Darlene later commented,

> Gabriel ... got upset because they weren't following. Like, he got all choked up and ready to cry and then he pulled himself back together.... The children seemed very self-regulated to respond to Gabriel the way they did, too. You could tell they just pulled themselves down. They listened, most of them followed his direction and listened to his idea. He came on strong with confidence, and he did very well. I thought it was just amazing.

Darlene provided Gabriel with just the right amount of support to ensure that he could manage his emotions.

Sharon and Mikayla found that most of the problems in their classroom came down to communication. One child would be trying to express something, and the other child did not understand, so the problem escalated. The teachers said that they would try to figure out the issue and then model for the child possible language to use. For instance, when the children were playing with the spinners at the Light Table, a conflict arose, so some children went to Sharon for guidance. She found that often when the children came to her, they told her about what had happened between two other children. Sharon sent them back

Photo 5.12: Gabriel Explains Where to Line Up

with some ideas about how to solve the conflict. She gave the children suggestions about questions they could ask, like "Do you know why they said that.... Maybe go back and ask them why they said, 'Don't do that....' So I am trying to get them to have those conversations amongst themselves." Sharon felt that it is only after a lot of modelling and coaching through role-play, having conversations using positive language, sharing relevant books, and teachers playing with the children at their level that children can solve conflicts on their own.

Mikayla said it depends on the children. Some children can solve conflicts, so she encourages them to come up with a solution on their own. She explained,

> There are other kids that I know do not have those tools and so I'll step in and just talk it through, ask questions. If the emotions are running too high ... I don't think you can ask children to talk it out when they are [upset].... I don't think it's fair to, you wouldn't ask an adult to do that. So, if they are in that mode, I'll just read a book with one of them or redirect, something to just diffuse and then we can revisit it later, not necessarily with those specific children but as a group, role-playing and that kind of thing.

Mikayla thought it was important to let children calm down first because they cannot manage their emotions and talk through conflicts when they are really upset.

CHAPTER SUMMARY

This chapter has focused on self-regulation and the conversation component of emergent curriculum. Oral language is fundamental for learning how to self-regulate. When children use it as a self-regulatory tool during conversations, this helps them to intentionally regulate their own emotions and behaviours. During inquiry-based learning, teachers use different strategies to encourage children to participate in conversations. They scaffold conversations so children can express their own ideas and theories about the inquiry. Effective questions are reflective and encourage more elaborate responses. This is an effective process to strengthen executive functions in the cognitive domain. Executive functions like reasoning and problem-solving are especially important for self-regulated learning. During inquiries, children share their ideas and theories in a logical way and find solutions to problems. Conversations help them understand, clarify, and focus their thoughts. Children becoming more aware of when and how to regulate their emotions is key to their ability to learn. Conversations during inquiry-based learning can provide many opportunities for children to share their emotions. The support teachers provide during conversations helps children better understand their own emotions and strengthens their ability to self-regulate.

REFLECTIVE QUESTIONS

1. When oral language is delayed, how might this impact the development of a child's self-regulation skills?
2. What scaffolding techniques do you use during conversations to help children express their ideas and theories?
3. Why is it so important to nurture the reasoning and problem-solving capabilities of children during inquiries?
4. What examples come to mind when you think about how conversation is used to help children become more aware of when and how to regulate their emotions?

RECOMMENDED READINGS

Duckworth, Eleanor. (2006). *The having of wonderful ideas.* New York: Teachers College Press.

Gallas, Karen. (2017). *Talking their way into science: Hearing children's questions and theories, responding with curriculum.* New York: Teachers College Press.

Gussin Paley, Vivian. (2007). On listening to what the children say. *Harvard Educational Review, 77,* 152–163.

Jacobs, Brenda. (2008). Children's conversations about the sun, moon, and earth. In Carol Anne Wien (Ed.), *Emergent curriculum in the primary classroom: Interpreting the Reggio Emilia approach in schools* (pp. 82–95). New York: Teachers College Press.

Miller, Mary Jane. (2008). "Can weaving make a horse?" Kang as protagonist. In Carol Anne Wien (Ed.), *Emergent curriculum in the primary classroom: Interpreting the Reggio Emilia approach in schools* (pp. 126–143). New York: Teachers College Press.

ONLINE RESOURCES

Listening in on a Classroom Inquiry

http://www.edugains.ca/resourcesKIN/Video/Inquiry/mp4/Inquiry(08).mp4

Listening in on Children Sharing Their Inquiry

http://www.edugains.ca/resourcesKIN/Video/Inquiry/mp4/Inquiry(11).mp4

Chapter Six

Self-Regulation and Documentation

Documentation is the generating of observational data through using multiple tools for documenting—such as generating images, videotaping, audiotaping, note taking, collecting sample of children's work—and making it available ... for others to study and interpret.... When the material is studied collaboratively, to gain the ideas and interpretations of multiple participants, it has the potential to become pedagogical, that is, to teach us, because it opens us up to what others see that we did not see and to what we might see that we had not thought to see or to think about. It expands—both widens and deepens—our world of thought and feeling.

    —Carol Anne Wien, 2014, p. 4

This chapter focuses on the documentation component of emergent curriculum, which also supports inquiry-based learning. The first three aspects involve teachers revisiting documentation with the children to (1) keep them invested in the inquiry, (2) scaffold their thinking, and (3) help them better understand their own theories and ideas. The other aspect involves (4) the teachers studying the documentation to reflect on the children's thinking and their engagement in the inquiry. When these four aspects are considered together, they demonstrate that the documentation component enables children to become self-regulated learners.

In the early stages of the inquiry, teachers decide how the documentation will be generated and the possible forms the documentation will take. Documentation makes visible the process the children and teachers followed as they co-constructed the curriculum throughout the inquiry. It is a record that seeks to explain the children's ideas, theories, and learning experiences that took place in the classroom. When teachers revisit documentation with the children, they use photographs, transcriptions, and work samples to remind the children of their earlier ideas and theories about the emergent curriculum inquiry, which

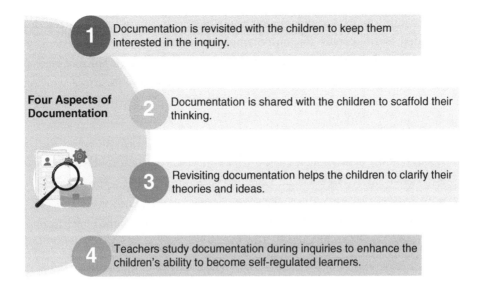

Four Aspects of Documentation

1. Documentation is revisited with the children to keep them interested in the inquiry.

2. Documentation is shared with the children to scaffold their thinking.

3. Revisiting documentation helps the children to clarify their theories and ideas.

4. Teachers study documentation during inquiries to enhance the children's ability to become self-regulated learners.

helps extend their understanding of the topic and come up with new or related ideas. When teachers study documentation, it deepens their analysis of the inquiry, which enables them to reflect on how children think and learn, their own teaching, and possibilities for the direction the inquiry might go. This pedagogical approach to documentation supports inquiry-based learning in the primary classroom. The four inquiries provide concrete examples of the relationship between self-regulation and documentation.

FOUR ASPECTS OF DOCUMENTATION

Documentation Is Revisited with the Children to Keep Them Invested in the Inquiry

When children revisit documentation, they feel like their contributions are valued, which encourages them to continue to participate in the inquiry. As noted previously, documentation holds children's ideas and theories in place so that when they revisit them, they can consider their logic and elaborate on their thinking as they discuss it with others. Through conversation, children begin to shift their thinking as they absorb and consider other children's ideas and theories. Dahlberg et al. (2013) note that children "can revisit what they did before and find new inspiration and become further engaged" (p. 157).

Rinaldi (2006) makes the connection between the act of listening and emotion, which is important for supporting self-regulation. For her, listening is "Being open to differences, recognizing the value of the other's point of view and interpretation ... giving meaning to the message and value to those who offer it" (p. 65). She explains that in a listening context, one learns to listen and to narrate. Rinaldi (2006) argues,

> Behind the act of listening there is often a curiosity, a desire, a doubt, an interest; there is always an emotion. Listening is emotion; it is generated by emotions and stimulates emotions. The emotions of others influence us by means of processes that are strong, direct, not mediated, and intrinsic to the interactions between communicating subjects. (p. 65)

In listening contexts, like when revisiting documentation, children feel permitted to express their theories and are open to listening to others' theories and offering their interpretation. Children from a young age demonstrate that they have a voice and that they know how to listen and want to be listened to. Rinaldi (2006) adds, "Listening that takes the individual out of anonymity, that legitimates us, gives us visibility, enriching both those who listen and those who produce the message (and children cannot bear to be anonymous)" (p. 65).

One of the insights about the relationship between self-regulation and inquiry-based learning is that inquiries promote positive emotions. Children are more likely to experience positive emotions when they feel calm and alert. When children are invested in the inquiry, their positive emotions lead to greater capacity for emotional growth. Children also have a greater ability to up-regulate or down-regulate strong positive and negative emotions, be resilient and move forward, learn on their own and in collaboration with others, and be proud of their own efforts and achievements as well as the efforts and achievements of others. Importantly, children need the energy associated with positive emotions (e.g., curiosity, interest, happiness) in order to explore more challenging emotions (e.g., honesty, compassion) and difficult emotional situations. Negative emotions drain the energy needed to navigate through new emotional territory.

Lauren reflected on the value of sharing documentation with children to keep them engaged in the inquiry:

> I think using the pedagogical documentation to reflect their own thinking back to them, that to them that's such a huge, huge—I don't want to call it an ego boost or a comfort—but that just demonstrates how important all of this

really is, and so they understand that. Not only did you just take a photograph or videotape of what I said and did there, but she actually went back and typed it up and put it all together and now you're reading it back to me. It's like this is something that's really, really important.

Lauren would sometimes share the documentation with all the children in the class even if they had not been directly involved in the inquiry. This way they would all know what everybody had been working on; as well it could provide an impetus for other children to join in and help think about what to do next. For example, Lauren shared the documentation of the Invisibility Inquiry by pointing to the pictures and reading highlights from the text. The class was focused and listened carefully to hear what happened next. Lauren talked about how Steven had made his mother invisible, and Deepa had made her jewel invisible, and that these ideas really got her thinking about what invisibility meant. Then she invited some children to see if they could make invisible drawings like Steven and use materials like Deepa did to make a gemstone invisible.

Lauren continued, "Then we did another fascinating experiment … where we put a [smaller] glass … inside the larger glass and then poured vegetable oil inside." At this point the children spontaneously started to join in and explain their thinking about the oil experiment.

> *Samantha*: Then you can't see it …
> *Lauren*: Then we talked about where the [smaller] glass might be and what happened to the glass. And so, the boys and girls … said that the glass was gone, it was nowhere. It was invisible you couldn't see it at all, and so it wasn't inside the big glass anymore …
> *Samantha*: The little flask goes in and when you pour it in you can't see it anymore, but it is still there it's just because the oil makes it that you can't see it there …
> *Tagwen*: When you're doing it, it is the same colour as the glass but you pour oil inside it so you can't see it … it made one cup almost disappear …
> *Dhara*: It [the small glass] might have been on … the bottom of the other glass.

This led to a further discussion about what it means to be invisible.

Kathryn wrote about her experience revisiting the Office Inquiry documentation with the children:

Reviewing the process with them by asking them what was happening in the photographs, reading their theories aloud, and even some of our own thoughts, proved to be a rich opportunity for engaging them in pedagogical documentation. It appeared that when the students heard our own insights into their thinking, they felt valued and important. This experience allowed them the venue to be able to articulate their thinking, reflect on how it has changed, and build on their own and others' ideas.

Kathryn believed that when you share documentation with the children and it includes the teacher's voice, it shows that the teacher honours their thought process and has thought deeply about it. It also enables a child to clear up any misunderstandings the teacher might have about their learning, and they feel more connected to the inquiry.

One day, Victoria started to read a few documentation panels from the Office Inquiry that had been turned into a book. She paused to ask the children where they were.

Sally: In the office.
Victoria: Who's there?
Sally: Ms. Harland and Ms. Winters.
Nikki: I just realized I see the computer … and a jar.
Victoria: A jar of what?
Nikki: Candies?

Victoria continued with the story by asking the children what they did when they got back to the classroom. The girls talked about making a list of things they saw in the office and how they had made nametags. They also talked about what Olive had discovered.

Victoria: What is Olive looking at?
Olive: The printer.
Victoria: We called it a printer. It is an old-fashioned typewriter, isn't it? What did you discover Olive? You were the typewriter discoverer.
Olive: It printed.
Victoria: Yeah, and what did you do with the paper?
Olive: I writed THE K.

When the story ended, Victoria explained to the children that the book wasn't finished and there would be more pages added to show their new learning. This reminded them that they had been thinking about security and how they would continue working on that.

Photo 6.1: A Child Is Looking at the Office Book

Darlene shared documentation with the children to keep them focused on the inquiry and thinking about how to move it forward. She explained, "I want to see them looking at that. I want to see if that tweaks any more interest." For example, when Darlene asked the children what they had to say about all the documentation on the table, Michael took the group's thinking in a new direction by suggesting that they could connect all their running ideas and make them into one big idea. The other children were then invited to share their ideas and build on what Michael was thinking.

Michael: Okay … so for example if me and Connor were the only ones here, we would make a big circle and run with one person at a time …

Darlene: Okay, so keep going, ask the next person.

Gabriel: My idea was the teacher could hold two clocks up and then you would try to run with another person and then when you come back you would try to beat your time. If you had a big one then you would have to try to get it lower. Like if I had 15 that the next one I would have 10. So, I would beat my score …

Michael: Adele.… What was your idea?…

Adele: There would be a big line at one side of the hall and then another at the other side and then two people would be running from this side or this side and touching hands and then whoever was going this way would go here and whoever was going this way would go here …

Michael: Adele, so what you are saying is one goes on this side and one goes on that side. They run at the opposite direction and they high five and then go to the other end. And the [other] person goes to that end …

Darlene: Why did you like it that way instead of two people running side by side? Why in the other direction?

Adele: Because they didn't want to bump into each other …

Michael: But Adele if you missed the person, no high five, they would crash so that is why it is not so safe. Because like if I missed you say I was here and you were there and we didn't high five than I would like go like (crash sound). And you would be hurt.

This initial discussion about the documentation led to a lot of excitement about the inquiry, and the children were very enthusiastic about going out into the hall and trying out their running ideas.

Sharon reflected on how revisiting documentation kept the children invested in the Community Inquiry:

Students have to feel safe to take risks, ask questions, and think critically. It is when they have that foundation of safety, with an environment that reflects

Photo 6.2: The Children Look at the Documentation on the Table

themselves and their real lives that they engage with that documentation (the binders, the photographs) because it's about them and their ideas. Not simply a retelling of an event. It is the changes and the transformations of their ideas and meaning making over the process that come out in the documentation.

On one occasion, Sharon showed a group of children a photograph of the valley with a building in the background. She asked the children if the picture was a place in their community.

Adhita: Yes.
Mahdi: I think it is nature.
Sharon: Is nature different than community?
Mahdi: I think a friend of the community. Nature is a friend of the community.
Sharon: Can you explain what you mean to us?
Mahdi: Because community and nature has the same things.
Sharon: Like what?
Mahdi: Like trees and sometimes crabapple trees … and sometimes it has some rivers … and some buildings … [and] sometimes we see the forest in nature like today.

Mahdi was sharing his thinking about nature being a friend of the community and how nature and community are the same. This led to a further discussion about how nature is a friend to us. For instance, Mahdi said, "Nature shares butterflies and that makes me happy." Anan said, "Nature shares sticks, rocks, and leaves." Amina said, "Nature helps us grow things like flowers, trees, and animals." Then the children went off to draw pictures of how nature is our friend. This work, as well as other documentation related to the valley, were put in a binder called "Nature Is a Friend of the Community," which Sharon shared with the children at various points as the inquiry progressed.

Documentation Is Shared with the Children to Scaffold Their Thinking

The scaffolding process during inquiry-based learning, I believe, significantly reduces children's stress levels so they are calm, alert, and ready to learn. Bruner (2006) explains that the scaffolding process is most effective when children are focused and interested in an activity that is manageable. The teacher's assistance reduces the children's potential for frustration, so they are more willing to take risks. Teachers use scaffolding strategies when revisiting their documentation, and this enables children to become self-regulated learners.

When teachers and children revisit documentation of earlier experiences together, the children are moved to a higher level of cognitive functioning where they are encouraged to focus their attention and remember previous experiences in detail (Fraser, 2012, citing Bodrova & Leong, 1996). The source of our strong emotions and urges is located in the limbic system, also known as the "emotional brain," which plays a critical role in the formation of memories and the positive and negative emotional associations that get attached to those memories (Shanker, 2016). The role of memory can be connected to revisiting documentation. Memory-enhancing materials strengthen the capacity for concentration and interpretation (Rinaldi, 2006). Different forms of documentation, such as photographs, videos, transcriptions, and drawings, can support a child's memory as they review previous thinking, self-correct, find confirmation and denials, and make comparisons with the theories and ideas of others. A child can see herself in a "new light," comment on herself, and listen to the comments of others. When teachers scaffold those memories during inquiry-based learning, this leads to a transformation in the co-construction of knowledge.

Lauren, for instance, showed the children photographs and a video of them making sounds with drumsticks and pots and pans. The photographs and video brought back memories of these experiences; then Lauren provided verbal reminders of what was said before and asked the children questions leading to new insights about invisibility. After the children described what they could see in the photographs and the video, Lauren asked them to think about what was missing from the photographs that was in the video. She showed the children the video a couple of times to prompt their thinking; however, they were not sure what Lauren meant. She said, "I might leave this for a while and just let them think about it because I can tell them, but I don't want to tell them … you just have to kind of sit with the uncomfortableness and just wait and wait and wait and just be patient." Lauren didn't want to ask the children about movement and sound directly because she felt like it would be leading them too much. She considered leaving it for another day but then suddenly said, "Let's watch the video again.… You have to really use your thinking brain.… What is in the video that is not in the picture?" Because Lauren gave the children another opportunity to watch the video, it gave them more time to think about her question and come up with the ideas that movement and sound were missing from the photographs.

On a different occasion, Lauren shared the photographs of the water experiment with the children.

Lauren: So, Daryl, why don't you tell us what is happening here?

Daryl: I am pouring the water inside a big glass cup [vase].… It gets higher.…
More water comes inside because it goes up.

Lauren: And what do you see right here?

Daryl: Bubbles go in at the bottom of the water …

Lauren: What's inside the bubbles …

Samantha: More bubbles …

Lauren: What's inside the bubbles inside the bubbles? What are bubbles made out of?

Daryl: Water and soap.… There's air inside the bubbles.

Lauren guided the children's thinking by asking them questions about the bubbles. Similarly, the children looked at a photograph where the table was covered in water. Lauren asked them what they were doing in this photograph.

Daryl: Blowing the table off …

Rory: We were blowing the water because we were thinking if it was moving.

Lauren: And I think that someone said the water was bending.

Daryl: Yeah, that's Rory …

Lauren: When you were blowing it was bending.

Samantha: Yeah, and I said they make these little pools.

In both water examples, Lauren was able to scaffold the children's thinking by first using the photographs to bring back the children's memories of the water experiment and then prompting their thinking by asking questions and using verbal reminders like "bending."

Kathryn shared the Office Inquiry book with the children so they could look at the new pages that had been added.

Kathryn: I want to share some of your great thinking and learning.… I am going to read you what the top says. It says an outing is organized to take pictures of the outside doors because you were so interested in looking at the security and how to get into the school. And then you took pictures of five different doors to make what?…

Girls: The screen.

Kathryn: The screen. That's right, remember the screen?… Nikki, can you turn the mirror around so we can all see the screen please.… Does it look very similar to the TV in the [school] office?

Girls: Yeah.

Then the children recalled the different ways you can enter the school and how the head of security monitors who comes in.

> *Kathryn*: Alright so then we got up to the door … what happened first?…
> *Anna*: We pushed the button and …
> *Kathryn*: What did we all say?…
> *Girls*: Ms. Harland, it's JK…. She let us come in …
> *Kathryn*: Who was waiting for us when we got in there?
> *Liza*: The security man.
> *Kathryn*: But then we went back outside, and we got in a different way. How did we get in the second time we came through? Vicky, do you remember?
> *Vicky*: We got in from a different door …
> *Anna*: We put the card on the red thing and then we pulled it and then it opened.

Kathryn continued by explaining that Rachel was really inspired by that idea. She asked her what she did when she came back to the classroom.

> *Rachel*: Make something in case the door is locked so you go over and they know it is you …
> *Kathryn*: You used paper to make your own card, and can I read you Rachel's words? Okay I'll read Rachel's words. We make four red squares. Can we count the red squares that she used?
> *Girls*: One, two, three, four.
> *Kathryn*: We need four red squares for the security: it goes on the door. You hold the card up like this. [Rachel held up her swipe card and used the mirror to show the door swinging open.] What would happen on [the head of security's] computer when Rachel went into the school?
> *Girls*: He sees it.
> *Kathryn*: He sees it on his computer and that helps him keep the place safe.

Kathryn scaffolded the children's thinking by reading some of the text, having them help her read parts of it, and asking them questions. She also had Nikki move the mirror to show the TV screen and Rachel use her swipe card to get into the office. At the end, the girls counted the squares aloud that were on the monitor that they used for their swipe cards. Kathryn even made gestures and sound effects to help prompt their thinking.

Darlene showed Gabriel and Michael pictures they had drawn of how they felt before and after they ran. Gabriel was having difficulty recalling what he said about his pictures.

Photo 6.3: Kathryn Revisiting Documentation with the Children

Darlene: I think we wrote on the back of it. It says when we couldn't run it felt like my heart was melting.… Can you explain that feeling of a melting heart?

Gabriel: Because I was very hot when I couldn't run, and I couldn't get any energy.

Darlene: So, you feel hot when you don't have energy.… Is it something that builds up inside you Gabriel?… You're a boy that likes to move a lot. How does it feel to you when you don't get to move a lot?…

Gabriel: Bored.

Darlene: And this one says, "When I could run my heart was beating really fast and I was happy.…" Why are you feeling your heart now?

Gabriel: Because it is not beating fast.

Darlene: So, what do you want to do about that?

Gabriel: Run.

Darlene guided Gabriel's thinking by first showing him his pictures and reminding him of what he said previously. She then prompted further thinking by asking Gabriel to explain what he meant by a melting heart. Darlene also connected with Gabriel on a personal level because she knew him so well, which also helped her scaffold his thinking. Michael also shared his thinking about the pictures he had drawn.

> *Michael*: This is how my heart was beating before and this is how my heart was beating after.
>
> *Darlene*: And … can you tell me the difference?
>
> *Michael*: Because this one is taking less air in my throat and this one is taking more air to get the energy.
>
> *Darlene*: … in the picture it looks like the heart of you in red looks bigger.
>
> *Michael*: That is because it is getting more air in it.
>
> *Darlene*: So, when it gets more air it expands?
>
> *Michael*: Yeah…. It is like a sponge.

Once again, Darlene asked questions to prompt further thinking. She also highlighted what she saw in the pictures, and this led to Michael responding with an explanation of how he thinks the heart works. The pictures helped the boys remember how they felt, and the writing helped Gabriel recall what he said.

Sharon shared photographs of the valley and the collaborative valley paintings with the children to bring back memories of these experiences. Revisiting documentation to scaffold the children's thinking was especially important in her class because the children were English Language Learners. She showed the children photographs that she took in the valley that morning and asked the children to explain what they were doing in them.

> *Adhita*: We're going down the steep road …
>
> *Sharon*: Yeah. Into the …
>
> *Adhita*: Valley …
>
> *Sharon*: What was this part of our trip? Mahdi?
>
> *Mahdi*: We were having some fun and we were playing.
>
> *Sharon*: Anybody else want to share what they were doing in this part?
>
> *Esita*: Me and Abeedah were sliding down [the hill] …
>
> *Ehsan*: We were having so much fun.
>
> *Sharon*: Yeah, what was fun about it?
>
> *Ehsan*: We were climbing up the hill and then we were rolling down.

Sharon used different strategies to prompt the children to elaborate on their experience in the valley. She asked questions, added connectors between sentences, invited other children to share their thinking, and had them add more detail to their responses.

In another example, Sharon shared the collaborative valley paintings that some of the children had worked on with the rest of the class. She invited the children to look at one of the paintings and tell her what they saw.

Alma: I see water …

Sharon: Where do we see the water in the valley? Adhita?

Adhita: The … river … it's underneath the bridge.

Sharon: Oh, where's the bridge? [Adhita points.] Can you describe it?

Adhita: It's the brown thing …

Sharon: Brown thing.… I see something else on the bridge. What do you see on the bridge?…

Amina: I see people. I even see lots of different leaves and lines, even I see rocks and suns and aeroplanes and lots of things.

Sharon was able to scaffold the children's thinking by asking them questions and having them point to different features in the painting.

Photo 6.4: Sharon Sharing Documentation of the Watercolour Pictures

Revisiting Documentation Helps the Children Clarify Their Theories and Ideas

As children share their theories with others, they reflect on those theories, modify and enrich them, and develop a more conscious vision of them. Children's theories evolve during inquiry-based learning when they have opportunities to listen and be listened to, to express their differences and be receptive to the differences of others (Rinaldi, 2006). Documentation makes visible how the children's ideas and theories change over time. When teachers and children revisit documentation together, the children draw on their cognitive processes to clarify their thinking. This involves thinking about their ideas and theories in a logical, sensible way; using multiple concepts simultaneously; finding solutions to problems; considering other perspectives; and keeping all kinds of information in their mind so they can draw on it when needed. It also involves being able to multitask by looking at different pieces of documentation and listening to others while not being distracted by things going on in the background.

Cognitive processes of metacognition and executive functions are highly relevant for successful self-regulated learners (Blair & Diamond, 2008; Bodrova & Leong, 2008). Executive functions are cognitive processes such as reasoning, problem-solving, flexible thinking, multitasking, and working memory. Metacognition is an awareness and understanding of one's own cognitive processes or thinking. The more self-regulated the child, the better they can develop or exercise their executive functions, and the better a child's executive functions, the more they can reduce the arousal created by stress. Revisiting documentation to help children better understand their ideas and theories in this way supports their ability to self-regulate.

When Lauren shared documentation with the children, it helped them to clarify their ideas and theories. After Lauren showed a group of children a video of Samantha talking about invisibility, Samantha explained her thinking: "When you camouflage the colours you blend in ... and then I said invisibility is ... white, it's not colours." Lauren wanted to see if she could clarify her thinking about invisibility being white by comparing it to Daryl's idea of invisibility.

> *Lauren*: Now Daryl you said something last time about water being see-through ... so you can see-through it. Is that what you are kind of talking about Samantha?... So is the water in this vase white or is it see-through?
>
> *Daryl*: I know the water's clear. It's not white, it's clear.... White is ... a bit darker so we can't see through it so then water is see-through so we can see through it. It's clear ...

Lauren: So, when you are invisible are you clear?

Daryl: Yes.

Samantha: No…. Like nobody can see you…. If something was invisible … you couldn't see it … you could see through it if it was see-through. If it wasn't see-through then you wouldn't be able to see any part of it.

Lauren: Daryl said if you are invisible then you're see-through. Right. You're clear. Samantha, you said you're not see-through if you are invisible. What would you look like if you are invisible? What would you be like?

Samantha: You would just be white.

During the conversation, it was clear that Samantha believed that invisibility is white and not transparent. Lauren followed up by holding up a white piece of paper in front of Kaitlyn's face and then holding up a piece of acetate. This demonstration seemed to help Samantha understand that invisibility is transparent rather than white.

On a different occasion, Tagwen revisited a picture she had drawn of a girl sitting with her back against a tree. She described what she had drawn to show her theory of invisibility. Tagwen said, "She has black skin and black clothes … that's why and then she is blending into the tree." Lauren asked, "So, is she invisible right now?" Tagwen responded, "Yeah." In the picture the girl was hidden because she blended into the shade of the tree. She then decided to use a piece of acetate so that she could draw black all over the top of her picture.

Lauren: All black on top?

Tagwen: Yeah, and then she would be invisible …

Lauren: So, you would make her even more invisible than she is now?

Tagwen: Yeah … because … if you colour all black and then if you colour your skin black you can't see one part of their skin.

Later that day, Lauren asked Tagwen how she could make the person in her picture visible, and Tagwen said she could use coloured markers on top of a new piece of acetate. When using the markers, Tagwen discovered that she could see the clothes and the inside of the girl's body when she added colour. If she added colour everywhere, she would be able to see everything in the drawing, even the tree's body. Tagwen said, "Black won't work because it will just make it darker then these [light] colours." Tagwen thought that darker colours like black, purple, blue, brown, and grey camouflage the picture. The documentation helped Lauren see how Tagwen's thinking evolved from drawing something that is invisible, to making it more invisible, to making it visible.

During the Office Inquiry, Kathryn revisited the transcription of "Why the Doors Are Locked" with the children.

> *Kathryn*: Liza said they don't want the cold to come in. And Susan said, I saw in the office they were checking for people coming in and coming out and Alia said, yeah, it's for safety.... Does anyone have any other ideas or thinking to add to that?
>
> *Nikki*: They keep the doors locked because they don't want any people to maybe think ... that maybe the cars has to go inside.
>
> *Laura*: Strangers.
>
> *Kathryn*: Okay so it's so the cars stay out and Laura you think it's so strangers stay out.... Great, good thinking. Does anyone have another idea to add? Sally, is your thought ready now? Go ahead.
>
> *Sally*: They will lock the doors because they don't want anything to blow away.
>
> *Kathryn*: Now if the door was just closed and it wasn't locked, it was just closed would things blow away?
>
> *Sally*: Um hum.
>
> *Kathryn*: Do you think that is the real reason that they want the door to be locked?...
>
> *Laura*: If the door is unlocked and you think it's locked, we give it a try and you find out it's locked.
>
> *Kathryn*: So, if you were walking down the street and you go up to the door and you pull it and you'd find out right away wouldn't you whether it was locked or unlocked. What a great thought, Laura.

Kathryn reflected on how the children's thinking about the doors being locked had evolved over time. She observed that sharing the documentation with the children provided them with a "venue to be able to articulate their thinking, reflect on how it has changed, and build on their own and others' ideas."

Darlene and the children looked at the ovals that recorded their running times to help clarify their thinking about who were the fastest and slowest runners. In the first example, we can see that Michael just needed a bit of time to think through his original theory.

> *Michael*: The smallest number is ... the fastest and whoever had the biggest number was the slowest ... we were using a stopwatch and if you were so fast you would only be seconds and if you don't want time in your score you want

no time, so like you run and challenge yourself … so whoever has the lowest
number wins.

Darlene: Good explanation so you must of left and thought about that a lot
because at the beginning you thought that the highest number was the
winner.

Michael: Yeah. But I forgot that we used the stopwatch.

Darlene: Aw so this is what helped you decide the right way.

Michael now understood that the person with the most time was the slowest
runner.

Evan, on the other hand, who is a year younger than Michael, was still
struggling to figure out who the fastest runners were and why.

Darlene: Tell me which one is the fastest runner, is it Connor or Adele?

Evan: Adele.

Darlene: What about you Evan? You got 21. So, are you faster than Connor or
slower than Connor?…

Evan: I guess if Gabriel and Connor have the same number they are both faster
than me because Gabriel's faster than me.

Darlene: So, these three got the same number so we will put them here, then
Michael came with the next highest number and then you got the highest out
of all of them. Connor, Zara, and Gabriel got 17, Michael got 19, and you got
21. So, who is the fastest out of this group?

Evan: I guess these three are not the fastest and I guess me and Michael are the
fastest.

Darlene: Because why?

Evan: Yes, so Max and me are both not the same number but we're both fast.

Darlene did not try to correct Evan's misperception; she was using documentation to clarify what he was thinking.

On a different occasion, Darlene was looking at a transcription of an earlier
conversation she had with Connor.

Darlene: Connor I have a question for you.… You say that when you run with
somebody else, it's too fast. You have to run too fast. When you run by
yourself you don't have to run as fast. Why is this?

Connor: It's not like a race and if somebody wins it is not fair …

> *Michael*: Is what you are saying is when you're racing you have to go as fast as you can to win, but when you're not racing against someone, you don't have to go as fast because you're not worried about losing?
>
> *Connor*: Yeah, and because like, so it is fair.

Darlene also invited other children to contribute their thoughts when trying to clarify someone else's thinking. Michael here articulated what he thought Connor meant, pinpointing his concern about winning and losing.

For Sharon, studying documentation with children is "not simply a retelling of an event. It is the changes and the transformations of their ideas and meaning making over the process that come out in the documentation." For example, Sharon revisited Mahdi's idea that nature is a friend of the community, and then asked the children to first clarify what they meant by friendship.

> *Adhita*: They help each other ...
>
> *Mahdi*: They play with each other ...
>
> *Dea*: Friends always work together ...
>
> *Mahdi*: They make things together.
>
> *Sharon*: I wonder if the community and nature make things?
>
> *Adhita*: Yes, they do.... Leaves. They make some food.
>
> *Mahdi*: They do. Actually, I agree with you.

Through this discussion, Mahdi was also able to clarify his own thinking about how nature is a friend. Sadi then returned the group to Mahdi's bigger idea that "nature is a friend of the community." He said, "Nature is our friend because he helps us a lot." Sharon replied, "You're right, Sadi. When we are talking about nature is helpful, that's one of the things that we said makes a good friend. They help us, right?" The children continued to think through the connection between nature and friendship.

In a different example, Anan explained in detail his theory about the origin of water. He said,

> Water comes from the sky and then it goes down the drain and the drain is so dark and it's so far down ... when water comes down that means it's raining and if you have a thunderstorm people have to [go] inside because [a] thunderstorm has so much rain and it's dark.

The following week, Sharon read Anan's theory to the class and invited other children to contribute their thoughts to help Anan clarify his thinking. Alma built on to Anan's theory by saying, "Rain comes from clouds." Sadi added that "The rain from the clouds it falls everywhere on the roof even on sidewalks even on the river." This helped Anan to better understand that rain comes from the clouds. Other children also built on to Anan's explanation of where water comes from by adding their theories. Aasfa commented, "Water comes from a water-fall." Eshan observed, "I went to Niagara Falls and I saw some waters and they were moving." Mustanjid said, "Water comes from the lake." Mahdi added, "I think the water comes from Niagara Falls then it goes to Oshawa and then to Toronto."

Teachers Study Documentation during Inquiries to Enhance the Children's Ability to Become Self-Regulated Learners

Documentation provides teachers with the unique opportunity to study the events and learning processes that took place during the inquiry so they can make sense of what happened and create shared meanings and values. Taguchi (2010) reminds us that documentation is not just a record of the children's learning but also "in itself an active agent in generating discursive knowledge. It is part of the process of constructing meaning about children's learning" (p. 63). Documentation becomes "pedagogical" when it is studied with others, leading to a deeper analysis of the inquiry and enabling teachers to reflect on how children think and learn as well as their own teaching and planning. Through collaborative discussions, teachers share their interpretations of the documentation and consider next steps (Fraser, 2012; Jacobs, 2008; Stacey, 2015; Wien, 2008). This kind of flexible planning enables teachers to think about possibilities for provocations and activities. Teachers plan by making hypotheses and predicting future experiences based on their relevance to the learning processes and interests of the children (Rinaldi, 2006).

Studying documentation is a mode of professional development for teachers. For instance, Lauren explained that she uses it as a form of assessment for herself to inform her own teaching: "I think that's when it's at its most valuable. That's the whole purpose of it, right?" Lauren believed that when teachers are working with children, they sometimes interpret what a child has said one way but then when they listen to it on the tape, they might realize that was not what the child meant. Lauren said,

> So then ... I like to go back [to the child] and say, you know yesterday, "I thought you said this, but you actually said this. Can you tell me more?" Because you really have to honour what their original thoughts and ideas are.

If Lauren did not transcribe the audiotapes, she would not have realized that her perception had changed the direction of the conversation. This process allows teachers to correct those kinds of miscalculations when they occur. Having multiple forms of documentation including ones that capture children's voices ensures that these types of miscalculations are less likely to occur.

This pedagogical approach to documentation enhances children's ability to become self-regulated learners. Documentation makes visible the children's engagement and thought processes during the inquiry. When teachers reflect on the children's engagement—confident, focused, thoughtful, driven, purposeful—it gives them insights into the children's self-regulation, which informs their hypotheses and predictions. The better we understand children's engagement, "the better we can design classroom practices that will enhance a student's self-regulation" (Shanker, 2013b, p. xxi). Similarly, when teachers study documentation, it deepens their understanding of the children's cognitive processes, such as reasoning, problem-solving, and flexible thinking. When teachers study documentation it slows down time so they can consider the children's ideas and theories in a more thoughtful way. Shanker (2013b) emphasizes how valuable it is for teachers to understand these processes: "a better understanding of the nature of these core processes helps us to devise classroom activities that will enhance our students' ability to focus attention and become self-regulated learners" (p. 46). Documentation enables teachers to reflect on how children use oral language during private speech as a tool for self-regulation. Private speech allows children to communicate to themselves, to regulate their own behavior and thinking. Children use private speech to think out loud and organize their thoughts while they work through problems independently. Private speech for children has been found to increase as tasks become more challenging and stressful (Diamond et al., 2007).

When Lauren reflected on the children's engagement in the Invisibility Inquiry, she studied a set of three photographs that showed the children banging on pots and pans with drumsticks and their hands as they explored what sounds they could make. Tagwen was the child most interested in this provocation. When looking at her photograph, Lauren said, "She looks like she's comfortable and enjoying herself and she looks focused. And she also looks like she's in control of the drums.... She's using it [the drums] in a deliberate manner."

In another photograph, Tagwen has taken on a leadership role with her peers. She is showing Emma how to tap the pot with her hand. She carefully points out to Emma that she should hold the pot to keep it from sliding off the bench. Lauren commented,

> It looks like she's showing her … where to hit it to get the best sound…. She doesn't have her own drumstick so it's almost like she's beyond participating … like she's almost sort of demonstrating or helping to support Emma. It seems like that because Emma's really watching what she's doing.

Lauren thought that Tagwen had explored the pots and pans on her own, was feeling very confident, and now was sharing her advice with a friend.

In the last photograph, Tagwen is showing Daryl how to hold the drumstick. She gently held the end of the stick while Daryl started to tap. Lauren found this to be an interesting photograph because Daryl looked a bit tentative, which is not like him. She thought that because Tagwen was taking charge, Daryl deferred to her. Lauren commented, "I love that she's holding it from behind so that as

Photo 6.5: A Child Helps Another Tap the Pot

he's looking at his hand, he's not seeing her hand ... he doesn't need to notice her guidance if he doesn't want to. It won't interfere with his enjoyment."

When Lauren analyzed both a photograph and a work sample together, she got an even deeper understanding of the children's engagement in the inquiry. For example, looking at the photograph of Iliana representing high and low sounds with the coloured markers, she said, "She's very focused ... and I don't know, it's not even just that she's looking down at it, because there's something more there.... She almost has that little smile of accomplishment or 'I'm getting my intention across.'" When Lauren zoomed in to look at the photograph more closely, she said, "You can almost hear the conversation she's having with herself in her head about what she's doing." Looking at Iliana's work sample, Lauren commented,

> Even though ... she's put a lot of things on the page, it's got some kind of an organization, so it doesn't look hectic. And it doesn't look like there's too much. Like these things, I'm imagining are ... almost like a bass sound, a deep sound. And then, I mean, just to sit there and to actually put all those little marks in that way, it looks like a piece of fabric or a weaving of some kind. Which would have taken her forever to do.... She's very thoughtful. Like you can tell she spent some time thinking about this theory.... She really thought about ... how she was going to make that look in order to be understood.

Iliana explained her own drawing by saying, "I am drawing the noise.... That's noise coming from the pot.... A banging noise."

While Lauren and Vanessa studied the documentation of Samantha trying to make a gemstone invisible, they both reflected on what she was thinking, feeling, and doing. In one photograph, Samantha is looking at the gemstone she has hidden by wrapping it up in green felt. Lauren said,

> She's totally focused ... her eyes are so focused on what she's doing that you can just see like all her energy is going into watching what she's doing with her hands and trying to figure out how to make that thing [gemstone] invisible.

Vanessa added, "She looks excited but again, still maintaining that focus and looking at the felt." While Samantha problem-solved how to make the gemstone disappear, she talked aloud to help clarify her thinking. She thought the gemstone was kind of invisible. She said, "When you put a gem in, and you fold it up you might kind of see it still because I see a little part of it."

In another photograph, Samantha has found a way to make the gemstone invisible. As she placed the green felt on top of all the other materials, she said, "If I go like that now I can't see it." Vanessa commented, "She's showing her excitement, but still her eyes and her hands are focusing." Lauren added, "She looks satisfied there. It's like okay, done. There."

In a final photograph, Samantha is trying to figure out how to make her gemstone the most invisible by using all the materials. Lauren noted that Samantha was thinking through each step in a methodical way. First, she put the gemstone on top of the green felt, then she placed the bottle cap and glass container on top, and finally she covered the whole thing with the black material. Samantha explained that the gemstone is really invisible because you can't see it. She said, "I can just feel it.… I can feel it a lot.… I can hear it. Aw, shake, shake, shake." Lauren said, "I'm really drawn to her mouth. Like, she's almost got a line—like set in the line of determination. She's determined to make her point somehow.… It's almost like she's happily determined." Lauren also noticed Samantha's hands. She said, "It's like she's got them set in a purposeful way. But it's not like she's clutching anything or grasping. She's very gently, almost gingerly, keeping her idea in place." Lauren noticed how Samantha's eyes showed just how absorbed she was as she completed the task.

During the Office Inquiry, Victoria studied two photographs of the children "working" as office workers in the Construction Centre and thought about how engaged they were in their play. She explained that the girls used the chairs as desks and were concentrating on drawing and writing in their I Wonder books. Victoria commented, "They are totally engaged … they've provided themselves with the equipment that they need. Nobody provided it for them … they are totally self-directed." She observed, "They are all in close proximity but working very individually really, although collaboratively. They are all on the same mission but there's not any interaction between each other. They are all self-motivated." Victoria added that the children were very independent and didn't want any help from the teachers, "They just want to be left on their own."

Kathryn and Victoria also shared their reflections about two photographs taken in the junior school office. In the first photograph, Liza and Vicky are talking to Ms. Harland at her desk. Kathryn recalled how Vicky was doing all the talking, as Liza waited patiently for Ms. Harland to type up their request to revisit the junior school office. Ms. Harland then printed the confirmation slip and handed it to Liza. In a second photograph, the girls have just returned to the junior school office for a visit with the rest of the class and Liza hands Ms. Winters the confirmation slip. Kathryn and Victoria remembered how surprised they were. Kathryn said,

Victoria and I didn't even know where that piece of paper was.... But we came back and they were like, do you have the confirmation of your appointment and Liza is like yep, here it is! And we were like whoa, where did that come from?... She had it! She had brought it with her. It was incredible.

Victoria added, "The fact that she took it to the office, and we didn't even know she got it." Liza had independently taken responsibility for the confirmation slip and kept it in a safe location until it was needed. These photographs made visible how engaged Liza was in the inquiry and her ability to think through a quite complex task in a logical way.

Kathryn and Victoria studied photographs to interpret what the children were thinking as they played in the classroom office. Victoria recalled that Olive had written "THE K" on a piece of paper and then run it through the roller on the typewriter over and over again. Olive was focused and followed through the process methodically step by step. She was intent on finding a way to make the typewriter work. Kathryn and Victoria were thinking about Olive's understanding of how a typewriter worked because this one was broken. Did Olive really understand that if you press the keys on the typewriter the letters should appear on the paper? Victoria said, "Well, I think Olive did. When she put THE K into it, she obviously was figuring that when you press those, it would print. Because it wasn't doing that, she printed it herself." Did this mean that Olive understood that if she touched the keys with the THE and K on the keyboard, it would have spelled that on her sheet of paper? Kathryn said, "I think she did." Victoria thought, "No, I don't think that far.... I think she knows that when you press those buttons, not the specific ones, that the printing comes up." Although Victoria wondered if they should tell the girls that there was a part missing on the typewriter, Kathryn was not that concerned. Kathryn later said, "Well, it's not a real office, you know. It's very developmentally appropriate."

Victoria and Kathryn continued to document Olive throughout the inquiry to see if they could clarify her thinking about how the typewriter works. On a different occasion, when Victoria was looking at the Office Inquiry book, she reflected on what Olive was thinking when she told Kathryn the typewriter was printing something. Kathryn asked Olive what the print said, and she responded, "It says THE K. We didn't know it would actually work. I printed something, look it actually works.... This actually works.... It prints in real life. It printed out for real life." Victoria didn't think that Olive really believed that the typewriter printed THE K. She said, "I feel that they [the children] fuse fantasy and reality quite strongly. Fantasy is very close to reality for them." Kathryn noted,

"What they [the children] articulate might be different than what they believe."
She speculated that Olive had put a blank piece of paper in the typewriter and
saw that it didn't work. She thought about that and then went through the slow
process of writing THE K.

On a different occasion, for the purpose of getting a clearer picture of what
Vicky and Kristina were thinking and doing in the classroom office, Kathryn
studied both photographs and work samples. In a series of photographs, Vicky
and Kristina are working together side by side and collaborating with one another as they use sticky notes to make nametags for all their friends. Kathryn
recalled that Vicky watched Kristina write down some names and then Kristina
shared the materials with Vicky and invited her to write names. Vicky said,
"Kristina how do you spell your name?" Kristina spelled her name aloud as Vicky
carefully held the sticky note with one hand and the marker with the other as she
recorded the letters. Vicky also spelled her name for Kristina. Kathryn explained
that then the girls took turns helping one another to spell their friends' names.
For example, Vicky started to write Angie's name as Kristina held Angie's plastic nametag for her. Vicky also wrote the names of her family members independently on the same sticky note. She said, "These are my family's names. Papa,
Mama, and Owen." When looking at the work samples, Kathryn could see how

Photo 6.6: The Typewriter Is Working!

both Kristina and Vicky took their time as they carefully wrote out the names. They didn't rush their work, but instead they focused on their goal, which was to make sure that all the girls had nametags. Vicky also wanted to make sure that her family had a nametag as well. Kathryn gained a deeper understanding of the children's cognitive processes by looking at both types of documentation.

When Darlene and Kerri looked at Connor's and Michael's work samples and photographs, it gave them a richer understanding of the children's engagement in the Running Club Inquiry. In a series of photographs of Connor, he is explaining what he has drawn in his picture about how his body feels when he runs. In the first photograph, he is leaning forward on his chair with his head bent and is pointing to his knees in the picture. In the second photograph, he is standing and leaning over with a smile on his face, pointing to the line he has drawn beside his knees. In the third photograph, he is back to leaning on his

Photo 6.7: The Children Writing in the Classroom Office

chair while he looks towards Darlene and points to the line beside his ribs. In the fourth photograph, he is hunched over as he writes *knees* on the line in his picture. Kerri thought that Connor seemed very interested in explaining the ideas in his drawing. She said, "He was obviously very interested in what he was doing, and he had control … he's clearly explaining everything and wanting to express himself. So, he needs to really concentrate and focus." Darlene thought that Connor seemed very excited and proud of the work he did drawing his picture. When looking at the work sample, she noted that Connor drew both the inside and outside of his body in great detail:

> So, he's looking at what makes a body work. He's showing different parts of the body, especially in the movement area…. It's all about the bones and I think that the time he took in doing this and the detail he put into this picture shows how important it was for him to show what his thinking was and his knowledge and understanding of the human body.

Connor had used different colours to accentuate different parts, like dark green for the heart. He had written his name in big capital letters and drawn a large arrow towards his body. Darlene felt that it was important to Connor to take his

Photo 6.8: Connor Is Pointing to His Knees in the Drawing

Photo 6.9: Connor Points to the Line Where He Will Write Ribs

work a step further by labelling the body parts with some help from her so that other people understood what he was thinking.

In the other example, Darlene was reflecting on a series of photographs of Michael. In the first photograph, he is waiting with his hand raised as the children are sharing their thoughts about the documentation sitting on the table. Darlene said, "He wants to say something…. I mean, he's dying to say something." She commented, "That's such a big step in self-regulation too. Like a huge step." She speculated that Michael realized that his friends wanted to share their ideas and that he just needed to wait his turn. In the second photograph, he is still waiting with his head resting on his hand. Darlene commented, "I think he's really listening to somebody and interested in what they're saying." Darlene also thought that Michael was already starting to think about how to connect the running ideas as he waited patiently for there to be a pause in the conversation so he could have his turn to share his thinking. She commented, "Yeah … so that brain was just connecting everything together and listening and paying attention." In the third photograph, he is standing as he looks at all the work on the table. He seems delighted that it is his turn to share his idea, and he knows that everybody will be listening to him. Darlene said, "Oh, here he goes … he's going for it…. He's got to stand and share it." She felt that he looked confident and proud as he shared his thinking. In his work sample, Michael has divided his paper into quarters so that he can draw his running idea. In the first square, he has drawn the runner racing by himself. In the second square, he has drawn two runners racing against each other. In the third square, he had drawn the runners in a line and in the fourth square he has drawn the runner being timed. Darlene thought that Michael had to do a lot of problem-solving to show how to combine everyone's running idea. She said,

> I see a plan, like a big plan in his mind and I see that he was able to show that in his drawing. To me, like, he had a vision and … this was a way of Michael being able to show that and get it out to other people and get them to understand exactly what he was thinking through, like a storyboard.

Darlene was able to more thoroughly analyze Michael's engagement with the inquiry by studying the photographs and work samples together.

Darlene also studied the documentation to see how the children's theories were evolving while she analyzed the children's drawings of their running ideas. When she looked at Gabriel's first drawing, she could see that he had drawn two people holding clocks so that two runners could run at the same time. Then each runner was supposed to try and beat their own time. Darlene recalled that Gabriel was very excited to show the other children his running idea. He took the stopwatch from the running box into the hallway and had the children line up so that he could tell them exactly when to start. Gabriel had each child run twice, so that their scores could be compared. Zara assisted Gabriel by recording each child's times on a clipboard. Darlene reflected on how Gabriel's second drawing was different from the first. In the second drawing, he had drawn himself holding the stopwatch and he had recorded Michael's running times to show how Michael beat his time. His second drawing more accurately represented what had happened during the run.

Adele's first drawing showed children lined up at either side of the hall and two children high fiving in the middle. Darlene remembered that when it was Adele's turn to share her running idea, she had Rose help her set up the hall. After the rest of the Running Club joined them, they formed a circle and Adele explained how her running idea worked. While Adele was demonstrating her idea, she spontaneously added warm-up exercises. Adele organized the children in pairs and the running idea unfolded. In Adele's second drawing, Darlene noted that Adele had added the idea of doing exercises to warm up and having the tape clearly show where the runners should begin. She speculated that because Adele is a hesitant drawer, she only drew the exercise piece because it was a new idea.

Darlene could see that, in Evan's first drawing, he showed the boys on one side of the hall and the girls on the other so they could race against each other. Darlene recalled that she helped support Evan when he shared his run by setting up the hallway for him. Everyone gathered into a circle, and Evan explained his idea. He chose a boy and a girl and lined them up. He told the boy when it was his turn to run and then a few seconds later he would tell the girl to run. In his second drawing, Darlene reflected on how Evan drew exactly what happened, which showed how his thinking had evolved. He had the boy slightly ahead of the girl so that it was not a competition. They ran simultaneously but the girl ran a bit behind the boy. When Darlene asked Evan why he changed his mind, he said that he didn't want anyone to get hurt.

In her first drawing, Rose drew a line, and the children who didn't want to race could go on one side, and the children who did want to race could go on the other side. Darlene remembered that when it was Rose's turn to share her running idea, she announced that she had a new idea. She had the children who were not racing on the far side of the hallway as spectators and the two children racing against each other on either side of the line. Rose had pairs of children race against each other. In her second drawing, Darlene observed that she had only focused on the children who wanted to race. Even though Rose didn't time the runs, she still drew a clock on the wall. Darlene speculated that Rose had been influenced by Zara's run and how the fastest runners had the shortest times. Darlene explained, "She was still thinking about the times and how it didn't make sense to her, I think, and that's why she wanted to race them against each other." By studying the documentation, Darlene gained insight into how the children's cognitive processes were developing, which is an important part of helping children become self-regulated learners.

When Sharon looked at the documentation of the children in the valley during the Community Inquiry, she first studied a photograph of Ehsan lying on the grass in the meadow to reflect on his engagement. Sharon said, "He's having a moment to himself, away from everybody else. He's lying down. So, it's a different position for his body to rest. He's looking up at the sky. His hand is over his heart area." She speculated about whether Ehsan was making a connection to his heart, perhaps feeling his heartbeat slow the longer that he lay there. She added, "You can tell like even the tilt of his feet, he's relaxed. His feet aren't upright. He's [in] that yoga pose … it's a very relaxed posture. He is sunk into the grass." Sharon thought that Ehsan seemed very focused and intent on what he was doing even though in the distance there were children moving around, laughing, and playing with one another. She observed, "You can see in his face he's very peaceful and calm. There's no tension. No tightness." Similarly, in a photograph of Amina, she is lying on the grass with her hands behind her head and her legs bent with one foot on the ground and one in the air. Her eyes are shut, and she has a big smile on her face. Sharon said, "I think she's just so happy. She is just enjoying life and enjoying the sunshine and being outside." She commented that, even though there were lots of other children running around her, Amina was totally focused and in her own space.

In a different set of photographs, Omja is looking through the magnifying glass into a container. He is experimenting with moving his head and the magnifying glass so he can see the snail at different angles and distances. Sharon commented,

> He has got something that he's looking at very intently. Like look at his head bent there … and he's not distracted, and he's definitely focused on something…. He's a kid that has very little English so a lot of it is through demonstration … what he would show me. So, it's interesting to see him so intense

and focused on this. Because he's clearly more interested in seeing it for himself than bringing it to my attention at this point in the year.

Sharon felt that Omja no longer needed to confirm what he was looking at with her; he was confident in his own abilities to explore and problem-solve on his own. Similarly, in another set of photographs of Ehsan, he is holding a magnifying glass as he looks around the valley to see what he can find. In the first one, he is holding the magnifying glass right up to his eye. In the second one, he has lowered the magnifying glass to look at something off in the distance. In the third one, he has raised the magnifying glass up to his eye once again. Sharon said, "He's definitely investigating and very curious about something … he's in the moment." She thought Ehsan looked happy, engaged, and full of joy as the sunshine crossed his face.

When Sharon looked at both the work samples and photographs, she could reflect more deeply on the children's thinking. In one photograph, Bihar and Adhita are sketching the collaborative building project. Bihar sits with his knees crossed to steady the clipboard. He is hunched over as he focuses his eyes on what he is drawing. He uses one hand to hold the clipboard and the other to hold the pencil. Beside him sits Adhita, her knees also crossed, one hand holding the clipboard while the other rests on top. She is observing her peers as they build. Sharon said,

> I see a lot of focus. I see a lot of calm, intention, [and] patience.… When I look at Adhita's face, for example, she is pausing in the activity to really observe and look at the landscape that she has helped to co-create.

When looking at Bihar, Sharon said that he was always eager to draw pictures, and when he saw what Adhita was doing he wanted to join her. She noted, "He wants to get down on his clipboard what he's seeing." Sharon said that both Adhita and Bihar were very absorbed in their work—there was a lot of activity in front of them, but they were able to stay focused for an extended period of time. When she looked at Adhita's detailed work sample, she observed how patient Adhita was when thinking about the directionality of all the different shapes and words she used to label her drawing. Sharon explained, "So she's trying to label the actual physical material as well as the imaginative part of it." She thought that Adhita labelled her work carefully because it was important to her that

Photo 6.10: Children Drawing on Clipboards

Photo 6.11: Anima Is Looking at the Tree

Photo 6.12: Anima Is Making an Observational Drawing of the Tree

others understand what she was trying to show: "It's almost like she has drawn it … for an audience. Like she had made this to share with somebody else."

When Sharon was looking at a series of photographs of Amina, she reflected on how Amina's sketches of the tree evolved. In the first photograph, Amina is sitting by herself on a cement wall looking at a tree in front of her as she thinks about how to begin sketching it. Amina looks intently at the tree, sitting in a moment of stillness as she soaks it all in. Sharon commented, "It just speaks to stillness and calmness and [being] present in the moment outside in nature.… She has a design, a very clear plan in her mind about how she's going to start." In the second photograph, Sharon observed that Amina used one hand to hold the clipboard while the other hand held the marker in a resting position. Amina looks at the tree through her hair, purses her lips, and pauses in deep concentration. She has placed a lot of importance on this task. In the third photograph, Amina has her head tilted and is looking at what she is drawing. One hand holds the marker as the other steadies the clipboard that is now turned purposefully in a different direction on her lap. Sharon pointed out, "She's tilted this clipboard … she's very mindful and focused." Here again we can see how studying documentation enables teachers to reflect on the link between children's cognitive processes and their ability to self-regulate.

CHAPTER SUMMARY

This chapter has focused on self-regulation and documentation. I have argued that when children feel valued and are invested in an inquiry, they learn to listen to others and have a greater ability to modulate their emotions, work collaboratively, and take pride in their achievements. During inquiry-based learning, positive emotions lead to a greater capacity for emotional growth and the ability to be resilient and move forward. Teachers use scaffolding strategies when revisiting documentation, and this enables children to become self-regulated learners. Children are moved to a higher level of cognitive functioning where they are encouraged to focus their attention and remember previous experiences. When teachers and children revisit documentation, the children draw on processes such as reasoning, problem-solving, flexible thinking, multitasking, and working memory to clarify their thinking. This helps strengthen the children's executive functions so they can reduce their stress load. When teachers study documentation to deepen their own analysis of the inquiry, it gives them insight into the children's self-regulation, which informs their hypotheses about how children think and learn and enables them to make predictions about future classroom experiences that will further develop these skills.

REFLECTIVE QUESTIONS

1. During inquiries do you revisit documentation with the children to keep them interested in the inquiry? If not, why not?
2. Why do you think that sharing documentation with children is an effective way to help them recall and build onto their ideas and theories?
3. How does providing children with opportunities to clarify their own thinking support their ability to self-regulate?
4. Do you feel that studying documentation informs your understanding about how children think and learn? If so, does this help you to plan future classroom experiences that will further develop their self-regulation skills?

RECOMMENDED READINGS

Anderson, Doug, Chiarotto, Lorraine, & Comay, Julie. (2017). Carol's story. In *Natural curiosity 2nd edition: A resource for educators* (pp. 168–177). Toronto, ON: OISE.

Berdoussis, Noula. (2008). The stretching starfish: Children's theories. In Carol Anne Wien (Ed.), *Emergent curriculum in the primary classroom: Interpreting the Reggio Emilia approach in schools* (pp. 96–110). New York: Teachers College Press.

Halls, Deborah, & Wien, Carol Anne. (2013). "The wind goes inside of me": Kindergarten children's theories about running fast. *Canadian Children, 38*, 4–10.

Tarr, Patricia, Bjartveit, Carolyn, Kostiuk, Lana, & McCowan, Daina. (2009). Supporting imagination in play through pedagogical documentation: Haunted houses; fairies and goblins; pirates and islands. *Canadian Children, 34*, 21–28.

ONLINE RESOURCES

Carla Rinaldi on Documentation
https://youtu.be/hUVi-fLc0zA

Carol Anne Wien Habits of Documenting
https://youtu.be/Q8aaxrHQG4o

The Sky Inquiry Project
https://youtu.be/QgoE7bOwNOM

Sky Inquiry Filming Series Video 3—Documenting and Sharing the Learning
https://youtu.be/NLdTrmM6HL0

It's about Documenting: Documentation Panels
https://vimeo.com/91973048

Reflections on Inquiry: Observations and Making Learning Visible
http://www.edugains.ca/resourcesKIN/Video/Inquiry/mp4/Inquiry(09).mp4

Reflections on Inquiry: The Power of Inquiry—Co-constructing and Making Learning
   Visible
http://www.edugains.ca/resourcesKIN/Video/Inquiry/mp4/Inquiry(10).mp4

Chapter Seven

Conclusion and Future Directions

In the quotation that opened this book, Charles Pascal (2009) states that self-regulation is "the cornerstone of development and is the central building block of early learning" (p. 4). It has come to be recognized as fundamental to learning in the primary years. Self-regulation is a reflective learning process where children become aware of what it feels like to be overstressed, recognize when they need to up-regulate or down-regulate, and develop strategies to reduce their stress and restore their energy. This process enables children to see themselves as self-regulated learners in a manner that has long-term implications for their capacity to learn. Self-regulation is a prominent issue because children are experiencing much more stress than in the past, especially since the COVID-19 pandemic, which has resulted in many more social, emotional, behavioural, cognitive, physical, and mental health problems.

This book focuses specifically on how inquiry-based learning helps children to become self-regulated learners in the primary classroom. Inquiry-based learning is an approach to teaching and learning that places students' observations, questions, ideas, and theories at the centre of intellectually stimulating learning experiences. It encourages active learning and critical thinking through collaborative student-led investigations guided by interesting questions or problems. Emergent curriculum is a particular type of curriculum planning or teaching practice that supports inquiry-based learning through inquiry design, design of the environment, conversation, and documentation. Emergent curriculum focuses on what the children are learning, while the inquiry-based approach explains how the children will go about it. Given the current educational crisis precipitated by the COVID-19 pandemic, when so many children have been in virtual classrooms, the epilogue that follows addresses how inquiry-based learning can be facilitated in online environments.

In this book, I have shown in innovative and unanticipated ways how inquiry-based learning helps children to become self-regulated learners. These efforts have uncovered an even greater potential for inquiry-based learning in the primary classroom than often appreciated. I have identified four fundamental insights about how inquiry-based learning supports self-regulation. The first insight is that children learn how to self-regulate during inquiry-based learning in the same way they do during play. The second insight is that teachers use scaffolding strategies during inquiry-based learning to support children as they become self-regulated learners. The third insight is that inquiry-based learning promotes positive emotions, which are important for the development of social and emotional learning (SEL). The fourth insight is that during inquiry-based learning children use oral language as a self-regulatory tool to help them regulate their own emotions and behaviours. I hope these insights will help teachers, Early Childhood Educators, parents, administrators, and policy makers to better appreciate the important contribution of inquiry-based learning to self-regulation in the primary classroom.

FUTURE DIRECTIONS

Self-Regulation and Exceptional Learners

Can these four compelling insights about how inquiry-based learning supports self-regulation inform our thinking about exceptional learners in the classroom? First, we must consider how self-regulation plays an especially critical role in helping children with exceptionalities address their needs (Shanker, 2013b). Difficulties in self-regulation can exacerbate the problems of a child with exceptionalities and, in turn, their ability to self-regulate can help mitigate these problems. These children often need to work much harder to block out stressors such as hypersensitivity to noise or visual stimuli. Focusing attention over a long period of time drains children's energy, which diminishes their ability to sustain their attention. The harder children with exceptionalities have to work, the less energy they have left over to learn. By reducing the stressors on their nervous system, they have more resources to control their impulses and can access the arousal level appropriate for the learning situation.

In the cognitive domain, students need to maintain their attention, deal with the demands on their working memory, process various kinds of information, and manage their time (Shanker & Hopkins, 2020). When students with exceptionalities experience chronic stress and anxiety, it seriously constrains their ability to learn. It makes it difficult for them to pay attention, which leads to avoidance, affects their working memory, which is essential for planning, reasoning, and problem-solving, and slows down their brain's ability to process information. These factors, as well as time management issues, exacerbate problems in curriculum areas like math. When teachers detect their students' stress in the cognitive domain, it can help them to support students with math problems who are not meeting expectations and learning outcomes. To meet our students' individual needs, we must constantly ask ourselves why a student is acting or reacting in a particular way, how we can modify things so that the student is eager to learn, and whether this modification is helping a student to be calmly focused and alert. When teachers better understand their exceptional students' cognitive processes, they can create activities that will enhance their students' ability to stay focused and become self-regulated learners.

For children with exceptionalities, self-regulation supports a growth mindset, to use Dweck's (2007) term, as it fosters the belief that intellectual and academic abilities are not fixed but can be developed. Montague (2007, 2008) argues that students with Learning Disabilities (LD), for example, have difficulty with memory, attention, and self-regulation, which adversely affects their performance in mathematics and problem-solving. These students tend to have limited strategies, immature metacognitive abilities, and low motivation, and fail to monitor their own performance. She found that children with LD must be explicitly taught self-regulation strategies like self-instruction, self-questioning, self-monitoring, and self-assessment as they engage in tasks that they find academically challenging. Self-regulation strategies enhance learning by helping students with exceptionalities take control of their own actions and become more independent. Butler and Schnellert (2015) argue that students bring motivationally charged beliefs to contexts. When students believe they can improve their ability by using learning strategies effectively, they view errors as opportunities to learn and will persist when challenged. In contrast, students can feel anxious and disengaged from learning if they think they have little control over the outcomes. Students with exceptionalities need self-regulation support in order to develop metacognitive knowledge about their strengths and needs so they can navigate expectations effectively. It enhances their executive functioning capacities, fosters self-awareness, and develops strategies to overcome difficulties with academic work. Self-regulating strategies have been found, for example, to improve on-task behaviour, preparedness, productivity, and academic accuracy in math. The connection to a growth mindset highlights that, for children with exceptionalities, poor academic achievement is not a fixed outcome but can be avoided through the development of their self-regulation skills so they experience success and take control over their own learning (Ruttenberg-Rozen & Jacobs, forthcoming).

It is also important to note that teaching students with exceptionalities can be very challenging at times because there are a wide range of issues that teachers need to address. When children with exceptionalities are overstressed and dysregulated, their emotions and behaviours can become overwhelming for teachers. Educators need to be able to recognize when they themselves have become overstressed so they can regulate their own emotions and cope with a child's anger, anxiety, or frustration. Shanker (2013b) thinks that teachers need to remain calm when a child, including a child with exceptionalities, is having difficulty modulating their emotions, as the teacher's response can have a dysregulating effect on the child. When teachers can maintain or quickly restore their own equilibrium, they are better able to help a child become calmly focused and alert. One of my observations is that, during inquiry-based learning, teachers become more aware of their own ability to self-regulate and how it affects their teaching.

Exceptional Learners and Inquiry-Based Learning

Can these four compelling insights inform our thinking about exceptional learners? Children with exceptionalities learn how to self-regulate during inquiry-based learning in the same way they do during play. Inquiries support these children's ability to self-regulate because they are pleasurable, self-motivated, and child-initiated and they offer children with exceptionalities the freedom to make their own choices, which can enhance their concentration and school performance (O'Brien, 2010). Choice-making enables students to tailor tasks to their own learning needs, build metacognitive knowledge, experience autonomy, control the level of challenge, participate more effectively, and reduce their anxiety. Children feel empowered to take control over their own learning during an inquiry in terms of the problems posed and the questions asked, as well as the investigations pursued. This enables them to stay focused, consider other perspectives, and figure out their own thinking. O'Brien (2010) believes that children with exceptionalities need to and may benefit the most from inquiry-based learning as it is essential to their development and stretches their current social and cognitive abilities. It is essential to create collaborative, inclusive environments where children develop authentic personal relationships where they feel valued, find their own voice, are treated with respect, and are supported in their knowledge construction with others. The ideas and theories of every student, including students with exceptionalities, help propel the investigation forward. Teachers and students become co-learners, celebrate and build on each other's strengths, and accommodate a diversity of needs. Mastrangelo (2017) explains that inquiry plays a critical role in helping children regulate their emotions, make plans, and solve problems. During inquiry, children with exceptionalities can practice their self-regulation skills in a natural, enjoyable, and motivating fashion. She notes that children with exceptionalities often need direct intervention on how to engage in inquiry-based learning. Difficulties related to their exceptionalities can be obstacles that hinder the quality of their inquiry experience because of the variability in their symptoms. Inquiries might need to be modified according to the capabilities of each child.

Teachers use scaffolding strategies during inquiry-based learning to support children with exceptionalities as they become self-regulated learners. Scaffolding provides these students with the initial support they need to learn and master new tasks, and then the teacher will pull back as the child becomes skilled enough to manage on their own (Bruner, 2004). Scaffolding during inquiries is an important way to reduce the stress load on children with exceptionalities. It also reduces their aversion to risk-taking so they can move to a higher level of cognitive functioning. Children with exceptionalities often need more scaffolding than other children to develop the skills needed for optimal self-regulation. Scaffolding for these students needs to be more carefully designed and adjusted to address the additional challenges they face. Gradually raising the bar during scaffolding can be an effective way to support children with exceptionalities (Shanker, 2013b). Reciprocal actions that are challenging but not overwhelming, such as introducing a provocation, support self-regulation because they enable children with exceptionalities to feel more confident and stay focused on the investigation.

Inquiry-based learning promotes positive emotions, which are important for the development of SEL in children with exceptionalities. In the social domain, children function optimally when they experience positive emotions like inspiration, curiosity, excitement, enthusiasm, interest, confidence, pride, and happiness, which generate energy so students will seek out interactions and concentrate for longer periods of time. On the other hand, negative emotions consume energy, making it difficult for children with exceptionalities to concentrate and pay attention. Many children with exceptionalities find social interactions stressful because of biological deficits or serious challenges in emotion regulation. Their stress load is often particularly acute, which predisposes them to want to avoid social interaction and engagement, and this can impede their ability to learn. When children with exceptionalities have mastered the nuances of social interaction and understand the meaning of communicative behaviours, they experience less stress. As these children begin to self-regulate, they demonstrate the desire and ability to engage socially (Shanker 2013b). When children with exceptionalities develop authentic relationships, they feel like they belong, and this creates the capacity for empathy, which promotes positive behaviours in the prosocial domain.

Many children with exceptionalities use oral language as a self-regulatory tool to help them regulate their own emotions and behaviours. Oral language enables their thinking to become more complex and flexible and allows them to imagine, manipulate, and create new ideas, as well as to share their ideas and theories with others. When exceptional children express their thinking during inquiry-based learning, speech is used to help them understand, clarify, and focus their thoughts. When children draw on their cognitive processes, this strengthens their executive functions so they can reduce the tension created by stress. Greenspan and Shanker (2004) point out that some children with exceptionalities are unable to engage in back-and-forth emotional gesturing, such as tone of voice, body posture, or facial expressions, and have difficulty keeping up with a longer conversation. When these children are not tuned in or responsive to others, it is difficult to remain creative and logical in the conversation. It is the continuous flow of emotional gesturing that organizes and maintains these high-level symbolic exchanges and provides a constant source of new emotions that stirs up the next sequence of ideas or words. Therefore, it is important for these children to have opportunities to experiment with emotional exchanges so they can engage in inquiry-based conversations that require them to be able to make inferences and use higher-level abstract thinking. All of this suggests that inquiry-based learning has extraordinary potential to help children with exceptionalities become self-regulated learners, but more research needs to be done.

REFLECTIVE QUESTIONS

1. When working with a child who has exceptionalities, have you had difficulty modulating your emotions and, if so, how did this affect the child?
2. Why is it important to provide inquiry-based learning opportunities for children with exceptionalities?

3. How can you use what you have learned here about self-regulation and inquiry-based learning in your own classroom environment?

4. How will the four inquiries in this book guide you as you undertake inquiries in the future?

5. What are your next steps when thinking about expanding your knowledge of how to support children as they become self-regulated learners?

Epilogue

Inquiry-Based Learning in an Online Primary Classroom

Over the past two years, we have experienced a major disruption in education around the world because of COVID-19. Canadian children are being educated online and attending virtual classrooms at a scale that was previously unimaginable. There are many indicators that some young children will continue to be educated online in the future. For Davies and Aurini (2021), this causes considerable concern, as they found that online learning was less effective than face-to-face learning, particularly among younger and vulnerable students. They estimate that some Canadian children have lost a full year of learning during the pandemic. According to Hargreaves (2021), many teachers found teaching online reduced their effectiveness because it was difficult to engage children online. One American study found that 42 percent of teachers felt that their students' engagement had declined during the pandemic. Hargreaves (2021) also found that 75 percent of Alberta teachers reported that they did not have the same emotional connection with their students and that the children were struggling with learning.

As online learning for some students is here to stay, this has left many teachers scrambling to come up with innovative ways to deliver curriculum that keeps them emotionally connected to their students and that keeps children engaged and focused on their learning. Hargreaves (2021) argues that when children learn in online environments, they need to become self-directed and self-regulating learners. Self-directed learning environments are child-centred in the sense that they are led by the children and scaffolded by the teacher in their role as a facilitator. It is about children having voice and choice in their learning. He observes that many learners developed these skills and habits during the pandemic out of necessity.

How can children become self-regulated learners in online classrooms? We have seen in this book that inquiry-based learning is an effective way to support children becoming self-regulated learners. Currently, there is very little concrete information and practical guidance on how to implement inquiry-based learning in a virtual classroom, which is a disadvantage for educators teaching their students online. An inquiry-based approach to teaching and learning in an online world is certainly possible, but what does it look like and sound like in a primary classroom?

Four key elements must be present in a virtual classroom setting to enable educators to implement an inquiry-based approach to teaching and learning that helps students become self-regulated learners:

1. Teachers must ensure that inquiries are built around the children's interests.
2. Virtual classroom environments must be designed to support the children's learning during inquiries.
3. There must be opportunities for students to engage in conversation throughout the inquiry.
4. The children's learning must be documented and made visible to others.

There exists a range of online educational platforms available that address one or more of these elements.

How can we use the ClassDojo platform (https://www.classdojo.com) for the inquiry design component of emergent curriculum? ClassDojo offers multiple tools that help teachers build inquiries around the children's interests. The Class Story is an interactive feed that allows the teacher to prompt discussion with photos, text, and video. Students can respond in a comment thread and interact with each other. The teacher can follow up by asking students questions to expand their thinking. This generation of rich conversation is an excellent way to collect data on students' initial interests and wonderings. The Portfolio feature gives students the choice and freedom to express their interests by using a multitude of "upload" tools, such as photos, videos, files, journaling, voice notes, captions, annotations, and drawings. Teachers can spark interest in an inquiry by introducing a provocation or allowing students to post about what they are curious to explore further. This enables the teacher to cluster students who have similar interests and provide relevant resources so they can pursue their inquiry together. ClassDojo supports the collaborative nature of inquiry-based learning among teachers, students, and their families as well.

How can we use the Google Classroom platform (https://classroom.google.com) for the design of the environment component of emergent curriculum? Google Classroom offers numerous possibilities to design an environment that supports the children's learning during inquiries. When thinking about the design of the environment, teachers must focus on equipping students with rich, open-ended materials and tools, and creating a positive social environment where students can form authentic relationships. Students can engage with each other and their teacher through discussion posts and comments on shared documents to create a collaborative and social learning environment where inquiry can thrive. Material folders and a Class Drive make it simple to provide students with rich resources in various modalities so they can pursue their inquiry interests. The multitude of applications available gives teachers the flexibility to create a space that suits their students' specific needs. Google Classroom easily blends with the rest of the G-Suite tools and add-ons, such as Google Slides, Blogger, Nearpod, and Pear Deck. It is a rich learning environment that can sustain the children's interest throughout the inquiry.

How can we use the Seesaw platform (https://web.seesaw.me) for the conversation component of emergent curriculum? Seesaw provides many opportunities for students to engage in rich conversations during inquiries. In the Journal feature, students can record their thinking through various creative means, including pictures, drawings, videos, and text, which enables students to demonstrate their learning in multiple ways. Teachers can respond to students' ideas and theories with prompts using the same tools. As teachers engage students in conversations, students can hear each other's theories and build on their previous thinking. Because the platform encourages parent engagement, student conversations regarding the inquiry extend beyond the classroom and follow them into their homes. Parents can communicate with the teachers through the messaging feature. This application is particularly beneficial for English Language Learners and parents who may have difficulty communicating in English, as teacher and parent communication can be translated into 55 different languages.

How can we use the Google Keep platform (https://keep.google.com) for the documentation component of emergent curriculum? Google Keep can be used to document the children's learning and make it visible to others during inquiries. It is a G-Suite feature that has four useful note add-on elements: lists, drawings, photos, and audio. Teachers can create notes combined with images and captions to document student ideas, theories, and questions. Audio clips of conversations between peers or teachers and students may be added to a note as well. A desirable feature is the labels tool. Labels may "tag" student names to inquiries. When one wants to look back at a specific student's progress, clicking on that student's label will compile and display all the documentation that has been created throughout the year. Tags are not restricted to student names as labels may be created for whatever the educator requires, such as curriculum expectations, frames, or inquiry topics. Tags are useful for reflecting on one's teaching practice, analyzing topics that inspired the most student interest or engagement, and more. Google Keep can also be used to manage group inquiries while providing real-time documentation co-constructed between the group of students and the teacher. Using the available features, students can reflect on their prior theories and build on their knowledge as the inquiry unfolds. The Google Keep platform is an organized way to keep documentation in one place.

These technology-enhanced virtual platforms do not just provide benefits for a specific component of emergent curriculum. I have highlighted them because they are comprehensive. Therefore, during inquiry-based learning they can be used on their own or grouped with another platform. This way educators who are teaching in virtual classrooms can select which platform works best for them and the students in their class. These online platforms make it possible for teachers and students to engage in inquiry-based learning, which is an effective way to keep teachers emotionally connected to their students and support children becoming self-regulated learners in a virtual classroom.

The four compelling insights about how inquiry-based learning supports self-regulation can also be applied to online learning. Children learn how to self-regulate during online inquiries in the same way they do during play. Teachers use scaffolding strategies during online inquiries to support children as they become self-regulated learners. Online inquiries promote positive emotions, which are important for the development of social and emotional learning (SEL). During online inquiries children use oral language as a self-regulatory tool to help them regulate their own emotions and behaviours. Given the uncertainty we face because of the pandemic and its lingering effects on children, it is even more important for teachers to adapt their practice to ensure that all students become self-regulated learners.

ONLINE RESOURCES FOR VIRTUAL CLASSROOMS

Apple Schoolwork

https://www.apple.com/education/k12/teaching-tools

Artsonia

https://www.artsonia.com

AudioNote
https://luminantsoftware.com/apps/audionote-notepad-and-voice-recorder

Biblionasium
https://www.biblionasium.com

Brightspace Portfolio
https://www.d2l.com/brightspace

Buncee
https://app.edu.buncee.com

ClassDojo
https://www.classdojo.com

Edmodo
https://go.edmodo.com/teachers

Edwin
https://edwin.nelson.com

Evernote
https://evernote.com

Floor Books
https://docs.google.com/document/d/1_RqirFqi_a52eNR7ZUYQkxSkZYG8cxkn
    RR14oPYdDOQ/edit

Formative
https://goformative.com

Google Classroom
https://classroom.google.com

Google Keep
https://keep.google.com

Himama

https://www.himama.com

Karizena

https://www.kaizena.com

Lino

http://en.linoit.com

Nearpod

https://nearpod.com

OneNote

https://www.onenote.com/classnotebook

PicCollage

https://pic-collage.com

Seesaw

https://web.seesaw.me

REFERENCES

Banchi, H., & Bell, R. (2008). The many levels of inquiry. *Science and Children, 46,* 26–29.

Barnes, D. (2008). Exploratory talk for learning. In N. Mercer & S. Hodgkinson (Eds.), *Exploring talk in schools* (pp. 1–16). London, UK: Sage Publications.

Bauer, I. M., & Baumeister, R. F. (2011). Self-regulatory strength. In K. D. Vohs & R. F. Baumeister (Eds.), *Handbook of self-regulation: Research, theory, and applications* (2nd ed., pp. 64–82). New York: the Guilford Press.

Berger, A. (2011). *Self-regulation: Brain, cognition, and development.* Washington, DC: American Psychological Association.

Biemiller, A. (2013). Vocabulary development and instruction: A prerequisite for school learning. In D. Dickinson & S. Neuman (Eds.), *Handbook of early literacy research* (Vol. 2, pp. 41–51). New York: Guildford Press.

Blair, C., & Diamond, A. (2008). Biological processes in prevention and intervention: The promotion of self-regulation as a means of preventing school failure. *Development and Psychopathology, 20,* 899–911.

Blair, C., Protzko, J., & Ursache, A. (2011). Self-regulation and early literacy. In S. B. Neuman & D. K. Dickinson (Eds.), *Handbook of early literacy research* (Vol. 2, pp. 20–35). New York: Guilford Press.

Blair, C., & Razza, R. P. (2007). Relating effortful control, executive function, and false belief understanding to emerging math and literacy ability in kindergarten. *Child Development, 78*(2), 647–663.

Blair, C., & Ursache, A. (2011). A bidirectional model of executive function and self-regulation. In K. D. Vohs & R. F. Baumeister (Eds.), *Handbook of self-regulation: Research, theory, and applications* (2nd ed., pp. 300–320). New York: Guilford Press.

Bodrova, E., & Leong, D. J. (2007). *Tools of the mind: The Vygotskian approach to early childhood education* (2nd ed.). Upper Saddle River, NJ: Pearson.

Bodrova, E., & Leong, D. J. (2008). Developing self-regulation in kindergarten: Can we keep all the crickets in the basket? *Young Children* (March), 1–3.

Boe, M., & Hogenstad, K. (2010). Critical thinking in kindergarten. *Childhood & Philosophy, 6,* 154–165.

Brooker, L. (2011). Taking play seriously. In S. Rogers (Ed.), *Rethinking play and pedagogy in early childhood education: Concepts, contexts and cultures* (pp. 152–164). London, UK: Routledge.

Bruner, J. (2004). *Child's talk: Learning to use language*. New York: W. W. Norton.

Bruner, J. (2006). *In search of pedagogy volume I: The selected works of Jerome S. Bruner*. Abingdon, UK: Routledge.

Butler, D., & Schnellert, L. (2015). Success for students with learning disabilities: What does self-regulation have to do with it? In T. J. Cleary (Ed.), *Self-regulated learning interventions with at-risk youth: Enhancing adaptability, performance, and well-being* (pp. 89–111). Washington, DC: American Psychological Association.

CASEL. (2022a). Transformative SEL. https://casel.org/fundamentals-of-sel/how-does-sel-support-educational-equity-and-excellence/transformative-sel/

CASEL. (2022b). What is the CASEL framework? https://casel.org/fundamentals-of-sel/what-is-the-casel-framework/

Chiarotto, L. (2011). *Natural curiosity: Building children's understanding of the world through environmental inquiry*. Toronto, ON: OISE University of Toronto.

Clinton, J. (2013). The power of positive adult child relationships: Connection is the key. In *Think, feel, act: Lessons from research about young children* (pp. 1–6). Toronto, ON: Government of Ontario.

Copple, C. (1994). Foreword to *Emergent Curriculum* (p. vii). Washington, DC: NAEYC.

Copple, C., & Bredekamp, S. (Eds.). (2009). *Developmentally appropriate practices in early childhood programs* (3rd ed.). Washington, DC: NAEYC.

Cost, K., Crosbie, J., Anagnostou, E., Birken, C., Charach, A., Monga, S., Kelley, E., Nicolson, R., Maguire, J., Burton, C., Schachar, R., Arnold, P., & Korczak, D. (2021). Mostly worse, occasionally better: Impact of COVID-19 pandemic on the mental health of Canadian children and adolescents. *European Child & Adolescent Psychiatry*. https://doi.org/10.1007/s00787-021-01744-3

Csikszentmihalyi, M. (1975). Play and intrinsic rewards. *Journal of Humanistic Psychology, 15*, 41–63.

Csikszentmihalyi, M. (2008). *Flow: The psychology of optimal experience*. New York: Harper Perennial.

Curtis, D., & Carter, M. (2003). *Designs for living and learning: Transforming early childhood environments*. St. Paul, MN: Redleaf Press.

Dahlberg, G., Moss, P., & Pence, A. (2013). *Beyond quality in early childhood education and care: Languages of evaluation* (classic ed.). London, UK: Routledge.

Davies, S., & Aurini, J. (2021). Estimates of student learning during COVID-19 school disruptions: Canada in international context. In T. Vaillancourt et al. (Eds.), *Children and schools during COVID-19: Engagement and connection through opportunity* (pp. 50–69). Ottawa, ON: Royal Society of Canada.

Diamond, A., Barnett, W. S., Thomas, J., & Munro, S. (2007). Preschool program improves cognitive control. *Science, 318,* 1387–1388.

Dickinson, D., Darrow, C., Ngo, S., & D'Souza, L. (2011). Changing classroom conversations: Narrowing the gap between potential and reality. In O. Barbanin & B. Wasik (Eds.), *Handbook of childhood development and early education: Research to practice* (pp. 328–351). New York: Guildford Press.

Dickinson, D., McCabe, A., & Essex, M. (2013). A window of opportunity we must open for all: The case for preschool with high-quality support for language and literacy. In D. Dickinson & S. Neuman (Eds), *Handbook of early literacy research* (Vol. 2, pp. 11–28). New York: Guildford Press.

Duckworth, A. L., & Carlson, S. M. (2013). Self-regulation and school success. In B. Sokol, F. Grouzet, & U. Müller (Eds.), *Self-regulation and autonomy: Social and developmental dimensions of human conduct* (pp. 208–230). New York: Cambridge University Press.

Duckworth, E. (2006). *The having of wonderful ideas* (3rd ed.). New York: Teachers College Press.

Dweck, C. (2007). *Mindset: The new psychology of success.* New York: Ballantine Books.

Edwards, C. (2002). Three approaches from Europe: Waldorf, Montessori, and Reggio Emilia. *Early Childhood Research and Practice, 4,* 1–14.

Fitzpatrick, C., & Pagani, L. (2013). Task-oriented kindergarten behavior pays off in later childhood. *Journal of Developmental & Behavioral Pediatrics, 34,* 94–101.

Florez, I. R. (2011). Developing young children's self-regulation through everyday experiences. *Young Children* (July), 46–51.

Forgas, J. P., Baumeister, R. E., & Tice, D. M. (2009). The psychology of self-regulation: An introductory review. In J. P. Forgas, R. F. Baumeister, & D. M. Tice (Eds.), *Psychology of self-regulation: Cognitive, affective, and motivational processes* (pp. 2–16). New York: Psychology Press.

Forman, G., & Fyfe, B. (2012). Negotiating learning through design, documentation, and discourse. In C. Edwards, L. Gandini, & G. Forman (Eds.), *The hundred languages of children: The Reggio Emilia experience in transformation* (3rd ed., pp. 247–271). Santa Barbara, CA: Praeger.

Fraser, S. (2006). *Authentic childhood: Experiencing Reggio Emilia in the classroom* (2nd ed.). Toronto, ON: Nelson Educational.

Fraser, S. (2012). *Authentic childhood: Experiencing Reggio Emilia in the classroom* (3rd ed.). Toronto, ON: Nelson Educational.

Gallas, K. (2017). *Talking their way into science: Hearing children's questions and theories, responding with curricula.* New York: Teachers College Press.

Gandini, L. (2012a). Connecting through caring and learning spaces. In C. Edwards, L. Gandini, & G. Forman (Eds.), *The hundred languages of children: The Reggio Emilia experience in transformation* (3rd ed., pp. 317–341). Santa Barbara, CA: Praeger.

Gandini, L. (2012b). History, ideas, and basic principles: An interview with Loris Malaguzzi. In C. Edwards, L. Gandini, & G. Forman (Eds.), *The hundred languages of children: The Reggio Emilia experience in transformation* (3rd ed., pp. 27–72). Santa Barbara, CA: Praeger.

Government of Alberta. (n.d.). *Social-emotional learning.* https://www.alberta.ca/social-emotional-learning.aspx

Government of British Columbia. (2021). *B.C. curriculum: Core competencies.* https://curriculum.gov.bc.ca/competencies

Government of Nova Scotia. (2015). *Action plan for education.* https://www.ednet.ns.ca/education-actionplan

Government of Nova Scotia. (2020). *Health education foundational outcomes.* https://curriculum.novascotia.ca/sites/default/files/documents/outcomes-indicators-files/Health%20Education%204-6%20Foundational%20Outcomes%20%282020-21%29.pdf

Government of Nova Scotia. (2021). *Social and emotional learning (SEL).* https://www.ednet.ns.ca/psp/social-emotional-learning-sel

Greenspan, S. I., & Shanker, S. (2004). *The first idea: How symbols, language, and intelligence evolved from our primate ancestors to modern humans.* Cambridge, MA: Da Capo Press.

Grolnick, W., Kurowski, C., & Gurland, S. (1999). Family processes and the development of self-regulation. *Educational Psychologist, 34*(1), 3–14.

Halls, D., & Wien, C. (2013). "The wind goes inside of me": Kindergarten children's theories about running fast. *Canadian Children, 38*, 4–10.

Hargreaves, A. (2021). What the COVID-19 pandemic has taught us about teachers and teaching. In T. Vaillancourt et al. (Eds.), *Children and schools during COVID-19: Engagement and connection through opportunity* (pp. 138–168). Ottawa, ON: Royal Society of Canada.

Hawes, Z., Gibson, A., Mir, S., & Pelletier, J. (2012). Children's experiences in full-day Kindergarten programs for 4- and 5-year-olds: Play and self-regulation. In *Toronto first duty: Phase 3 report* (pp. 33–54). Toronto, ON: OISE.

Heroman, C., & Copple, C. (2006). Teaching in the kindergarten year. In D. Gullo (Ed.), *K today: Teaching and learning in the kindergarten year* (pp. 61–68). Washington, DC: NAEYC.

Horner, S., & Shwery, C. (2002). Becoming an engaged, self-regulated reader. *Theory into Practice, 41*, 102–109.

Howard, J. (2010). Making the most of play in the early years: The importance of children's perceptions. In P. Broadhead, J. Howard, & E. Wood (Eds.), *Play and learning in the early years* (pp. 145–160). London, UK: Sage.

Jacobs, B. (2008). Children's conversations about the sun, moon, and earth. In C. Wien, (Ed.), *Emergent curriculum in the primary classroom* (pp. 82–95). New York: Teachers College Press.

Jones, E. (2012). The emergence of emergent curriculum. *Young Children* (March), 66–68.

Jones, E., & Nimmo, J. (1994). *Emergent curriculum.* Washington, DC: NAEYC.

Jones, S., & Doolittle, E. (2017), Social and emotional learning: Introducing the issue. *The Future of Children, 27*(1), 3–12.

Jones, S., & Kahn, J. (2017). *The evidence base for how we learn: Supporting students' social, emotional, and academic development.* Aspen, CO: The Aspen Institute.

Jones, S., Barnes, S., Bailey, R., & Doolittle, E. (2017), Promoting social and emotional competencies in elementary school. *The Future of Children, 27*(1), 49–73.

Kaufman, P. (1998). Poppies and the dance of world making. In C. Edwards, L. Gandini, & G. Forman (Eds.), *The hundred languages of children: The Reggio Emilia approach—advanced reflections* (2nd ed., pp. 285–294). Westport, CT: Ablex.

Kohlberg, L., Yaefer, J., & Hjertholm, E. (1968). Private speech: Four studies and a review of theories. *Child Development, 39*, 691–736.

Lewis, M. D., & Todd, R. M. (2007). The self-regulating brain: Cortical-subcortical feedback and the development of intelligent action. *Cognitive Development, 22*, 406–430.

Lillas, C., & Turnbull, J. (2009). *Infant/child mental health, early intervention, and relationship-based therapies.* New York: W. W. Norton.

Malaguzzi, L. (1994). Your image of the child: Where teaching begins. *Exchange, 3*, 1–5.

Mastrangelo, S. (2012). Can self-regulation create successful school communities? *Principal Connection, 16*(2), 8–11.

Mastrangelo, S. (2017). The promise of play as an intervention to develop self-regulation in children on the autism spectrum. In T. Bruce, P. Hakkarainen, & M. Bredikyte (Eds.), *The Routledge international handbook of early childhood play* (pp. 376–394). London, UK: Routledge.

McClelland, M., Acock, A., & Morrison, F. (2006). The impact of kindergarten learning-related skills on academic trajectories at the end of elementary school. *Early Childhood Research Quarterly, 21*, 471–490.

McClelland, M., & Cameron, C. (2011). Self-regulation and academic achievement in elementary school children. *New Directions for Child and Adolescent Development, 133*, 29–44.

Mercer, N., & Dawes, L. (2008). The value of exploratory talk. In N. Mercer & S. Hodgkinson (Eds.), *Exploring talk in schools* (pp. 55–72). London, UK: Sage Publications.

Montague, M. (2007). Self-regulation and mathematics instruction. *Learning Disabilities Research & Practice, 22*, 75–83.

Montague, M. (2008). Self-regulations strategies to improve mathematical problem solving for children with learning disabilities. *Learning Disability Quarterly, 31*, 37–44.

Montessori, M. (1964). *The Montessori method.* Trans. Anne George. New York: Schocken. (Original work published 1912)

Moss, P., & Petrie, P. (2002). *Children's services to children's spaces: Public policy, children and childhood.* London, UK: Routledge.

O'Brien, L. (2010). Let the wild rumpus begin! The radical possibilities of play for young children with disabilities. In L. Brooker & S. Edwards (Eds.), *Engaging play* (pp. 182–194). Maidenhead, UK: McGraw-Hill.

Offord Centre for Child Studies. (2020). *Impact of the COVID-19 pandemic on Ontario families and children: Findings from the initial lockdown.* Hamilton, ON: McMaster University.

Ontario Ministry of Education. (2011). *Inquiry-based learning.* http://www.edu.gov.on.ca/eng/literacynumeracy/inspire/research/CBS_inquirybased.pdf

Ontario Ministry of Education. (2014). *How does learning happen? Ontario's pedagogy for the early years.* Toronto, ON: Government of Ontario.

Ontario Ministry of Education. (2016). *The kindergarten program.* Toronto, ON: Government of Ontario.

Ontario Ministry of Education. (2020). *The Ontario curriculum grades 1–8: Mathematics 2020.* http://www.edu.gov.on.ca/eng/curriculum/elementary/math.html

Pacini-Ketchabaw, V., Nxumalo, F., Kocher, L., Elliot, E., & Sanchez, A. (2015). *Journeys: Reconceptualizing early childhood practices through pedagogical narration.* Toronto, ON: University of Toronto Press.

Pascal, C. (2009). *Every child, every opportunity: Curriculum and pedagogy for the early learning program.* Toronto, ON: Government of Ontario.

Pelletier, J. (2014a). *Key findings from year 3 of full-day early learning kindergarten in Peel.* Toronto, ON: OISE.

Pelletier, J. (2014b). Ontario's full-day Kindergarten: A bold public policy initiative. *Public Sector Digest* (June), 41–49.

Ponitz, C. C., McClelland, M. M., Matthews, J. S., & Morrison, F. J. (2009). A structured observation of behavioral self-regulation and its contribution to kindergarten outcomes. *Developmental Psychology, 45*, 605–619.

Porges, S. (2011). *The polyvagal theory: Neurophysiological foundations of emotions, attachment, communication, self-regulation*. New York: W. W. Norton.

Porges, S. (2015a). Making the world safe for our children: Down-regulating defence and up-regulating social engagement to "optimise" the human experience. *Children Australia, 1*, 1–9.

Porges, S. (2015b). Play as a neural exercise: Insights from polyvagal theory. *The GAINS Quarterly* (Fall/Winter), 1–4.

Project Zero, Cambridgeport School, Cambridgeport Children's Center, Erza H. Baker School, & John Simpkins School. (2003). *Making teaching visible: Documenting individual and group learning as professional development*. Cambridge, MA: Harvard University Graduate School of Education.

Rimm-Kaufman, S., Curby, T., Grimm, K., Nathanson, L., & Brock, L. (2009). The contribution of children's self-regulation and classroom quality to children's adaptive behaviors in the kindergarten classroom. *Developmental Psychology, 45*, 958–972.

Rimm-Kaufman, S., & Wanless, S. (2012). An ecological perspective for understanding the early development of self-regulatory skills, social skills, and achievement. In R. C. Pianta (Ed.), *Handbook of early childhood education* (pp. 299–323). New York: The Guilford Press.

Rinaldi, C. (2001). Document and assessment: What is the relationship? In C. Giudici, C. Rinaldi, & M. Krechevsky (Eds.), *Making learning visible: Children as individual and group learners* (pp. 78–89). Cambridge, MA: Reggio Children.

Rinaldi, C. (2006). *In dialogue with Reggio Emilia: Listening, researching and learning*. London, UK: Routledge.

Ruttenberg-Rozen, R., & Jacobs, B. (Forthcoming). Considerations of equity for learners experiencing mathematics difficulties. In Y. P. Xin, H. Thouless, & R. Tzur (Eds.), *At the nexus between mathematics and special education*. Berlin, DE: Springer.

Schunk, D. H., & Zimmerman, B. (2007). Influencing children's self-efficacy and self-regulation of reading and writing through modeling. *Reading and Writing Quarterly, 23*, 7–25.

Shanker, S. (2010). Self-regulation. *Education Canada, 50*(3).

Shanker, S. (2012a). Emotion regulation through the ages. In A. Foolen, U. Luedke, J. Zlatev, & T. Racine (Eds.), *Moving ourselves, moving others: Motion and emotion in intersubjectivity, consciousness and language* (pp. 105–138). London, UK: John Benjamins.

Shanker, S. (2012b). *Report of the 2012 thinker in residence Western Australia*. Subiaco, AU: Commissioner for Children and Young People WA.

Shanker, S. (2013a). *Calm, alert and happy*. Toronto, ON: Queen's Printer for Ontario.

Shanker, S. (2013b). *Calm, alert, and learning: Classroom strategies for self-regulation*. Toronto, ON: Pearson.

Shanker, S., with Barker, T. (2016). *Self-reg: How to help your child (and you) break the stress cycle and successfully engage with life*. Toronto, ON: Viking/Penguin Canada.

Shanker, S. (2020). *Reframed: Self-reg for a just society*. Toronto, ON: University of Toronto Press.

Shanker, S., & Hopkins, S. (2020). *Self-reg schools: A handbook for educators*. Toronto, ON: Pearson.

Stacey, S. (2009). *Emergent curriculum in early childhood settings: From theory to practice*. St. Paul, MN: Redleaf Press.

Stacey, S. (2015). *Pedagogical documentation in early childhood: Sharing children's learning and teachers' thinking*. St. Paul, MN: Redleaf Press.

Statistics Canada. (2020). *Impacts of COVID-19 on Canadian families and children*. Ottawa, ON: Government of Canada.

Taguchi, H. L. (2010). *Going beyond the theory/practice divide in early childhood education: Introducing an intra-active pedagogy*. London, UK: Routledge.

Tarr, P. (2004). Consider the walls. *Young Children* (May), 88–92.

Timmons, K., Pelletier, J., & Corter, C. (2016). Understanding children's self-regulation within different classroom contexts. *Early Child Development and Care, 186*, 249–267.

UNESCO. (2021). *Culturally responsive curriculum*. Paris, France: International Bureau of Education.

Vaillancourt, T., McDougall, P., Comeau, J., & Finn, C. (2021). COVID-19 school closures and social isolation in children and youth: Prioritizing relationships in education. In T. Vaillancourt et al. (Eds.), *Children and schools during COVID-19: Engagement and connection through opportunity* (pp. 70–88). Ottawa, ON: Royal Society of Canada.

Vaillancourt, T., Szatmari, P., Georgiades, K., & Krygsman, A. (2021). The impact of COVID-19 on the mental health of Canadian children and youth. In T. Vaillancourt et al. (Eds.), *Children and schools during COVID-19: Engagement and connection through opportunity* (pp. 9–29). Ottawa, ON: Royal Society of Canada.

Vecchi, V. (2001). The curiosity to understand. In C. Giudici, C. Rinaldi, & M. Krechevsky (Eds.), *Making learning visible: Children as individual and group learners* (pp. 158–212). Cambridge, MA: Reggio Children.

Vohs, K. D., & Baumeister, R. F. (Eds.). (2011). *Handbook of self-regulation: Research, theory, and applications* (2nd ed.). New York: the Guilford Press.

Vygotsky, L. S. (1978). *Mind in society: The development of higher psychological process.* Cambridge, MA: Harvard University Press.

Wasik, B., & Herrmann, S. (2004). Family literacy: History, concepts, services. In B. Wasik (Ed.), *Handbook of family literacy* (pp. 3–22). Mahwah, NJ: Lawrence Erlbaum.

Wells, G. (2011). The social context of language and literacy development. In O. Barbanin & B. Wasik (Eds.), *Handbook of childhood development and early education: Research to practice* (pp. 271–302). New York: Guildford Press.

Welsh, J., Nix, R., Blair, C., Bierman, K., & Nelson, K. (2010). The development of cognitive skills and gains in academic school readiness for children from low-income families. *Journal of Educational Psychology, 102,* 43–53.

Whitebread, D. (2010). Play, metacognition and self-regulation. In P. Broadhead, J. Howard, & E. Wood (Eds.), *Play and learning in the early years* (pp. 161–176). London, UK: Sage.

Wien, C. (2006). Emergent curriculum. *Connections Journal, 10*(1).

Wien, C. (Ed.). (2008). *Emergent curriculum in the primary classroom.* New York: Teachers College Press.

Wien, C. (2014). *The power of emergent curriculum: Stories from early childhood settings.* Washington, DC: NAEYC.

Wien, C., Comeau, A., Keating, B.-L., & Bigelow, B. (2014). Designing the environment to build connection to place. In C. Wien (Ed.), *The power of emergent curriculum: Stories from early childhood settings* (pp. 25–34). Washington, DC: NAEYC.

Wien, C., Guyevskey, V., & Berdoussis, N. (2011). Learning to document in Reggio-inspired education. *Early Childhood Research and Practice, 13*(2).

Wien, C., Jacobs, B., & Brown, E. (2015). Emergent curriculum and the tension between relationship and assessment. In O. Saracho & B. Spodek (Eds.), *Educational assessment and evaluation in early childhood education: Contemporary perspectives in early childhood education* (pp. 93–116). Charlotte, NC: Information Age Publishing.

Wien, C., & Stacey, S. (2014). Untiming the curriculum: A case study of removing clocks from the program. In C. Wien (Ed.), *The power of emergent curriculum: Stories from early childhood settings* (pp. 13–20). Washington, DC: NAEYC.

Zins, J., & Elias, M. (2007). Social and emotional learning: Promoting the development of all students. *Journal of Educational and Psychological Consultation, 17,* 233–255.

INDEX